Déjà Viewed

THE SUNY SERIES

HORIZONS OF CINEMA

MURRAY POMERANCE | EDITOR

RECENT TITLES

Stanley Cavell, *Cavell on Film*

Saverio Giovacchini, *The Celluloid Atlantic*

John Caps, *Overhearing Film Music*

Hannah Holtzman, *Through a Nuclear Lens*

Benedict Morrison, *Eccentric Laughter*

Matthew Cipa, *Is Harpo Free?*

Daniel Varndell, *Torturous Etiquettes*

Seth Barry Watter, *The Human Figure on Film*

Jonah Corne and Monika Vrečar, *Yiddish Cinema*

Jason Jacobs, *Reluctant Sleuths, True Detectives*

Lucy J. Miller, *Distancing Representations in Transgender Film*

Tomoyuki Sasaki, *Cinema of Discontent*

Mary Ann McDonald Carolan, *Orienting Italy*

Matthew Rukgaber, *Nietzsche in Hollywood*

Jason Sperb, *The Hard Sell of Paradise*

William Rothman, *The Holiday in His Eye*

David Venditto, *Whiteness at the End of the World*

Fareed Ben-Youssef, *No Jurisdiction*

Tony Tracy, *White Cottage, White House*

Tom Conley, *Action, Action, Action*

A complete listing of books in this series can be found online at www.sunypress.edu.

Déjà Viewed

Nation, Gender, and Genre in
Bollywood Remakes of Hollywood Cinema

Gohar Siddiqui

SUNY PRESS

Cover credit: [top] Sonia hiding behind Kabir's apartment door to avoid being seen by Vishal and Siddharth (*Jism*, Amit Saxena, 2003). [bottom] Phyllis hiding behind Walter's apartment door to avoid being seen by Keyes (*Double Indemnity*, Billy Wilder, 1942). Cover design by Dan Ruccia and Sherry Freyermuth.

Published by State University of New York Press, Albany

© 2025 State University of New York

All rights reserved

Printed in the United States of America

No part of this book may be used or reproduced in any manner whatsoever without written permission. No part of this book may be stored in a retrieval system or transmitted in any form or by any means including electronic, electrostatic, magnetic tape, mechanical, photocopying, recording, or otherwise without the prior permission in writing of the publisher.

Links to third-party websites are provided as a convenience and for informational purposes only. They do not constitute an endorsement or an approval of any of the products, services, or opinions of the organization, companies, or individuals. SUNY Press bears no responsibility for the accuracy, legality, or content of a URL, the external website, or for that of subsequent websites.

EU GPSR Authorised Representative:
Logos Europe, 9 rue Nicolas Poussin, 17000, La Rochelle, France
contact@logoseurope.eu

For information, contact State University of New York Press, Albany, NY
www.sunypress.edu

Library of Congress Cataloging-in-Publication Data

Name: Siddiqui, Gohar, 1978– author.
Title: Déjà viewed : nation, gender, and genre in Bollywood remakes of Hollywood cinema / Gohar Siddiqui.
Description: Albany : State University of New York Press, [2025]. | Series: SUNY series, horizons of cinema | Includes bibliographical references and index.
Identifiers: LCCN 2024049472 | ISBN 9798855802955 (hardcover : alk. paper) | ISBN 9798855802931 (ebook) | ISBN 9798855802948 (pbk. : alk. paper)
Subjects: LCSH: Motion pictures—India. | Film remakes—India. | Motion picture industry—India—Mumbai. | LCGFT: Film criticism.
Classification: LCC PN1993.5.I8 S53324 2025 | DDC 791.430954—dc23/eng/20241216
LC record available at https://lccn.loc.gov/2024049472

Contents

List of Illustrations	vii
Acknowledgments	ix
Introduction	1
1 Indianization and the Bollywood Family Film	25
2 The Vamp and the Femme Fatale: Defamiliarized Femininities in the Bollywood Remake	59
3 From Remake to Pastiche: Bollywood, Hollywood, and Noir Masculinity	99
4 "Lihaaf Maang Le" ("Ask for the Quilt"): Queerness in the Cross-Cultural Remake	133
Conclusion	169
Notes	179
Bibliography	197
Filmography	213
Index	217

Illustrations

1.1a–b	Caricaturized people in the song "Jo Hona Hai So Hona Hai."	28
2.1	Phyllis hiding behind Walter's apartment door to avoid being seen by Keyes.	60
2.2	Sonia hiding behind Kabir's apartment door to avoid being seen by Vishal and Siddharth.	60
2.3	Sonia's control is suggested as her hands run over the crisscross pattern of a makeshift hut in the song "Jadoo Hai Nashaa Hai."	77
2.4	Theme of entrapment continues as Kabir kisses Sonia behind the crisscrossed wall.	78
2.5	Noir aesthetic as vertical blinds cast shadows behind Phyllis's head.	78
2.6	Neo-noir aestheic of imprisonment is suggested by the patterns in the doorways.	79
3.1	Opening scene of *Johnny Gaddaar* that pays homage to classic film noir.	100
3.2	Scene from *Chinatown* (with Polanski's cameo) plays on the TV in Satyaveer's home.	121
4.1	The kiss between Kunal and Sameer in *Dostana*.	134
4.2	Ving Rhames singing and dancing in *I Now Pronounce You Chuck and Larry*.	141

4.3a–b	"Beedi" song-and-dance number from *Dostana*.	148
4.4a–b	Radha and Sita dancing in *Fire*.	160
4.5	*Dedh Ishqiya*, Begum Para dancing a *mujra*.	162
4.6	*Dedh Ishqiya*, Munniya joins Begum Para and they dance together.	164
4.7	*Dedh Ishqiya*, Khalujaan watching from outside.	164
4.8	*Dedh Ishqiya*, Babban watching from outside.	164

Acknowledgments

I have been joking with friends about the validity of an antiacknowledgements page along with the acknowledgments page so that authors can call out and name everything that came in the way of their project ("hello, imposter syndrome and its friends"). So, here I am feeling extremely grateful to every single person mentioned below and countless more who supported and encouraged me and, in the process, undid all that would otherwise permeate my imaginary antiacknowledgments page.

This book would not exist without the guidance and mentorship of Steve Cohan. Steve encouraged me in pursuing this project more than a decade ago when I was a graduate student at Syracuse University. He and Roger Hallas, who also read countless drafts of my dissertation, continue to be mentors and friends. Rashna Richards and Tejaswini Ganti provided me with valuable information that helped me start my research for the project. I'm indebted to Monika Mehta for her generosity and conversations about remakes, Hindi film, and SRK. I would like to offer special thanks to Carol Fadda-Conrey, Chandra Talpade Mohanty, Coran Klaver, Crystal Bartolovich, Dana Olwan, and Robin Riley for their friendship and input on the theoretical stakes of my project when I first started this work.

I'm in the company of brilliant and funny people in the Visual and Performing Arts Department at Clark University; I'd like to thank these incredible colleagues for their encouragement and support these past few years as I juggled work and parenting during a pandemic. Hugh Manon, Kristina Wilson, and Toby Sisson have been wonderful mentors and have had faith in me when sometimes I didn't. Jed Samer and Soren Sorensen have been therapists and my go-to people for all questions film related. Hugh, Ben Korstvedt, Kristina, and Soren, in their capacities as department chairs and program directors, ensured that I had time to devote to my research. Chris Ruble's help with my work on this book almost makes him a fellow contributor—he has helped me over the years with accessing films, with getting clips and images for my various presentations on remakes, and in capturing and processing the frame captures for the book. Sherry Freyermuth's expertise as a graphic designer resulted in the cover design, which I love. The infectious and uplifting enthusiasm of Stephen DiRado is unmatched, and Christina McGovern and Naomi Pitamber have been willing victims of my venting. I'm thankful for the warmth and support provided by Cailin Marcel Manson, Gino DiIorio, James Maurelle, Jessie Darrell-Jarbadan, John Aylward, John Freyermuth, John Garton, Kevin McGerigle, Matt Malsky, and Yelena Beriyeva.

Betsy Huang's leadership for the Center for Gender, Race, and Area Studies and the initiatives started by Esther Jones for faculty and staff of color at Clark have been instrumental in helping faculty to succeed in their research and teaching, and I'm grateful to them for looking out for early career faculty. Asha Best has taken up Betsy's role, and her friendship has been invaluable in times of struggle as I tried to complete this book. My thanks to Stephen Levin and the English department for inviting me to their colloquium and for discussing remakes along with nation and gender with me. Elizabeth Imber, Marianne Sarkis, Nina Kushner, and Wiebke Deimling have been my writing partners over the past few years, and their company has made writing enjoyable and nonsolitary. My lovely students, especially those in my international-cinema and transnational-film-remakes courses (you know who you are!), have been the most enthusiastic and brilliant people I have had the pleasure to discuss films and remakes with.

Kamille Gentles-Peart and Tatiana Cruz have developed the impressive North Star Collective (NSC)—a consortium of colleges and universities committed to racial equity out of the New England Board of Higher Education—and the NSC Writing fellowship for BIPOC faculty. They created an antiracist and anticolonial space for healing that has been very generative for me. The revisions of this book would not have been possible without this fellowship, the writing retreats, and the support of my fellows. An extra-special shout out to members of my writing group—Ana Marcelo, Forrest Rodgers, Jimoh Fatoki, Jonix Owino, Melissa Colón, Nandita Gurjar, Suzanne Angeli, and Vanita Naidu.

I'd like to extend my deep gratitude to the impressive *jamghat* of South Asian film scholars who have been very welcoming since I was a fledgling grad student at my first Society for Cinema and Media Studies (SCMS) conference, offering guidance and advice and helping me find true joy in this work. My thanks to Anupama Kapse, Ashish Avikunthak, Corey Creekmur, Darshana Sreedhar Mini, Debashree Mukherjee, Iain Robert Smith, Jyotika Virdi, Koel Banerjee, Kuhu Tanvir, Meheli Sen, Neepa Majumdar, Nilanjana Bhattacharjya, Nitin Govil, Priya Jaikumar, Rajinder Dudrah, Salma Siddique, Samhita Sunya, and Sangita Gopal for conversations on Indian cinema and suggestions on paper presentations or research ideas that helped me develop my project. I have loved discussing my work with Pavitra Sundar and Usha Iyer across various conferences and dinners. Above all, along with other film scholars on Indian cinema, all these people have produced an impressive body of work and built the field in the past two decades. I cannot imagine writing this book without their work and commitment to film and to Indian cinema.

I cannot emphasize enough my appreciation of this manuscript's readers for devoting their time and energy to reading and responding to it. The anonymous reviewers of this book provided invaluable feedback that I hope they see in the revised version; their thoroughness, constructive criticism, enthusiasm, and positivity are worthy of emulation. One cannot ask for better editors than James Peltz, Julia Cosacchi, and Murray Pomerance. Their gentle patience, wit, and expertise in helping me navigate this book have been amazing. I'd also like to thank Ideas on Fire and Christine Crabb for helping me edit earlier versions of the book. Thanks to University of Hawai'i Press as well; parts of chapter 3 were originally published in *Pop Empires: Transnational and Diasporic Flows of India and Korea*, edited by S. Heijin Lee, Monika Mehta, and Robert Ji-Song Ku (University of Hawai'i Press, 2019).

My journey across various universities such as Delhi University, Bridgewater State, Syracuse, and University of Wisconsin-Platteville and outside of university spaces has provided me with mentors, friends, and colleagues who have ensured that I didn't fall through the cracks. I've been very lucky to have mentors such as Javed Malik, Lakhmir Singh, Lee Torda, Novy Kapadia, P. S. Siddhu, and Rahul Sapra. Thank you, Arati Tai, for always checking in on me while I worked on this book for supporting me with your constant encouragement. I treasure our conversations about Hindustani classical music, about

Hindi film, and about gender and ideology. I'm deeply appreciative of the friendship of Amanda Tucker, David Gillota, Mike Dwyer, Sara Koeller, Shan Sappleton, and Steven Doles that has resulted in conversations regarding food, film, Hollywood, Bollywood, systemic inequalities, literature, and international politics.

Who needs a pep squad when they have friends like Anuja Jain, Anupama Arora, Bek Orr, Jessica Kuskey, Nina Kushner, and Tanushree Ghosh? My thanks to Anuja, Anupama, and Tanu for their cinephilia, their knowledge of all things Indian film, for giving me feedback on ideas for this book, and for their unfailing love and support. I wrote some of these chapters in the company of Bek; we bond over food and feminism, and I have learned so much from them in our conversations about gender and feminist theory. Thank you, Nina, for our epic writing sessions and advice on all things life and academia. I am very grateful to Jessica Kuskey for her patience and friendship over the years as she read and reread several drafts of this project.

Some of the most enjoyable times I have had while working on this book have been conversations with my brother, Ajmal Siddiqui, about poetry and film. My introduction would look different without these marathon talking sessions, and I wouldn't have a perfect ending *sher* without him either. My sister, Kausar Ismail, with her infectious optimism and disregard for anything that even remotely resembles anxiety, was instrumental in keeping me sane throughout this process. Afnan, Ayush, Faris, Inaaya, Lubna, Nuqra, Rida, and Sumbul unfailingly make me smile. And my mom, my ammi, is the first feminist I encountered, just as my father, my abbu, was the first person who engendered in me the love of poetry, art, and critical analysis. Their faith in me makes me persevere when all else fails.

Finally, who am I kidding? There is no way I could have finished this book without Autif Khan, my partner in all things; he took care of everything, from cooking to childcare to making sure that I could work. There aren't enough words to convey his support that ensured that I ate, got enough sleep, and wasn't spinning out of control. Chunmun, Namir, Roman, and Zukie—my human and feline littles—are strong contenders against Autif because the cuteness they bring and the antidepressant work they do remain unmatched.

I dedicate this book to my *ammi* and *abbu*.

Introduction

haiñ aur bhī duniyā meñ sukhan-var bahut achchhe
kahte haiñ ki 'ġhālib' kā hai andāz-e-bayāñ aur[1]

—Mirza Ghalib

THIS *SHER* (COUPLET) BY Mirza Ghalib (1797–1869), an endearing earworm for me throughout the process of writing this book, was sung by Jagjit Singh as the theme song of a 1980s TV show based on Ghalib's life and works.[2] Ghalib was one of the greatest Urdu poets during Mughal and British rule in India; the simplicity of his poetry combined with the mastery of the *ghazal* style, as well as his deliberations on life via his poetry, are responsible for his continued popularity an entire century later. The TV series made him an even more beloved figure, and his poetry is part of the popular imaginary in Urdu- and Hindi-speaking India, especially as it was aired on the national television network, before there were cable TV channels.[3] This couplet, then, forms part of the fabric of popular memory.

These two lines by Ghalib link together the ideas of originality and repetition with those of art and the artist. The literal meaning of these words is:

There are many great poets in the world
But they say, Ghalib's way/style is quite something else

Ghalib's poetry is known, amongst other things, for his humor as well as for the playful rivalry with other poets. These lines that compose the *maqta*—the final couplet of a *ghazal* which contains the *takhallus* (penname) of the *shayar* (poet)—continue in that humorous vein of self-praise. However, as is true of any art, interpretations of these words are layered, polysemic, and they get at the heart of what constitutes art. At its most literal level, the couplet expresses the importance of expression over content—that there might be great poets conveying great truths through their poetry, but that what makes Ghalib great is his *andāz-e-bayāñ*, his style of expressing that which might be ordinary and not so great. Someone familiar with Ghalib's oeuvre and the density of allusions in his poetry might also realize that the first line of the couplet unconsciously admits to the possibility that there might not be anything original left to say: that every poet, every artist, is perhaps saying similar things but in different ways.[4] Ironically, or perhaps expectedly because of his habit of being contrary, Ghalib has also paid homage to Mir Taqi Mir (1722–1810), whom he considered one of the greatest poets of all time. His own poetry, which sometimes builds on the works of Mir and other poets, however, is simultaneously literarily derivative and original. His practice thus shows the happy coexistence of copying and innovation, thus underlining the point of his couplet. The second line draws attention to the importance of presentation, of style, of expression, of the "how" instead of the "what"—or rather, of how the "how" makes the "what" more palpable, philosophical, real, and new. The couplet is thus ostensibly about the poet praising his own work as extraordinary, while also exploring concerns of intertextuality, repetition, difference, and aesthetic expression and form. Ghalib's homage thus collapses the boundary between copy and original as his own poetry is both.[5]

Ghalib's *maqta* here is about a poet, an artist who was lauded for his work and became the poet laureate. It is about an art form that is often seen as free from the crass materialism and commodification of industrial reproduction, which is an inescapable part of other forms such as mainstream film. But it also underlines the fact that repetition is inherent to any aesthetic practice. Film remakes, the subject of this book, engage in a certain kind of repetition that belongs to the realm of commercial enterprise in mainstream filmmaking. But films are also aesthetic texts, and Bollywood remakes borrow from the aesthetic practice central to Indian art forms as well as from the industry's love for formulae. In "Remembering, Repeating, and Working Through *Devdas*," Corey Creekmur discusses the various kinds of repetitions attendant on cinematic avatars of Sarat Chandra Chatterjee's novel *Devdas*—the adaptations and remakes of the novel and the subsequent films (176); the unofficial remakes of the story in Guru Dutt and Amitabh Bachchan films (181); the repetitive narrative structure (181); the motif of going away and returning home that is evident in Hindi films from the 1950s, 1970s, and 1990s (182); and even the reoccurrence of specific words, scenes, shots, and so on in a film (181)—to argue that they articulate an Indian structure of feeling based in South Asian cultural practices and history. His discussion of *Devdas* dismantles the binary of original and copy as well and points to the nature of intertextuality resulting from this specific kind of repetition by suggesting, "If only for the last century, no Indian watches *Devdas* for the first time" (173).[6] He complicates this argument later while discussing Sanjay Leela Bhansali's *Devdas* and the historical amnesia of contemporary audiences, but his provocative suggestion here reveals an Indian or South Asian approach to repetition that is not based in a Western-individualist notion of ownership and property. The story of *Devdas* has intertextual resonance that is part of cultural memory, and therefore "suspense and revelation are not the pleasures offered by the narrative tradition in which *Devdas* is now embedded" (Creekmur, "Remembering" 179). Creekmur's point draws attention to noneconomic and non-Western ways in which pleasures accompany remaking and repetition in the Indian film.

In some ways, the emphasis on repetition and expression that we see in Indian Urdu poetry or Hindi film shows how remaking too can be an aesthetic act as repetition is inherent to Indian art forms historically. Repetition, in its various guises, as being foundational to art is about the centrality of intertextuality, a version of Mikhail Bakhtin's claim that all words carry ghosts of previous utterances of the word,[7] that newness is built on repetition and reference, whether explicit or implicit, or at a macro level (like genre or myth) or a micro level (like quotation or detail). Ghalib's poetry, in the genre of the *ghazal*, is also about mood and emotion and how the expressiveness of his words makes the listener inhabit and feel the palimpsestic meanings. Hearing or reading it is a bodily experience in addition to an intellectual one. A feeling of déjà vu accompanies these meanings as a listener's or reader's ear or eye meanders through the words.

This feeling, of course, changes based on the depth of familiarity with the text. What *Devdas* films may elicit for some viewers as part of cultural memory may be absent or not as strong for others. The pleasures vary, especially when the source material is foreign, as is the case with remakes of Hollywood films. Still, within the Indian context, there is a long history of both the use of repetition and its intertextual weight in undoing constructed oppositions between notions of original and copy.

It is this feeling evoked by memory—at times obvious to a viewer and yet at other times transient or murky—of an affective and intellectual engagement with repetition that sparked the idea for this book. While watching *Bonnie and Clyde* (Arthur Penn 1967), I experienced this feeling of déjà vu as I simultaneously tried to place where I had experienced something similar yet different. Pleasure, incredulity, and an intangible (to me) pursuit of moments that would get me that high of recognition again and again interrupted my immersion in the film, culminating in my realization that I was noticing story elements I'd seen in a Bollywood film, *Bunty Aur Babli* (*Bunty and Babli*) (Shaad Ali 2005). *Bunty Aur Babli* is a very loose comedic take on the story of Bonnie and Clyde but with a different *andāz-e-bayāñ*, or style of expression, that is as much rooted in the industry as in the individual filmmaker and creative unit. A focus on industry, history, ideology, and culture thus immediately accompanies the affective charge of the repetition. This book, as a result, is an exploration of the nature of intertextuality in certain kinds of repetitions and differences and develops its arguments about ideologies of gender, genre, and nation in Bollywood remakes of Hollywood films via close analyses of these repetitions.

In early 2013, the first hit on a Google search for "Bollywood remakes of Hollywood films" was an official-looking IMDb page, created in August 2012, listing Hindi films that are in varying degrees of intertextuality with Hollywood films.[8] SammyManiac, the creator, provides a disclaimer: "I have not distinguished between remakes/ inspired /copied/ adapted /legally acquired/stolen, etc. movies." This list is very similar to other user-created lists of Hindi remakes on blogs and film forums, and it shares certain characteristics with them. First, none of these lists is comprehensive. Second, most of these lists do not differentiate between loose remakes and close remakes.[9] For instance, SammyManiac's list fails to mention several close remakes of Hollywood films, including *Ghulam* (*Slave*) (Vikram Bhatt 1998), a remake of *On the Waterfront* (Elia Kazan 1954), and *Dil Hai Ke Manta Nahin* (*The Heart Is Such, It Disagrees*) (Mahesh Bhatt 1991), a remake of *It Happened One Night* (Frank Capra 1934), which enjoyed popularity in India and abroad. Third, barring a small number of examples of films from 1950 to 1990, the Hindi remakes their list mentions were all produced after 1990. Thus, despite its lack of comprehensiveness, SammyManiac's list still indicates a rise in the remaking trend in Bollywood in the 1990s, along with revealing viewer awareness of the fact that the listed films are remakes. Finally, the number of remakes of Hollywood films that appear here increases massively after 2000. In this list alone, out of a total of one hundred films, seven were produced before 1990 (five of them in the late 1980s), seventeen were produced in the 1990s, and seventy-six were produced between 2000 and 2014. While changes in the Bollywood film industry that have occurred since the 1990s—including its transnationalization, its corporatization, and the related ideological mobilization of gender—have received a lot of critical attention, less attention has been paid to the connections between these changes in the industry and the sharp increase in Bollywood remakes.

Déjà Viewed positions the post-1990s Bollywood remakes of Hollywood films as invested with polysemic significance pertaining to industry, culture, and transnational circulation of capital; the remake, then, as a textual and economic object of study uniquely reveals the ideological relay between the two industries and cultures. Online forums, reviews, and articles demonstrate audience awareness of unacknowledged remakes as copies of non-Bollywood plotlines that have been embellished and "Indianized." Economic liberalization and globalization in the 1990s opened the doors for the entry of Western programming into India, including Hollywood films on cable TV. I argue that this familiarity with the source texts contributed to the perception that there was an unprecedented increase in the number of remakes produced by Bollywood. The 1990s remakes mirror the problematic associations between gender and Indianness constructed by the genre of the Bollywood family film, which can be seen as the film industry's direct response to the globalization of the economy and the entry of foreign programming. As I argue in chapter 1, these remakes are involved in the process of Indianization, an industry term, also used by scholars, to explain the industrial and cultural makeover of the remakes produced by Bollywood. I build on their work to situate Indianization as a constantly shifting process that is implicated within the historical moment; in other words, the temporal aspect affects how and when the nation is connected to an idea of remaking. These remaking practices start to change at the turn of the century as the close ties to a notion of Indianness get splintered, and this shift in the industry is made apparent particularly via the remake: for example, domestic remakes often appeal to nostalgia for past Hindi cinema, and in the case of transnational remakes, filmmakers borrow the iconography of Hollywood films to introduce new aesthetic styles.[10] Farah Khan's *Om Shanti Om/OSO* (2007), is one of the most popular films that commodified this aesthetics of nostalgia via citation. While it references films such as *Singin' in the Rain*, *Coyote Ugly*, and *The Pirate* for the cosmopolitan cinephile viewer familiar with Hollywood films—and includes nods to South Indian film industries as well—it overwhelmingly remakes and pastiches films and dominant tropes of past Hindi cinema. *OSO* is not the first film to do so, but it is one of the first few A-list mainstream Bollywood films for which intertextual play is the dominant mode.[11] In doing so, it announces the postmodern sensibility not just of contemporary Bollywood but also of its audiences.

The post-1990 remakes under discussion here are all mainstream films, functioning within the popular idiom and therefore reflective of changing dominant ideologies as tied with industry and capital. They show the impact of liberalization of the economy, changing target audience demographics, and rising fundamentalist strains in the 1990s, as well as the effects of the corporatization of the industry in that decade.[12] *Déjà Viewed* looks at the remake as a register of these economic and cultural changes as they pertain to gender, genre, and national identity or Indianness. Instead of hiding the fact of its borrowing, as is true for many 1990s remakes, the post-2000 remakes display very confident relationships to Hollywood and the West, as well as to past Hindi cinema. Indianization, as a framework for understanding remakes in terms of cultural and ideological adaptation of the source text, gets fractured in this context; the connection between the Bollywood form (which transforms Hollywood film into a primarily melodramatic mode, adds family values, and inserts song-and-dance sequences) and the nation that dominates in the 1990s loses its stranglehold as the markers of Indianness keep changing. Post-2000 remakes engage with their source texts in increasingly palimpsestic ways that now include formal experimentations with the Hollywood form, including aspects as diverse as genres, character types, and film length (e.g., shorter-length films that no longer contain the staple, the song-and-dance number). The connection to the nation via the remake waxes and wanes because of the proliferation of formal changes in the Bollywood film, and gender remains central to these formulations. *Déjà Viewed* produces an in-depth analysis of Bollywood remakes as a gendered response to the economic and cultural changes that the globalization and corporatization of the industry brought to Indian film.

Hollywood Hegemony, Hollywood Remakes, and Bollywood Remakes

Despite recent scholarly attention to Bollywood and to transnational remakes, remake scholarship remains largely focused on Hollywood, and it explores issues of copyright and plagiarism or borrows from adaptation studies to interrogate concerns of homage, update, and anxiety of influence. Most work on transnational remakes discusses remaking in terms of Hollywood hegemony or in terms of postmodernism. Lucy Mazdon's study of Hollywood and French cinema as industries, *Encore Hollywood*, emphasizes the transnational and intertextual nature of cinema itself to contest claims regarding high art (French cinema) and commercial cinema (Hollywood) in Hollywood's remaking of French films. Mazdon argues that the real negotiation is about cultural identity and politics between Hollywood and French cinema: French films cannot compete with their remakes on foreign soil, especially when a popular version is present in an accessible language and culture (4). In *Double Takes*, Carolyn Durham focuses on culture and gender as they get transferred or transformed in the Hollywood remake when it crosses aesthetic and national borders from France to the United States (5). She situates remaking within the larger framework of the relationship between the two cultures and argues that the French antipathy to Hollywood partially emanates from the threat that Hollywood represents to the potential domination and hegemony of French culture in the international market and especially in Europe (7). More recent scholarship has shown attention to Hollywood and Asian cinemas. For instance, Yiman Wang's book *Remaking*

Chinese Cinema provides an approach that acknowledges Hollywood's hegemony given its borrowing from Asian cinemas (including Chinese and Hong Kong cinemas) but also discusses the historical and political ramifications of these remakings. The transnational remake, then, raises issues of globalization and neocolonialism.

Bollywood remakes of Hollywood films resist these kinds of theorizations mainly because the situation is reversed. Remakes by Hindi filmmakers did not really worry Hollywood studios until recently. The target audiences and industrial contexts were so disparate that there were no debates over ownership of property—that is, until Bollywood was granted industry status in 1998, which opened up India as a lucrative market for conglomerates such as Sony and Twentieth Century Fox Film Corporation (Twentieth Century Studios since 2020).[13] The changes in the industry have also affected the manner in which remakes are made in Bollywood: since 2001, Hindi remakes have become more daring and less prone to hiding the fact of the remaking through extensive changes to the storyline. As a result, scholarship on Hindi remakes is also split.

Early scholarship on remakes (see articles by Sheila Nayar, Rosie Thomas, and Tejaswini Ganti) was concerned with Bollywood's remaking practice in the 1990s, which is quite different from the changes after 2000. These theorizations, while still applicable in some capacity to later remakes, are attendant upon the nature of earlier remakes. The remakes in the 1990s are unacknowledged, don't involve the purchase of intellectual property rights, and exist on a broad intertextual spectrum with varying intensities of intertextual relationships with their source texts. That is, some remakes can only be called "loose" remakes because their intertextuality is either minimal or is dispersed across the multiple Hollywood films from which they borrow. Others clearly resemble their source texts but are considered to be merely inspired by their sources instead of remakes of them.

There are several reasons for these disavowals of sources. The three sectors in Bollywood—production, distribution, and exhibition—were run by independent family firms in the 1990s instead of being vertically or horizontally integrated in the manner of the corporations that run Hollywood (Ganti, *Bollywood* 59).[14] As a result, filmmakers often didn't have the corporate backing and power necessary to fight major battles over intellectual copyright.[15] Therefore, as the remake performed a cultural and industrial transformation of the Hollywood film, it also translated into a text that avoided violating international copyright laws. Beyond the economic explanations of such disavowals, the remake as a category did not really exist in Bollywood, although remaking as a practice informed the works of some filmmakers. Copying in the name of inspiration is an open secret in the industry. Vikram Bhatt, director of many Hindi remakes, claims that the ingenuity lies in hiding the fact that the film is not original (qtd. in Bannerjee, "Cloning Hollywood"). Finally, remaking and adapting texts is part of the industry's practice, as Hindi cinema has had a long tradition of recycling stories ritualistically.

This context explains why Bollywood remakes differ so much from their Hollywood sources; Nayar even asks for a consideration of Hindi films adapted from foreign works as "less remakes than extracted skeletons" because what is borrowed is at best the bare-bones plot from the source text (74). Rosie Thomas, while deliberating on the melodramatic codes and conventions of Indian cinema that contribute to a gendered imagination of national culture, talks about remaking as a process of Indianization ("Melodrama" 162). Ganti uses the term (H)Indianization in the title of her essay on remaking as Indianization to call attention to the problematic hegemonic positioning of the Hindi film industry ("And Yet My Heart" 140). She shifts the attention to industry as she looks at Indianization as a conservative process dependent on how filmmakers think about what their audiences will deem acceptable in adapting a Hollywood film, and she argues that remaking a Hollywood film "generates a self-consciousness about social norms and moral codes that can make filmmakers more cautious" ("And Yet My Heart" 143).

Bollywood remakes after the turn of the century, including remakes of films from regional cinemas, older Hindi films, and Hollywood films, establish a different relationship to their source texts. As I discuss in chapter 3, producer Sanjay Dutt was looking for an infusion of something new to appeal to audiences when he decided to remake Quentin Tarantino's *Reservoir Dogs* (1992) as *Kaante* (*Thorns*) (Sanjay Gupta 2002). Postmillennial remakes of Hollywood films, therefore, don't erase all signs of the Westernness of their source texts. In fact, now that they could get corporate backing, filmmakers experimented more with stylized special effects and new aesthetics and therefore were remaking films that allowed them to showcase these attractions.

New and exciting work by scholars such as Lucia Krämer, Neelam Sidhar Wright, Nitin Govil, Rashna Wadia Richards, Iain Robert Smith, and others adds to the handful of articles that existed when I started this project.[16] Krämer points to three other areas that need consideration as part of Indianization: the role of star actors, references to politics, and the borrowing from multiple sources (84). She argues that "the unacknowledged Bollywood remake [thus] emerges as a specific national variety of the remake as an industrial category" (90). Wright's book on postmodernism and Bollywood considers the remake as a twenty-first century phenomenon and analyzes the idea of repetition, and more specifically remakes, in two chapters. Blair Orfall's dissertation considers aspects of copyright and copying as well as Bollywood remakes within the larger context of adaptation studies. Govil's book, *Orienting Hollywood*, while not devoted to remakes, considers important aspects (like piracy, copyright, and the notion of the copy as central to Hindi cinema's relationship to Hollywood) that form necessary contexts for them. Both Govil and Richards draw attention to the globalization of the industry and do close readings of films to show how the transnational is central to the remaking of national cinemas. Smith's work places Bollywood remakes within the larger context of transnational studies and transnational remaking. I expand on these conversations by looking back, both to focus on how and where the nation and its connected ideologies are negotiated via the remake as the film industry goes through a period of rapid transition and to examine how the changes in the industry have affected and shaped the form of the remake and its ideological implications since that time. *Déjà Viewed* provides an in-depth historicized study of Bollywood remakes since 1990 and considers aspects that have been central to how films acquire meaning in Hindi cinema.

My intervention in these conversations is to examine the process across the two decades as the remake is shaped by the changes in the Bollywood industry, to historicize it within both Hollywood and Bollywood industries, and to do an aesthetic and ideological analysis that is attentive to cultural and formal concerns attendant on both industries. The cultural adaptations in the remake that participate in an idea of Indianness starting from the 1990s and the transnationalization of Bollywood in the twenty-first century result in self-aware (although still mostly unacknowledged) remakes; these two are not disconnected processes. My attempt here differentiates unacknowledged Bollywood remakes before 1990 and after, where I consider the post-1990 remake as affected by changes in the industry brought on by a plethora of cultural and economic upheavals. The ideological inflections in terms of gender and genre—both specific to the dominant ways in which the nation was imagined in the 1990s and to how New Bollywood registers postmillennial changes to the industry—necessitate a reckoning of these concerns with that of remaking.

The book, then, aims to historicize the Bollywood remake; looks at how the remake displays Bollywood's resistance to Hollywood's hegemony at the same time as it reveals the new ways in which Bollywood and Hollywood negotiate as industries under global capitalism; establishes and delineates the central connection between gender, genre, nation, and the industry; and articulates a need for a hybrid theoretical approach drawn from Indian scholarship on gender and Western theorizations to the study of not just remakes but to transnational cinema that is influenced by the global reach of both industries.

Why the 1990s?

The 1990s are an important decade in the history of popular Hindi cinema due to the major impact that globalization of the Indian economy had on film-production practices. These changes are discernible in three important events: the liberalization of the Indian economy in 1991, the introduction of satellite television in India in 1992, and the recognition of Bollywood as an industry by the state in 1998.[17] Ashish Rajadhyaksha coined the term Bollywoodization to describe the new practices and changes that define Bollywood after 1990 and even titled his essay "Bollywoodization of Indian Cinema."[18] Almost all scholars of Hindi cinema cite films like *Hum Aapke Hain Koun . . . !* (*What Am I to You*) (Sooraj Barjatya 1994) and *Dilwale Dulhania Le Jayenge* or *DDLJ* (*The Big-Hearted Will Win the Bride*) (Aditya Chopra 1995) as examples of the changing product, full of lavish spectacles and foreign locales and targeting an urban middle-class or diasporic audience. These two films, which are not remakes, were immediate hits in India and among the Indian diasporas. Further, they also spawned a spate of films that followed the formula that had resulted in their high profits, thus drawing much critical attention.

Once considered a derogatory term, Bollywood has been variously understood by diverse theorists of Indian cinema as Bombay-based Hindi cinema, as the style of masala movies after the 1980s, and as a culture industry that is distinct from actual film production.[19] It was a name used pejoratively earlier to convey a lack of originality in the industry and to assign it a secondary status in comparison to Hollywood. I'd argue that Bollywood is similar to Hollywood, but not because it is (wrongly) assumed to be nothing more than an industry that steals from Hollywood. Rather, the term indicates its geographical roots, its connection to the country and to the world, its industrial identity, and its ideological positioning. The term Bollywood is often used to indicate popular Hindi cinema produced in the city of Bombay. For example, Govil looks at the history of Hindi cinema, of Bombay as Hollywood-like, and of Bollywood as associated with copying and imitation (*Orienting Hollywood* 42). He uses this history of Hollywood and Bollywood to argue that "Bollywood needs to be understood as an expression of a relation, with the copy at its root" and then uses the remake to elaborate further on this relationship (*Orienting Hollywood* 60). The works of scholars such as Rajadhyaksha, as I mentioned above, have influenced the current use of the term Bollywood in academia, where it is meant to indicate films produced after 1990. My use of the term is aligned similarly, understanding it in its relation to globalization; Bollywood is thus distinguished from the umbrella term *popular Hindi cinema* to indicate its status as a subset encompassing films produced since the 1990s.

The twin impulses in the industry to reembrace a notion of nationness as well as to globalize itself differently than before are present in the genres of the war film and the Bollywood family film of the 1990s. It is in 1998 that Bollywood gets recognized as an industry, and we see how it had already started working like one in the ways in which certain formulae and genres become common similarly to Hollywood. Certain film directors refuse to call their films "Bollywood" precisely to differentiate their films from what they consider capitalist commodities in the marketplace. Bollywood therefore becomes, like Hollywood, a film industry that is associated with a country and with its globalization; an industry that relies on categories like genres and other kinds of repetitions to provide cinematic pleasure and to assure profits;[20] and one that is participant in various kinds of ideological mobilizations because it is a dominant cultural phenomenon.

The geographical marker of Hollywood is not real, as Hollywood films are produced all over the world, and Hollywood is understood to be equivalent to globalization. The relationship to Americanness and a certain national/cultural expression is therefore an ideological one. Bollywood, as a cinema from the third world is curiously located. It is one industry that punctures the easy equivalence of Hollywood with globalization, it is still implicated with the national along with the transnational, and, as Ravi Vasudevan has argued, as an industry from a third world country, it is also counter to the dominant and is anti-colonial in that sense.[21] Thus, Bollywood is at the nexus of both dominant ideology and hegemony as well as resistance and counterhegemony. The Bollywood remakes of Hollywood films, then, are important sites to study this expression of transnational relations that simultaneously convey aspects that transcend the national and yet are connected to the nation, especially during historical junctures when the nation is evidently discernible in ideological frameworks of the films.

This book aims to contribute to conversations about globalization and Hindi cinema. I argue that Bollywood's reactions to and against the globalization and liberalization of the economy include remakes. The remaking trend gained momentum starting right from 1991, the year Mahesh Bhatt directed *Dil Hai Ke Manta Nahin*, which is a remake of *It Happened One Night*.[22] Further, it is significant, according to one claim, that up to 90 percent of Bollywood films produced in 1993 were remakes (Nayar).[23] While this percentage might be overestimated, the claim itself underlines the growing awareness of audiences regarding the increase in remakes, which indicates both a change in how remakes are talked about by the press and the industry and a connection between the anxieties brought in with the entry of satellite TV and the remaking practice in Bollywood. In their discussion of Hollywood remakes during the studio era in *Dead Ringers: The Remake in Theory and Practice*, Jennifer Forrest and Leonard R. Koos state that the "remake has reappeared whenever audience attendance has been low or threatened because of rival technologies like radio, television, and video" (4). The exponential rise in the number of

Bollywood remakes of Hollywood films might seem to be a similar occurrence, but instead of being a reaction to a threat, as an analysis of these remakes will reveal, their increase is partly a result of how the effects of globalization have made it a new industrial and aesthetic category. As a renewed form, then, Bollywood remakes register the negotiation of culture between the two industries. These cinematic texts are markers of history and ideology as well as sites of transnational negotiations in terms of genre, mode, and industrial conventions. The remake is thus a crucial part of Bollywood's response to the impact of globalization on the Indian economy, a response that is apparent on the remake's form as well as on its content.

Hindi Cinema, Nation, Gender, and Genre

Indianization, the term used by filmmakers and almost all scholars discussing Hindi remakes, conveys how Bollywood remakes are often involved in cultural transformations connected with notions of Indianness, as the industry is associated with a national imaginary. Because it developed alongside "India's nationalist phase" and was then part of Nehruvian modernization, Hindi cinema was "implicated in debates regarding national identity" (Chakravarty 8). But with globalization's effects, and later corporatization, the industry's connections shift, and the remakes, because they translate into the industry's understanding of culture, display that. The paradox of an industry that is transnational and hybrid in nature and yet tries to maintain a sense of national identity has always existed in popular Hindi cinema. From its inception, Hindi cinema has been influenced by multiple factors: the melodramatic mode that it borrows from Parsi theater, the codes of *dharma* and *rasa* that come from Sanskrit theater and the epics, the influence of Hollywood, and other influences like mythologies and Sufism.[24] Hindi film, however, has its own codes and conventions that distinguish the industry from Hollywood. Jyotika Virdi argues that even though Hindi films "embrace Hollywood style elements of linear narrative, with closure and a strong hero who affects that closure, they are adapted to a local sensibility, are topical, and . . . will always exclude Hollywood" (21). Thomas, too, enumerates the elements that characterize Hindi films' distinctiveness from Hollywood films. The importance of emotion; incorporation of songs, dances, and fights;

and loose narrative structure in which dialogue is more important than realism are a few conventions that constitute this difference (Thomas, "Melodrama" 162). These formal differences from the Hollywood films occur due to the distinctive characteristics of what constitutes verisimilitude in the two industries. Hollywood narrative cinema is based in a continuity style that creates verisimilitude and an illusion of realism. Verisimilitude in Hindi cinema, on the other hand, is the product of adherence to the codes and conventions deployed within a melodramatic mode that binarizes good and evil as Indian and Western. In a newly decolonized state, modernization was accompanied by the anxiety of Westernization in the 1950s. Thomas argues that Hindi cinema responded to that anxiety by constructing "a cold, rapacious but exotic West/Other" ("Melodrama" 160). The industrial codes of representation are thus tied to the national and cultural values that Hindi cinema represents. The evil men or villains in the films were Westernized, and the evil women were sexualized (also read as Westernized) vamps.

The selective embrace of Western values by Hindi cinema was also gendered in other ways.[25] Women became the sites where anxieties of the nation got played out in postindependence India. Mehboob Khan's *Mother India* (1957) articulates the close association of nation with gender and popular Hindi cinema in postindependence India. The categories of gender and nation remain linked with popular Hindi cinema, especially regarding films produced after India gained independence in 1947. Sumita Chakravarty provides the first book-length study of postindependence films until 1987 that discusses national identity and Hindi cinema.[26] Jyotika Virdi borrows from Benedict Anderson's conceptualization of a nation as an imagined community and applies it to Hindi cinema in the twentieth century (*Cinematic ImagiNation* 6–7, 32–33). In her book, *The Cinematic ImagiNation*, Virdi argues that cinema offers a way to study the Indian nation not just because it is popular in India, but also because it projects the imagined nation in the terrain of the family, heterosexuality, and community (7). She focuses on gender as one of the key ideological nodes on which this imagined nation rests because ideas of gender, community, and the nation developed alongside each other. The figure of the mother becomes the icon for the national imaginary and becomes the image that is revered as a goddess, but it also becomes the bearer of the burden of Indian tradition by epitomizing values of domesticity, sacrifice, purity, and a great capacity for suffering hardship. Thomas emphasizes this sacred image of the mother as one of the unwritten codes in Hindi cinema. The examples she gives, however, include that of a mother being threatened by the villain as metaphor for tradition and the motherland being threatened by a Western other ("Melodrama" 158). The mother, therefore, is simultaneously a symbol of the nation and of the ideology of the ideal femininity embedded in the values of the woman as mother.[27] The conventions of Hindi cinema are thus closely tied with the melodramatic codes by which an embodiment of ideal femininity becomes the upholder of Indian tradition as the West gets "othered" through the figures of vamps and villains. The burden of representing ideal values as Indianness, however, is not limited to women in Hindi film. In addition to "othering" vamps and villains as Western, these films also present the hero as someone who follows the codes of dharma (duty to society and community) and is implicated in kinship relations.[28] Honor, love, and sacrifice are hallmarks of the hero as well, one who will always sacrifice their personal desires for the filial, familial, or communal good.

Virdi and Thomas are not alone in discussing the centrality of gender, especially via the patriarchal unit of the family, in Hindi cinema and in tracing the figure of the woman as an embattled site upon which colonial and communal battles have been fought (Virdi 13). Monika Mehta ("Globalizing"), Purnima Mankekar, and others refer to a heightening of gender politics in cinema since 1990 whereby the heroine again becomes the upholder of tradition and Indianness.[29] Considering this history in which Hindi cinema's codes of representation are involved in preserving a certain imagined notion of Indianness by creating the West and the Western as its antithesis, the remake of Hollywood film becomes a paradoxical cultural object. It displays an anxiety regarding the preservation of national and cultural traditions in a cultural object that is nonetheless dependent on and borrows from the West. At the same time, the remake represents a contemporary culture that is becoming increasingly globalized. However, with globalization comes a perceived threat to this imagined national consciousness that had been embodied in these traditions that had until this time safely "othered" the West. Delineating the Western as evil becomes increasingly problematic as more Indians travel west and Western industries enter the domestic market: the earlier opposition between tradition and modernity updates to one between Indianness and Westernness, where both are ideological constructions.[30] If the remakes of the early 1990s clung to the codes of verisimilitude that Hindi cinema established in the 1950s, each successive remake presents a more globalized idea of Indianness.

I discuss the case of the 1990s in detail in chapter 1 and argue how the genre of the family film is the perfect receptacle for the remake in that decade. It is in this chapter that I build on the notion of Indianization to define it in terms of industrial conventions, cultural codes, and ideology as these pertain to a notion of Indianness. I also emphasize the importance of Indianization's temporal dimension and therefore ask that it be understood as a process that is affected by both, changing notions of Indianness and a remake's context that affects to what extent it adheres to codes connected to an imagined idea of the nation. Thus, the Indianization of a film can be strongly connected to the nation or expressive of the industry's globalization (or, as is the case most of the time, can be an articulation of different degrees of this negotiation between the national and transnational and between the local and the global), but it needs to be attentive to the historical moment. How filmmakers imagine their audiences is dependent on a host of other factors, such as the regressive turn in the 1990s and the experimentation with gender and form in films after 2000. Changes in the industry in the new millennium shift its identity to what Sangita Gopal designates New Bollywood, thereby ushering in a plethora of new genres as well (*Conjugations* 2).[31] Gopal's book looks at the changes in the film industry in the postmillennial era via the change in the central couple. This ideological shift in mainstream films, but also in the industry itself—where several filmmakers are *hatke* (alternative) or on the fringes between *hatke* and mainstream cinema—takes place in a major way in the field of gender. *Bollywood's New Woman*, edited by Megha Anwer and Anupama Arora, examines the new femininity that is the result of changes in Bollywood after 2000, when the combination of gender and family with the nation is explored by several filmmakers. At times this combination is updated; at other times, it is rejected or ignored. In the introduction, Anwer and Arora build on Rupal Oza's discussion of the figure of the new liberal woman in the films of the 1990s to see how this figure hybridizes the traditional heroine with the vamp and yet to note how postmillennial new women at times represent extreme forms of newness that are disconnected from any Hindustani or Indian lineage (11). These changes in the industry are also felt in another area: that of genre. The ideological codes of existing genres are affected in post-2000 films as well, as filmmakers stretch the boundaries of cultural verisimilitude associated with a genre or just ignore many of the semantic elements that constitute them. These changes are felt even more so in the field of gender as it has been key to some of these codes.[32] Moreover, experimentation with new genres is made possible via the remake. In fact, what we have is similar to the chicken-and-egg question; what came first: changes in the industry or remakes? In other words, do the changes in the industry influence what films can be remade and how (the answer is yes)? And do the remakes introduce new genres, thus changing what the industry looks like (the answer is, also, yes)?

Intertextuality, Genre, and the Bollywood Remake

With genre, we get back to the sticky nature of intertextuality, which is at the heart of remake analysis. Most theorizations of the remake center on the intertextual relationship between a film and its remake that complicate the very notion of originality itself. Gérard Genette in his book, *Palimpsests*, provides a taxonomy that is dependent on the kinds of intertextuality between texts. Starting from intertextuality, which he associates with allusion, he qualifies four other relationships: paratextuality as a relationship between a primary literary text and its surrounding texts, like preface or subtitle, that create a setting for the primary text; metatextuality, where a critical distance and commentary mark the association between the first and second text; architextuality, which defines the intertextual closeness between texts belonging to the same genre; and hypertextuality, which comes closest to discussions of remakes that are near copies (2–5). Hypertextuality is about transformation of a text from a hypotext to a hypertext, what I have been calling a "source text" and its remake. Immediately after delineating these categories, however, Genette points to the blurriness between them. Certainly, the presence of hypertextuality does not automatically erase the presence of intertextual allusions, as I explore in my analysis of *Pyaar To Hona Hi Tha* (chapter 1) or *Kaante* (chapter 3), both close remakes of their source texts or hypotexts. Genres and remakes might seem distinct from each other, but industrial practices of using formulae point to the similarity between them and reveal that architextuality can exist within hypertextuality as well. My discussions of neo-noir in chapter 3 articulate the border crossings between the two categories of genres and remakes. Finally, Genette's isolation of allusions as intertextuality as opposed to hypertextuality, which would include parodies or close remakes, doesn't necessarily disallow nonclose remakes to be thrown out of consideration. Nowhere is this more marked than in cross-cultural remakes, which show the impossibility of the idea of a close remake. To be fair, Genette himself discusses the overlap between these categories in actual texts, thus pointing to the heuristic needs for this taxonomy instead of expressing a desire to force texts to fit certain categories. The taxonomy has proven useful in closely analyzing the aesthetic and ideological relay at work as is obvious from how influential Genette has been on remake scholars.

In *Play It Again, Sam*, one of the first collections seeking to theorize about and understand cinematic remakes, Andrew Horton and Stuart McDougal deliberate on the nature of intertextuality in these films and ask, "Do we simply watch or read these texts?" (2). Remakes thus require an immersive as well as intellectual engagement with similarity and difference. In *Dead Ringers*, another foundational collection of essays on remakes, Jennifer Forrest and Leonard Koos differentiate between different kinds of remakes, contextualize them within Hollywood history, discuss the relationship between remakes and genres, theorize the remake, and interrogate the ideological implications inherent in cross-cultural remakes (1–36). Within this collection, Thomas Leitch uses Harold Bloom's concept of anxiety of influence to point out the oedipal power dynamic inherent between a film and its remake, in which the remake seeks to both pay homage to and to annihilate its predecessor (50). It is this dynamic of intertextuality, through which the film references its source while also adapting to something more current, that is often relevant to a study of cross-cultural remakes. Forrest and Koos, too, differentiate the cross-cultural remake in terms of ideology that has to do with erasing the cultural and linguistic differences of the other as encapsulated in the source text (15).

The intertextuality in Bollywood remakes of Hollywood films and the negotiation of power they involve happen along two axes—one is with the Hollywood films/genres being remade, and the other is the Bollywood films and genres being remade. Therefore, in addition to the aspects of intertextuality, which have to do with defamiliarization, cultural translation and adaptation, and hegemony, examining remakes requires the approach laid out by Constantine Verevis in *Film Remakes*, in which he asks that a remake be understood as an industrial, textual, and critical category because remakes "depend upon a network of historically variable relationships" (2). My hope is that the close analysis of the remakes discussed in this book will provide one avenue into understanding Bollywood's relationship with Hollywood and with its own history. While several taxonomies of remakes differentiate between various kinds of remakes based on the intensity of intertextuality, I broadly follow Leo Braudy's attitude as to what counts as a remake; he argues that the "remake can exist anywhere on an intertextual continuum from allusions in specific lines, individual scenes, and camera style to the explicit patterning of an entire film on a previous exemplar" (327). Thus, the films discussed here are close remakes, loose remakes, and pastiches.

The chapters in *Déjà Viewed* present a historicized analysis of Bollywood remakes of Hollywood films from the early 1990s, when their Indianization is tied to concerns of the nation within a context of globalization and economic liberalization, into the twenty-first century, when the connection to a national imaginary gets splintered as the remake becomes a popular economic product generated by Bollywood filmmakers. Overall, *Déjà Viewed* examines how the remakes register the shifting ideological valences regarding nation, codes of gender, genre, and Hindi film conventions. Therefore, the book approaches remakes in two ways: by historically contextualizing the changing relationship between gender and nation resulting from the advent of globalization in the 1990s and the effect of subsequent changes after 2000 (such as corporatization of the industry, establishment and popularity of multiplexes, transnationalization of production, and mergers with Hollywood studios) and by analyzing through close reading the ideological tensions that the remake articulates. The chapters are chronological, thus charting the changing nature of the remake from unacknowledged imitation to self-reflexive pastiche. The first chapter analyzes the Bollywood remake as a metaphor for the industry's simultaneous embrace and rejection of westernization. The next chapter focuses on the translation of the femme fatale into the Bollywood vamp. The last two chapters analyze masculinity and queerness in remakes that also indulge in auteurist homage and postmodern intertextuality.

Chapter 1, "Indianization and the Bollywood Family Film," contextualizes the remake as an economic category and approaches remaking as Indianization by focusing on the connection between home, nation, and gender in Anees Bazmee's *Pyaar To Hona Hi Tha* (*Love Had to Happen*) (1998), a remake of *French Kiss* (Lawrence Kasdan 1995). I focus on *Pyaar To Hona Hi Tha* (a huge box-office success) because it deals with the West directly and therefore provides an example of the different kinds of films that Bollywood was churning out in the 1990s for its growing diasporic audiences.[33] The film thus ensures its success by borrowing from the Hollywood film, transforming it enough so that there are no copyright violations and then further transforming it within the current formula for success.[34] I explore the Bollywood remake as a site of anxiety about preserving Indian national identity in the context of globalization. The remake is thus proof of the westernization of the economy, the Hindi film industry, and culture. At the same time, the remake emphasizes the importance of traditional values located in kinship relationships and the figure of the woman; it displays the same impetus that characterized Hindi films in the Nehruvian era, by which popular Hindi cinema participated in the modernization of the nation-state in a gendered manner.

In this chapter, I look at Indianness as a gendered construction in 1990s films and analyze Indianization alongside the Bollywood codes that reproduce conservative notions connected with a national imaginary. I argue that Indianization needs to be understood as a process that is contingent on historically shifting understanding of Indianness and on the changing degree of connectedness between the films and an ideology of the nation. *Pyaar To Hona Hi Tha* remakes a Hollywood romantic comedy into the Bollywood family film, which has been a genre understood to project the family as representative of the nation. This close tie with the nation changes in postmillennial remakes; thus, the Indianization in the 1990s gives way in post-2000 remakes to a different kind of Indianization where the ideologies of inherited gendered Indianness are not as dominant in the remake. Even *Pyaar To Hona Hi Tha*, however, already reveals a negotiation between the local, the national, and the global. This chapter, therefore, also analyzes how the remake moves between these axes to produce the nation as transnational.

Chapter 2, "The Vamp and the Femme Fatale: Defamiliarized Femininities in the Bollywood Remake," examines the figure of the femme fatale as a transnational character type. Film noir is a genre that has enjoyed transnational appeal from its very beginnings and has been a dominant genre for Bollywood remakes. This chapter borrows from Carolyn Durham's discussion of the transference and transformation in a cross-cultural remake to analyze the femme fatale in Hollywood's own remakes, in its remakes of French noir films, and in Bollywood remakes of Hollywood noir.[35] I argue that *Jism* (Amit Saxena 2003) and *Murder* (Anurag Basu 2004) combine the noir femme fatale with the vamp of older cinema as a form of Indianization. Since the audiences themselves are now consumers of global products, including films, the remake does not necessarily conservatively cling to fixed ideas of cinematic conventions tied to Indianness. Indianization thus loses its ideological hold on the remaking process as these films produce an intertextual amalgam. The femininities transgress borders of nations, industries, and ideologies through the process of remaking. *Jism* borrows from two Hollywood noir films—*Double Indemnity* (Billy Wilder 1944) and its remake, *Body Heat* (Lawrence Kasdan 1981)—whereas *Murder* remakes the Hollywood thriller *Unfaithful* (Adrian Lyne 2002), which itself is a remake of French New Wave director Claude Chabrol's *La Femme infidèle* (*Unfaithful Wife*) (1969). Through their portrayals of women, these films provide the pleasure of what Horton and McDougal call "defamiliarization" in the remake, thereby engaging the audience in an intellectual "reading" of the character type as a signifier of cross-cultural and cross-industrial intertexts (2). Most significantly, the character type becomes a historical register as well, thus opening up the inherited fixed meanings surrounding the Bollywood vamp and the Hollywood femme fatale as already-transnational inheritances in both contexts.

Chapter 3, "From Remake to Pastiche: Bollywood, Hollywood, and Noir Masculinity," shifts the focus of this book from femininity to masculinity, from mainstream to *hatke* and auteurist cinema, and from remake to pastiche. In this chapter, I analyze masculinity in Abbas-Mustan's *Baazigar* (*Gambler*) (1993), Sanjay Gupta's *Kaante* (*Thorns*) (2002), Navdeep Singh's *Manorama Six Feet Under* (2007), and Sriram Raghavan's *Johnny Gaddaar* (2007). This trajectory reveals how the changes in the industry from the liberalization to the post-liberalization period affect the varying degrees of intertextuality that these films have with their sources.

The cinephilic imagination of Singh and Raghavan in the latter two films and the nod to the source texts set them apart from the previous remakes. *Om Shanti Om* (*OSO*) is another mainstream Hindi film—produced around the same time—that is a postmodern experimentation with intertextuality and pastiche, but where *OSO*'s quotations of the past are always reshot, thus complicating the film's homage to Hindi cinema's past, these two films as noir pastiches quote directly. Instead of discussing them as part of Bollywood (which *Baazigar* and *Kaante* are), I argue that they are examples of *hatke* (alternative) cinema and announce their connections to noir and its notions of masculinity through their cinephilic invocations.

The final chapter, Chapter 4, "'Lihaaf Maang Le' ('Ask for the Quilt'): Queerness in the Cross-Cultural Remake," investigates the intersection of gender and sexuality and the translation of queer identity and desire in comedy remakes that are from two transnational contexts. The comedic mode in the two films (*Dostana* and *Dedh Ishqiya*) is politically charged as it creates a space for the articulation of nonnormative sexuality through a carnivalesque subversion, one made possible through the remake. In both cases, the heavily suggested queer subplot gains dominance over the ideologically heteroconservative main plot. As a remake of the Hollywood film *I Now Pronounce You Chuck and Larry* (Dennis Dugan 2007), *Dostana* (*Friendship*) (Tarun Mansukhani 2008) is placed at the intersection of the Indian and Western ideologies. I engage with the arguments made by many scholars who either view *Dostana* as an example of gender discrimination, in which men are allowed sexual license, or view it as a film that presents homosexuality as a Western construct or even as one that neutralizes the queer readings through the ending, which reveals it to be a mere performance of homosexuality. While these concerns are valid and indicate the political conservatism of this film, I draw attention to the queer politics that are simultaneously at work in it. *Dedh Ishqiya* (*Passionate 1.5*) (India, Abhishek Chaubey 2014), on the other hand, plots a triangulated relationship with Deepa Mehta's *Fire* (Canada, 1996) and Ismat Chughtai's short story "Lihaaf" (Pakistan, 1942). While *Fire* was heavily criticized by right-wing groups for its portrayal of same-sex desire as Indian, and the director was blamed for imposing morally depraved Western constructs on Indian culture, *Dedh Ishqiya* draws attention to the source text of the film as a Pakistani short story, thus indicating a transnational South Asian–inflected context for queerness that actually does not align with Western constructions of queer identities.

1

Indianization and the Bollywood Family Film

> No successful Bombay film-maker ever simply "copies" Western films. Of course, most borrow openly . . . but borrowings must always be integrated with Indian film-making conventions if the film is to work with the Indian audience: no close copy of Hollywood has ever been a hit.
>
> —Rosie Thomas, "Indian Cinema: Pleasures and Popularity," *Screen*

ANEES BAZMEE'S *Pyaar To Hona Hi Tha* (*Love Had to Happen*) (1998) is an unacknowledged close copy of Lawrence Kasdan's *French Kiss* (1995). Despite the disavowal of its source text, the remake's resemblance to the Hollywood film reveals the continuation and transfer of *French Kiss*'s visual and narrative aspects. Although *Pyaar To Hona Hi Tha* does copy plot and images, it transforms the source text in significant ways. In fact, the film is what Thomas Leitch would perhaps call an "update" or "true remake" (48–49) and what Rosie Thomas would call "Indianized" to indicate the text's cultural, industrial, and ideological transformation ("Melodrama" 162).¹ The updating in the film, however, occurs mostly because it crosses cultural and industrial boundaries. An analysis of the film's Indianization reveals how Hollywood and Bollywood function similarly as financial and cultural industries. At the same time, the transformation in this close remake points to the ways in which the two industries are different, particularly as the remake articulates anxieties about gender and nation in the 1990s. The two films, in short, serve different ideological functions in registering the historical moment particular to each film and its respective industry's response to it.

The Bollywood remake of the 1990s is an example of the industry's complicated response to the influence of globalization via the influx of Western programming, economic liberalization, and the large-scale exodus of Indians to the West during the software boom. The Bollywood remake is therefore an industrial category, like genres and sequels, that functions to secure profits. It is an aesthetic commodity that is a product of global capitalism. However, it also dramatizes the perceived threat of the westernization of Indian culture that was particular to the 1990s because of the effects of globalization. For this reason, the Bollywood remake of the Hollywood film represents internally what the culture is experiencing externally—that is, infiltration by the West and India's effort at incorporating Western culture within an ideology of Indianness, that is largely a gendered projection onto, rather than a representation of, society. As a result, Hollywood becomes synonymous with westernization and globalization, and the remake becomes an analogy for the contradictory nature of India's participation in globalization.

Pyaar To Hona Hi Tha aggressively engages with global as well as nationalistic aspects at several levels: through the process of remaking a film from Hollywood; by invoking the genre of the Bollywood family film; and through its first (and very unusual) song number. While most of the film, like other family films of the decade, papers over any inconsistencies between the local and the global, the irreconcilable contradictions erupt at several moments. Nowhere is this more obvious in the film than in its bizarre first song, which occurs on an airplane. "Jo Hona Hai Woh Hona Hai" ("What will happen will happen)" is a stand-alone number. The airplane encounters turbulence, people are frightened, and a song expressing a *que será será* mood fills in the time until the worst of it is over. The visuals, however, are anything but calm. Technically, the song-and-dance number functions as a distraction as the airplane goes through turbulence and then rights itself. In terms of tone, it ostensibly sets the stage for a happy film and assures the viewers that the ending won't be tragic because of how comic the number is. It is a spectacle and is excessive, thus fulfilling the parameters of cinematic appeal for a particular kind of song-and-dance number, but it repels more than it attracts.

Nevertheless, ideologically, it marks the film's transnationalism while defining India as encompassing a variety of types. The passengers on this British Airways flight enroute from France to India hail from various regions of India and from other countries. The plane, then, contains a microcosm of India and the globe marked by different religions as well as races. These variations are often signaled in the song via stereotyped costuming and makeup and through manipulation of sound and iconic images. The passengers seem to be caricatures of their culture and are reduced to visible markers that function as metonyms for their identity—for example, there are a few Hindu pundits with big tilaks on their foreheads; the Muslim man is wearing a traditional cap, has a beard, and is accompanied by wives in burqa; and the Sikh family is signaled by the turbans worn by the man and his kids. The repetition of the costumes here in the several pundits or the women in black burqas, or the five yellow-turbaned kids makes it the stuff of comedy. The international culture is indicated by one person with an Afro and blackface makeup and another person who is a Michael Jackson lookalike (see figures 1.1a and b). The song is also a medley of different flavors: it starts as a typical Hindi song, uses the rhythms and meter of a *qawwali* when it is focused on the Muslim family, and switches to the music of "Macarena" when it shifts to the global passengers.[2] The strange pastiche of song genres and the costuming presents a cultural mixing that celebrates globalization and Bollywood and, significantly enough, occurs in a space that can be seen as a symbol for transnationalism—an airplane. Setting aside the importance of international airlines in attracting diaspora and tourists through product placement, or the obviousness of the airplane in the air in transnational space, the song itself functions to underscore the cross-cultural product that it is bringing to its audiences. Perhaps the song is also welcoming these globalized diasporic Indians and foreigners to Bollywood while simultaneously othering and treating these identities as stereotyped commodities in the global marketplace.

Figures 1.1a and b. Caricaturized people in the song "Jo Hona Hai So Hona Hai." *Source: Pyaar To Hona Hi Tha* (Anees Bazmee 1998).

At the same time, the song appropriates well-known visual and aural signs in a parodic remix of cultures, religions, races, nationalities, songs, and musical genres that are exaggerated for recognition. It is here that the film performatively draws attention to various kinds of borrowings that are otherwise largely hidden in the plot, even though it borrows from the Hollywood film. The song also draws attention to the form of the film that replicates and joins disparate things to make them appear seamless. The parody at its heart indicates a mismatch either via excess (*qawwali* style) or contradiction (macarena music for Michael Jackson/American pop). The song even breaks the illusion of synchronous conjoining of sound and image necessary for spectatorial immersion when the camera focuses on a man crying because he is terrified but the sound that accompanies this image is of a crying baby. It is this act of putting unrelated things together that the film's plot also does—an activity at the heart of a transnational remake—but this strange song performatively highlights the transnational borrowing the film itself is involved in. What we get is a mish-mashed medley of national and global stereotypes, and the rest of the film presents a much more muted form of this combination of a Hollywood genre with a Bollywood one. The film, in a sense, Indianizes from a Hollywood romantic comedy to a Bollywood family film; the song draws attention to the disparate parts as disparate; and the film creates a seamlessness in how it retains and remakes aspects of the American film.

Indianization and Globalization

Indianization has been variously approached by different scholars working in the field of Indian cinema studies. Thomas, while writing about the masala films of the 1970s and 80s,[3] considers Indianization in terms of codes and conventions associated with the melodramatic mode that is dominant in Hindi cinema ("Melodrama" 162–65). Sheila Nayar sees this cross-cultural translation in terms of adaptation and says that these films, "adapted from foreign works, are less remakes than extracted skeletons: plot repositories, molded and shaped for a more sufficient and efficient cultural refilling" (74–75). Tejaswini Ganti discusses remakes in terms of audience desires, rather what filmmakers ascertain would be acceptable to mass audiences ("And Yet My Heart" 143). What we have here are three separate things—one relating to the form (production), second to content (text), and the third to audiences (reception). In each case, culture and ideology accompany the process of cross-cultural remaking. When considering cross-cultural remaking, the form is essential especially if the film crosses industries as disparate as Hollywood and Bollywood. These scholars draw attention to aspects such as mode, characteristics of Hindi film that differentiate it from Hollywood, and cinematic conventions tied to culture.

While the melodramatic mode operates in Hollywood as well, it is an overwhelmingly dominant mode in Bollywood and has its own history of cultural codes associated with it. Other conventions of the Hindi film that remain central despite several changes since 2000 include the following: multiple plots and storylines unlike the linearity of Hollywood plots; song-and-dance numbers that are not relegated just to a single genre; and combination of aspects such as comic interludes, action sequences, tragedy and pathos, and emotional conflicts, in a single film. When Thomas discusses the aspects that underwrite the melodramatic mode in Hindi cinema, she states that what breaks verisimilitude for the audience is cultural conventions connected with the melodramatic universe of the films.[4] Amongst the conventions that she lists are kinship values, emotions, controlled female sexuality, and *usool* ("moral code"). She focuses particularly on the figure of the mother and the villain, one who is sacrosanct and the other who is known for uncontrolled sexuality, but later adds the vamp as a character type similar to the villain (Thomas, "Melodrama" 167–69). The melodramatic universe functions on oppositionalities that align villainy with sexual freedom. These conventions are historically dependent and influence as well as are affected by changing socioeconomic contexts, which have repercussions for the industry, audiences, and the aesthetic form of the films. For example, the target audience in the 1990s was no longer the masses but the diasporic Indians, and the rise of multiplexes beginning in late 1990s and other changes in production shifted that primary audience to urban cosmopolitan crowds after 2000.[5] The exhibition space in terms of multiple screens, smaller seating capacity, and expensive tickets also produced fractured audience groups so that there were different markets for different producers/filmmakers.[6] The form and address of the films before, during, and after the 1990s underwent radical, visible transformation. Globalization of the industry in the 1990s is the catalyst for these changes.

Drawing attention to the hyperglobal influence on remakes, Rashna Wadia Richards' insightful essay complicates the idea of Indianization as understood solely in terms of cultural transformation or as a transformation into Bollywood's cultural codes. She reads several contemporary (post 1990) Bollywood remakes in terms of a radical hybridization of culture and sees them as a coming together of the global and the local. For example, she examines *Kuch Kuch Hota Hai* (Karan Johar 1998) for how it borrows from Hollywood films—including *Some Kind of Wonderful* (Howard Deutsch 1987), *Sleepless in Seattle* (Nora Ephron 1993), and *The Parent Trap* (Nancy Meyers 1998)—but also includes other instances of borrowings that we see in the films from the 1990s to discuss how the film complicates any easy separation of the local from the global and India from the West. She argues against reading the film in terms of mere gendered conservatism or Indianness by noting that when Tina (Rani Mukerji), the diasporic woman, sings a Hindu religious prayer, "Om Jai Jagdish Hare," a Pepsi vending machine is simultaneously visible in a corner of the frame, thus suggesting the coexistence of "the traditional and the modern" ("Glocal Masala Film" 348).

In this chapter, I want to interrogate the nature of this coexistence of the traditional and the modern, which often is the equivalent of the national and the transnational or the local and the global. I build on these approaches to Indianization to anchor it in its historical and industrial context. A remake such as *Pyaar To Hona Hi Tha* uses the form of the family film, a Bollywood genre understood as a response to globalization in the 1990s. However, since the genre also projects the notion of a certain kind of family as a microcosm of the nation, the Indianization in the remake is associated with the ideology of India as a nation. I look at precisely how the global is invoked and how the local is used to produce an idea of the nation as a transnational entity, particularly via the remake. The nation is resurrected as one with malleable borders via this negotiation, and the coexistence of the global/transnational with the local/national can be seen as one of postmodern coexistence or one where the modern and the traditional successfully mingle. However, there are ideological stakes involved in how the global redefines the local and vice versa via this hybridization. It is in the projection of the nation that gender becomes key to understanding how tradition and modernity coexist, and therefore, the national and the global as connected to gender remain central to my inquiry on Bollywood remakes. How is the diasporic woman both a global icon and locally situated in the remake, both a cosmopolitan mobile woman and one who assures the presence of Indianness? In other words, how gender is deployed in this Indianization and how it is constantly redefined and contained anew by a certain projection of Indianness in the remake is a necessary extension of my study.

Indianization, then, is historically contingent on the particular matrix of this negotiation, which is affected by cultural and industrial factors. The next few chapters show how the remaking practice is influenced by the corporatization of the industry, by new auteurs and changes in exhibition spaces that also affect the genres that are introduced, and by changing cultural registers regarding gender and sexuality, as they lose the close ties to the nation. Thus, the "Indian" in Indianization is not geographically bound as the imagined nation is always produced by what lies outside of it; *Pyaar To Hona Hi Tha* indicates how globalization in the 1990s promotes a certain notion of Indianness. An examination of *Pyaar To Hona Hi Tha* also reveals how the remaking itself betrays an idea of Indianness, via the specific cultural codes that it transforms from the Hollywood film. Indianization, then, is also not a static cleaving to an idea of the nation via the remake; rather, it is a production of the nation in global flux. The remake then becomes participant in this discursive construction of the nation.

While I was intrigued that many remakes in the 1990s align well with the genre of the family film, it is my interest in gender that brought me to the topic of Bollywood remakes. An essay I wrote in 2013 addressed the domestic-abuse cycle, which encompasses several Bollywood remakes of *Sleeping with the Enemy* (Joseph Ruben 1991) produced within a short period of time in the early 1990s.[7] Two factors affected these films—influence of the (waning) feminist impulse of the 1980s in India as well as the avenging women cycle of films.[8] But where the energy of these remakes was inward in terms of critiquing patriarchy, I realized that the focus of the majority of 1990s remakes was outward in terms of embracing global capitalism, which has historically aligned well with heteropatriarchy, racism, and colonialism. Religious fundamentalism has also been a vector in the production of Indianness in the 1990s given the rise of Hindu fundamentalism or Hindutva; its influence extends to the seemingly benign Hinduism that permeates the family film.[9] Madhavi Murty argues that "Hindu nationalism in India . . . is sometimes conceptualized as the ideological façade of global capital" (3). She sees its ascent in the 1970s, 1980s, and 1990s, before it gets consolidated in the new millennium (3). There is a sharp difference between the Hindu cultural dominance of earlier films and those of the 1990s. The family film, in particular, erases other religions from the plot of the film. The world of these films remains populated by upper-class, upper-caste, and Hindu characters. The neoliberal turn in the industry then includes religion and conservative religious ideology in connection with gender and patriarchy. However, even as the industry embraces neoliberalism when the state favors global capitalism by allowing development of the free-market economy, it simultaneously underlines that impulse by an ideological (patriarchal) anchoring via the woman, very much opposite to what the domestic-abuse cycle did. While the domestic-abuse cycle looked back to older forms of Hindi cinema, the family film remakes of the 1990s expressed this remaking as part of Bollywoodization, indicating aspects and functions of the industry connected with its globalization. An analysis of *Pyaar To Hona Hi Tha*'s remaking shows the negotiation between gender, nation, and globalization.

The Melodramatic Mode: From Hollywood to Bollywood

As a family film and as a remake, *Pyaar To Hona Hi Tha* emphasizes Bollywood's paradoxical relationship with globalization. Although it clearly profits from remaking *French Kiss*, *Pyaar To Hona Hi Tha* ostensibly rejects globalization and influence of Western values on Indian culture. The film deals with the local/global binary in three ways. First of all, by remaking the popular romantic comedy into a family film, it functions as an industrial product that is involved in attracting the domestic as well as foreign markets. Second, as a remake, the film borrows from a Western text, and the resultant industrial and cultural transformations of the plot resonate with the preservation and maintenance of so-called Indian culture and traditions that the state-sponsored family films were also doing. The choice of this genre to inculcate Indianness is significant because it depends on gendered divisions of the domestic sphere versus the public sphere and because it aligns with patriarchal notions of behavior. Finally, in both *French Kiss* and *Pyaar To Hona Hi Tha*, the melodramatic mode is used to present a utopia that critiques global capitalism even as that utopia cannot be sustained without capitalism. *Pyaar To Hona Hi Tha*'s remaking at the level of industrial codes and generic codes therefore displays the cultural anxiety about globalization and gender while its own diegesis and its status as a global product borrowing from a foreign text undercuts this melodramatic move to reject global capitalism.

Remakes, argue Jennifer Forrest and Leonard R. Koos, can cross genres and are therefore different from genre films (6). When remaking happens across industries as distinct and different as Hollywood and Bollywood, a generic transformation becomes highly likely. In the absence of a genre clearly defined as romantic comedy in Hindi cinema, the Bollywood remakes of romantic comedies usually get transformed into the general masala films that have a little bit of everything—action, romance, comedy, and musical numbers. But *Pyaar To Hona Hi Tha* takes the form of the Bollywood family film, which was a very specific and new Bollywood genre that was dominant in the nineties. Interestingly enough, the melodramatic mode often operates in romantic comedies and is also the dominant mode in popular Hindi cinema and has similar ideological valences. Thus, even though the Bollywood remake crosses genres in this example, it remains within the same mode.

Such a formulation complicates the modal polarity established between Hollywood and popular Hindi cinema by (primarily) scholars of Hindi cinema. Hollywood has been categorized as an industry that functions within the realist mode and has the classical narrative structure. In contrast, scholars of Hindi cinema, including Ravi Vasudevan, use Peter Brooks's conception of the melodramatic mode to argue how it is dominant in Hindi cinema. There are two problems with such a point of view. One has to do with how the realist mode is assumed to indicate immersion into the world of the film versus melodrama, which is known for its potential for a subversive viewing practice. Much scholarship on Hollywood melodrama talks about its excess, which can rupture the narrative and therefore audience immersion in the film (Kristin Thompson 517). Auteurs, known for their mastery of the melodrama genre, such as Douglas Sirk, were heavily influenced by German expressionism, which is visible in the campy surfeit of their style. Even women's films from the 1930s produce emotional excess via pathos, suffering, tears, and incongruity, thus separating melodrama as a genre from other Hollywood films, which are argued to function within the immersive realist mode. Hindi cinema still shows up as Hollywood's opposite because of the various ways in which emotion and excess saturate the films. But Hindi cinema also draws attention to how immersion is also an effect of codes of viewing that get naturalized over time, including the conventions of the realist as well as melodramatic mode. The melodramatic excess is not jarring for an Indian audience in the same way as it would be if it were included in an otherwise mostly realist Hollywood film. Unlike in Hollywood films, immersion here is not necessarily because of transparency—or tight continuity editing and storyline—but exists despite the excess that makes the audience aware of being the audience.[10]

Second—and this is true for how melodrama and realism have been both theorized and contested by scholars of Hollywood cinema—seeing melodrama in terms of excess and realism in terms of immersion pits the two modes as mutually exclusive. However, the presence of a realist mode does not in fact cancel out the presence of a melodramatic mode or vice versa; the two modes can coexist within one film, as is the case with many Hollywood films.[11] Linda Williams argues that the melodramatic mode has always been present in Hollywood films (*Playing the Race Card* 54). The commonality of mode between the Hollywood rom-com and the Bollywood family film, then, points to the shared aspects, thus undoing understandings of the two as aesthetically opposite.

The Bollywood remake facilitates a nuanced understanding of the similarities and differences between the two industries. For instance, the genres of Hollywood romantic comedy and the Bollywood family film borrow from melodrama the will to resolve all contradictions in a perfect ending. A rom-com often ends with a marriage or a coming together of the (usually heterosexual) couple that promises a wedding as a future next step. The family film uses the marriage of the hero and heroine to emphasize the importance of the patriarchal family unit. This seeming similarity in the two films because of mode and genre, however, still allows for widely disparate films. For example, *Kuch Kuch Hota Hai* is a very loose Bollywood remake of *Some Kind of Wonderful*, as compared to *Pyaar To Hona Hi Tha*, which is much more similar in plot to *French Kiss*. Yet, *Pyaar To Hona Hi Tha* resonates very differently from its Hollywood source despite its closeness to the Hollywood film. The necessary industrial and cultural transformation points to the insufficiency of the critique leveled at Bollywood remakes as mere imitations. Not every Hollywood film can be remade, and the producers often choose a film that can be easily realized and sold.[12] For most remakes, this selection by the producers is significant in revealing how the two industries understand and hail their audiences. Furthermore, the genre and the mode of the source text and the remake highlight their global appeal as well because the two industries target both national and international markets.

That being said, the cultural differences in the two industries affect the conventions within which the melodramatic mode operates in *French Kiss* and *Pyaar To Hona Hi Tha*. In *French Kiss*, the moral legibility of melodrama is clearly discernible in how the film separates vice from virtue and ends in a space of innocence. *Pyaar To Hona Hi Tha* translates the Hollywood film very carefully but also adds moments of excess. These additions to the remake, however, do not produce a difference in the degree of the melodramatic mode. Rather, the cultural contexts and history of the development of melodrama in the two industries are the reason for the variations between them.

The melodramatic mode in Hindi cinema borrows from Parsi theater as well as from forms of classical dance and the theories of dharma and *rasa*. The moral legibility of Western melodrama that Parsi theater brings in combines with the personal moral codes of dharma that underwrite virtue in Hindi cinema. Furthermore, cultural verisimilitude, which is important in Hindi cinema, includes certain melodramatic codes: the importance of kinship relations, brotherly love and respect, and the importance of sacrifice of personal desire for something higher.[13] Individualism is usually seen as selfish and self-aggrandizing, and it is often associated with Western values, against which Indian values are defined. In *French Kiss*, Luc and his brother are at odds with each other because Luc had slept with his brother's fiancée. He had also lost his lands to his brother in a gambling bet. So, when Luc returns from Canada, his brother welcomes him with a punch, and the two scuffle. *Pyaar To Hona Hi Tha* changes this filial situation completely while retaining the visual similarity of the scene: Shekhar's brother punches him when he sees him, and the brothers grapple with each other. However, their interaction is viewed by the village people with a certain indulgence, thus presenting a preferred interpretation of the scene as an expression of love, as though they are reliving their boyhood memories by hitting each other. The brother hits Shekhar because he has missed him; Shekhar has been gone for a long time and hasn't really kept in touch. The same scene, while remade to look visually similar, rings in a brotherly bond quite opposite to the relationship between Luc and his sibling.

Since it is the dominant mode in popular Hindi cinema, the melodramatic mode is deeply implicated in the interconnecting ideologies about gender and nation that the industry has been associated with since before India's independence. It presents an ideal moral universe that associates goodness and morality with Indianness and evil and decadence with "rapacious" Westernness.[14] Often, the hero is allowed to move between these two poles because he is the symbol of modern Indian identity. The heroine, however, is not allowed the same freedom and has to embrace the role of the sacrificing, dutiful, and chaste wife. While these women seem modernized as well, anxiety about these mobile, modern women is often responsible for conservative endings even if the diegesis gives them the space to express their desires—sexual and otherwise. As a result, the films from the 1990s fall back into the colonial patterns that postcolonial theorist Partha Chatterjee has laid out. In discussing these films' diasporic heroes (as wealthy and yet possessing the essence of Indianness), Priya Jaikumar mentions experiencing a sense of déjà vu while watching the films because they are "reminiscent of similar periods when the nation encountered the market forces and fashion of the West" (27). She uses examples from as far back as 1934 as instances of "when popular Hindi films responded with narratives where 'Indianness' was defined against a corrupt West, with the abstractions frequently embodied in female characters and their choices" (27). Gender was mobilized in the postindependence films of the fifties to resist the threat of westernization that modernization promised—the ideal Indian woman became the safekeeper of Indian traditions so that men could participate in the modernization of the nation-state.[15] Given that this argument has been made about preindependence films, postindependence films, and now again with the 1990s family films, the patriarchal and gendered manner of these responses perhaps now forms a myth of colonialism in India, a myth that gets renewed each time a certain notion of Indianness is engaged with by cultural texts. Each historical moment of excessive transnational activity with the West results in a conservative, though updated, turn.

Globalization in the 1990s renewed anxieties about gender and culture, and the remakes in this decade reveal the industry's mobilization of related tropes to produce a certain notion of an Indianness that is uncorrupted despite the danger of westernization. *Indianization*, the term I have been using for remaking in this time period, not only indicates the cultural transformation that is attendant in the remake, but also the close ties of the industry with an idea of Indian culture. The use of this term rests on the assumption that popular Hindi cinema attempts to be the national cultural industry of India and tries to represent the nation.[16] Therefore, the connection between nation, Indian culture, and the industry, while ideologically problematic, is not arbitrary. This connection, as mentioned previously, is not static and changes in intensity. Loosely speaking, it was very strong in the postindependence decade of the 1950s but then waned in the 1960s. The state was critiqued via the angry-young-man films of the 1970s, and Amitabh Bachchan's stardom therefore aligned the idea of the nation with the working class. Many radical films were released in the 1980s; these films questioned the dynamics of gender, class, and patriarchy that usually support the ideal of nationness. Several filmmakers were critiquing patriarchy; for example, Shyam Benegal, who is known for his middle cinema, was producing films, such as *Bhumika* (1977), that provoked questioning of the status quo.[17] While family and kinship relations continued to be important in Hindi cinema, the women's movement in the 1980s resulted in films that were quite antipatriarchal.[18] At another level, many directors started pushing the limits of the state censor board by producing films that showed too much skin and included extremely suggestive song-and-dance numbers.[19] The 1990s present the opposite via patriotic war films or family films, each portraying the nation explicitly or implicitly as Hindu, upper class, and patriarchal.

Family Film

In the 1990s, Bollywood started producing films that "wove a happy marriage between Indian 'traditions' and the global market" (Mehta, "Globalizing" 136). The melodramatic polarizations I mentioned in the previous section are revisited as well as updated in the 1990s through the family film in its presentation of a mix of global aspirations and emphasis on the importance of Indian traditions. These traditions, which stand in for Indian culture, restore parental authority (of fathers, in particular) and regress into gender divisions that are deeply problematic. These films reinstate the connection between the Hindi film industry and the nation, which had become tenuous. Monika Mehta's analysis of these family films echoes Sumita Chakravarty's argument about the gendered nature of postindependence films, where women become upholders of tradition and men are representative of modernizing the state. She says, "In these [family] films, women become pivotal for the production of the patriarchal Indian family and men are charged with spreading seeds of liberalization within and beyond the borders of the Indian national state" (Mehta, "Globalizing" 143). In the 1990s, the state actively renewed interest in the industry in order to attract foreign investment (by Indians who had settled abroad) in the country.[20] Radhika Desai argues that Bombay cinema had lost its feel for the national pulse in the 1980s and that in the 1990s, "when it found that pulse again, it poured everything it had into amplifying it, adopting new themes and tropes and even creating new genres" (44). She notes the emerging NRI (nonresident-Indian) genre, so called because it targets the Indian diaspora abroad. I prefer Mehta's term *family film* because of the importance given to a certain notion of family in these films, which has implications for the diaspora and for the audience at home who are in the process of understanding national and cultural identity within globalized modernity.

These family films share some traits with the Hollywood family film but constitute a very different category. Robert Allen defines the family film as "the discursive marker for a set of narrative, representational and institutional practices designed to maximize marketability and profitability across theatrical, video, licensing and merchandising markets by means of what we might call cross-generational appeal" (114). Hollywood family films occupy a broad spectrum of genres but share the ratings of G, PG, and sometimes PG-13. Designed to have mass appeal, these films were aimed at both children and parents and were made to be blockbusters in the 1960s and 1970s.[21] The rise in births in the 1980s and the popularity of the VCR made these films very lucrative for the studios as more and more parents were watching them at home with their children.

Bollywood family films are similar to Hollywood family films in so far as these are suitable for all ages; both tend to provide clean entertainment that can be watched by the entire family together. That, however, is not why the latter are called "family films." The Hollywood family film does not necessarily deal with the family, but the Bollywood family film is so named because of its ideological emphasis on family values rooted in a joint family system. While *Hum Aapke Hain Koun . . . !*, about a family located within India, is among the first few family films, most of these—such as *DDLJ*, *Kuch Kuch Hota Hai*, *Pardes (Foreign Land)* (Subhash Ghai 1997), or *Kabhi Khushi Kabhie Gham/K3G* (*Sometimes There's Happiness, Sometimes Sadness*) (Karan

Johar 2001)—are about the diaspora. In light of worries about the splintering of families resulting from the exodus of young Indians to Western countries, these films serve as reminders of the ideal family, in which the children love and respect their elders and happily coexist with the extended family, emphasized through celebratory events which bring the family together.[22] In addition, these family films have certain other tropes that privilege a classed notion of family. These tropes include diasporic Indians as models, upper-caste rituals, family as social institution, ideological valorization of certain kinds of émigrés, the cultural authenticity of these groups as the privileged form of nationalism, and the resurgence of the idea of the woman as the repository of tradition that is now upper caste and upper class (Desai 53–60). The Hindu family values that are affirmed here are both similar to earlier ways in which a gendered national identity was emphasized in postindependence films—*Shree 420* (Raj Kapoor 1955) is one such example—and also expressive of the 1990s assertion of nationalism through which other identity categories are either othered or erased altogether.[23] The genre of the family film re-creates the construct of the nation often through this Hindu family unit and gender plays a huge role in plugging the rift between tradition and modernity, and between the local and the global, that these films try to stitch together. The remakes of the 1990s were produced in this context and depend on similar gendered tropes to Indianize the foreign text.

Pyaar To Hona Hi Tha is similar to other family films such as *DDLJ* in defining the hero as one who respects Indian culture and in deploying the woman as the custodian of culture and tradition. By presenting the woman as an ideal because of her understanding and preservation of tradition or Indianness, *Pyaar To Hona Hi Tha* allays the twin anxieties brought in by globalization: anxieties about the loss of the imagined Indian culture and the corruption of women by Western values. The concepts of the home, gender, and the nation are brought together to articulate and dispel these anxieties but in a way that both continues and interrupts the family film.

From Rom-Com to Family Film: Politics of Gender and Nation

The generic characteristics of the romantic comedy are generally amenable to the codes and conventions of popular Hindi cinema and are the reason why this is one genre that was occasionally remade even before the 1990s.²⁴ *Pyaar To Hona Hi Tha* follows the story of *French Kiss* quite closely and was successful at the box office. In addition, as I briefly mentioned before, the genre of the Bollywood family film has a lot in common with the romantic comedy, and the plot of *French Kiss*, in particular, comes very close to the generic codes of the Bollywood family film. In these two films, the melodramatic mode operates to reveal the implication of the two genres with the ideologies about gender and space, particularly evinced through the endings. Often, the endings in melodramas are seen as false endings or false happy endings because they seem forced; they are unable to fully suture the gaps created by the ideological oppositions the films reveal. At the very least, they seem excessive and often lay bare the workings of dominant ideology. The endings in both of these films have progressive political potential because they critique global capitalism. At the same time, though, the gender politics the films employ to articulate this critique complicate that potential.

French Kiss is a romantic comedy starring Meg Ryan and Kevin Kline. The story follows Kate (Ryan) as she flies from Canada to France in an attempt to win back her fiancé, Charlie, who has been ensnared by a French siren, Juliette. Kline plays the role of Luc, a French thief who sits next to her on the plane and helps her forget her aerophobia by involving her in a verbal spat regarding her relationship with Charlie. Luc surreptitiously slips a diamond necklace into her bag to avoid being caught on arrival. From this point on, their encounters enact the convention of what Mike Bygrave calls the "meet cute," which is Hollywood's traditional way of getting two strangers together until they fall in love.²⁵ The pretext is Luc's need to retrieve the diamond necklace from Kate's bag; to facilitate the retrieval, he accompanies her and tries to help her win back Charlie. In the process, they walk around the streets of Paris, spend some time with Luc's family in rural France, and finally realize that they love each other, but neither of them admits it. Knowing that prison awaits Luc if he does not return the necklace, Kate pretends to sell it at Cartier (but actually returns it to the policeman who has been tracking Luc) and gives him her own savings instead so that he can buy a vineyard.

Pyaar To Hona Hi Tha follows the same plotline. Sanjana (Kajol) is presumably a second-generation Indian living in France. She has to overcome her fear of flying and travel to India to retrieve her errant fiancé, Rahul. On the plane, she meets Shekhar (Ajay Devgn), who tries to smuggle in a stolen necklace by putting it in Sanjana's purse. Bombay replaces Paris, a farm replaces the vineyard, and the film ends with Sanjana and Shekhar uniting. Apart from the changes in locations, there are changes at the level of form. The components of the masala in Bollywood include song-and-dance numbers and a little bit of everything that will appeal to most audiences. For example, the film adds a comic section in which Sanjana and Shekhar play a prank on Rahul by making him believe that Sanjana is about to inherit a fortune. Rahul, soon after, is rendered unsuitable because his sudden interest in Sanjana as a result of this fake information shows him to be motivated purely by greed and individual self-interest. This scene generates a lot of humor as Rahul makes a fool of himself in trying to pursue Sanjana. In another scene, robbers with a gun grab hold of Sanjana to ensure everyone obeys them, thus adding suspense and action. Shekhar jumps to rescue her and therefore resembles the character type of the hero. He may be on the other side of the law but morally behaves according to the codes of dharma and therefore is legible as a hero. Perhaps the most essential element that *Pyaar To Hona Hi Tha* borrows from the romantic comedy is the heterosexual couple's romance. This trope lies at the heart of romantic comedy and is a necessary component of the masala of popular Hindi film as well. In the Bollywood family films, however, it is not one of the elements; rather, it is the organizing trope that drives the narrative. The family film celebrates family through the marriage of the central couple. The narrative resolution in romantic comedy tends to lean toward marriage or the promise of marriage of the central couple after they overcome the obstructions they encounter. There are crucial differences—the romantic comedy locates the happy ending in the coming together of the couple and is very individualistic in that sense, whereas the family film propagates the ideology of the extended family as a unit through this union. Traditional family values get asserted when the family film restores parental authority; values kinship relations; and, through the couple, often brings together families and therefore presents the idea of a communal family unit.

That said, the importance given to family in the genre of the romantic comedy is of particular interest for Bollywood filmmakers because the family functions as a social and ideological institution in popular Hindi cinema as well as in family films. Romances arguably display the tension between individual desires and social obligations, and they validate the individual over the social and the communal.[26] The resolution of romantic comedies often promises a compromise through marriage, which is a social and legal contract. The romantic comedies of the 1990s emphasize the ideological weight that is attendant in the Bollywood films as well. Catherine Preston locates the rise in Hollywood romances from 1990 to 1996 in the political ascendancy of the Republican Right and the "new traditionalists" who wanted entertainment with family values (233). Among the conventions she lists are those that lend themselves particularly well to Bollywood family films: "assumption of marriage at the end, absence of sex before realization of true love," and "very little emphasis on the display of the female star's body" (233–35). Family films produced by Bollywood promised good, clean entertainment that promoted the sanctity of family and its hierarchies. Further, these family films also functioned to correct the individualism of the Hindi romantic films of the late 1980s, which were dismissive of the larger family unit.[27]

Meg Ryan films in particular are a good source for Bollywood family film. Evans explores the star-genre intertextuality between Meg Ryan and the romantic comedy to argue that her characters desire "deep confinement in the closet of family life" (191). As opposed to other romantic comedies, in which female desire for love often finds completion in the promise of a wedding, Ryan's characters want something more. In *French Kiss*, this is certainly true. The Meg Ryan character, Kate, mentions the existence of her own family in passing but behaves more like an orphan for whom the families of the two men are obvious attractions. In the case of Charlie, she seems to be an integral part of his family and even views their interference in her life as evidence of their love. She calls his mother "Mom," is best friends with his sister, and calls them for emotional support when she sees Charlie with Juliette. Where Luc is concerned, his family and the vineyard motif add to his charm and to his stability as her potential future life partner. Her stay with his family is a turning point in the narrative because she sees an aspect of Luc that she had not seen before: a depth to his character that is revealed when he interacts with his family and shows her the vineyard he wants to own.

Pyaar To Hona Hi Tha intensifies the importance placed on family in order to assert traditional values that are gendered. In *French Kiss*, Luc's suitability for Kate in the film depends on his closeness to nature and to the family (Evans 203). The scene in which he and Kate spend a few hours in his village is crucial for Kate to see him in a new light. However, where one scene in *French Kiss* suffices to show him as rooted in rural, family life, the remake expands this section of the film. It is not just family values that get conveyed in the Hindi film; rather, Sanjana's ability to fit in with the family and understand them becomes the focus. This aspect of the remake achieves the film's Indianization through Sanjana's "Indianization." The remaking, in turn, makes the woman the site for tradition because she is pivotal, and her character transforms and adheres to the Bollywood codes and conventions related to the Indian culture that is being propagated.

A song-and-dance number that takes place in Shekhar's village encapsulates this Indianization. The number functions industrially as a Bollywood convention and is in line with what can be considered a wedding song. The occasion is the engagement ceremony for Shekhar's sister, Chutki, and the number conveys multiple things: it reveals the unconscious articulation of desire between Shekhar and Sanjana, emphasizes the joy that attends the coming together of the community through song and dance, and shows Sanjana's comfort with Indian clothes and Indian values. Sanjana sings and dances with the entire extended family. The change in Sanjana's clothing from Western wear to Indian attire is accompanied by a change in character from shy, panicked woman to one who seems to have a newfound confidence through association with this family. At the same time, Sanjana becomes aware of her own femininity and gains an understanding of her position in the hierarchical unit of a family; she is now demure and more deferential. Her transformation then continues even when she switches back from traditional clothes to her own Western clothes; she retains the values, which include being respectful of elders in the family and caring about the problems that Shekhar's family is encountering. In other words, her movement from the beginning of the film to the end completes her development from an individualist to a person espousing a familial ideological position. Therefore, when she gives up all her savings for Shekhar and his family later, it does not come as a surprise. She fulfills the ideal of the sacrificing woman and the upholder of culture and tradition in Hindi films, albeit she makes this sacrifice in a very different way than Kate does in *French Kiss*. She uses her money—she is the agent of global capitalism here—to save the family and their rural land, not solely to support the dreams of her love interest.

The remake borrows from the source text the good/evil binary of the main characters. The perfection that the remake promises as its resolution and the creation of clear binaries betray the workings of the melodramatic mode in *French Kiss*. Peter Evans argues that "romantic comedy refuses to be exclusively sustained by reality principles—however much it is regulated by them—and, for all modernity's anxieties about commitment and the vicissitudes of desire, still seeks perfection" (197). According to Brooks, a Manichaean moral order characterizes the melodramatic mode (17). Ideologies about gender and nation are invoked in both as the films establish moral polarizations through the characters. The masculine hero Luc/Shekhar is pitted against the greedy and weak Charlie/Rahul, and the good woman Kate/Sanjana, against the evil sexualized predator Juliette/Nisha.

Melodramatic Binaries and Gender

Both films ensure that the men, like the women, are clearly recognizable as good and evil according to the particular generic and industrial conventions. Initial impressions of both Luc and Shekhar indicate their unsuitability—they are both crooks—but both films utilize the trope of conversion of the right man into the romantic hero. Part of Luc's charm is his sexual appeal, which is established by references to his sexual promiscuity; he is the conventional rake who gets reformed by true love. He has a devil-may-care attitude; his friends are petty thieves; he consorts with women; and he even sleeps with his brother's fiancée. His character undergoes a transformation when Kate enters his life. Luc gets established as the romantic hero of a Hollywood romantic comedy, but the same behavior would make Shekhar unsuitable as the hero of a Bollywood family film. In fact, it would make him resemble the villains of films from the 1970s and 1980s.[28] Other family films such as *DDLJ* and *Pardes* set up binaries of good and evil according to male sexual morality as well, where sexual looseness would associate a character with villainy. Therefore, the transformation of the hero in the remake of *French Kiss* deals with the way in which Shekhar's masculinity is made different from Luc's by deemphasizing the sexual innuendos that surround Luc.[29]

Luc's promiscuity establishes him as the naughty rake, in line with the genre of romance, but the remake transforms Shekhar into someone who will risk his life to protect Sanjana from a criminal. Both

Luc and Shekhar love their family and care about their land. Opposed to these two are Charlie and Rahul, who seem weak in comparison to Luc and Shekhar, respectively. Charlie is the genre's convention of the wrong man who needs to be discarded before the woman finds the right man. He fits Evans's description of the "secondary wooer" in Meg Ryan romantic comedies, who is "too colonised by consumerist ethos to earn the favour of a modern heroine" (203). Charlie is attracted by glitz and glamour, and, in many ways, Juliette is just another shiny new object for him; he seeks immediate gratification like the ideal consumer. Therefore, the difference between Luc and Charlie is also an ideological one. Where Luc stands for the pastoral world, family values, and love of land, Charlie represents selfishness and consumerism.

Rahul, the NRI, comes off even worse than Charlie. Where in one scene Charlie is annoyed by his family's constant interference in his life, Rahul seems not to have—and not to care that he doesn't have—a family. His lack of appreciation of family values is indicated by the fact that he doesn't mention his family in the film. Like Sanjana, he might be an orphan, but the film never mentions that. Therefore, he represents only individual and individualist desires. His desire for Nisha is based in both physical desire and material desire for the money and luxury she represents. That is why he is quick to transfer his attentions to Sanjana and beg for her forgiveness when (because of a trick played by Shekhar) he believes she is going to inherit a fortune. His greed makes him come across as completely self-serving and spineless. He is associated with the hedonism and self-aggrandizement that are also associated with Nisha. As a couple, then, they represent a lifestyle that is urban, cosmopolitan, and globalized, whereas Sanjana and Shekhar stand in sharp relief for their values associated with home and family, prized above any self-serving wants. The Bollywood film has updated the older conventions of Indian and Western, but whereas the NRI hero is usually the prized protagonist in films such as *DDLJ*, here the protagonist is rooted within the geographically bounded space of India, and the NRI Rahul is discredited as someone with Western values. On the other hand, Nisha, who lives in India, is presented as westernized, while Sanjana, who is the NRI woman, is seen as more Indian. In some ways, then, the remake splinters any easy understanding of Indianness as located within a certain space; rather, it aligns Indianness within inherited patriarchal conventions of gender. However, unlike most Bollywood films, this remake translates the central role of the heroine of the romantic comedy even as it updates the oppositionalities of the rom-com into those of Hindi cinema conventions.

In the Hollywood film, France is both the exoticized other and the place for romance. Juliette is French, and her sexualization and objectification are contrasted against Kate, who appears as naïve and innocent. Robert Shandley sees *French Kiss* as a reappearance of the runaway romances that Hollywood produced in the late fifties and sixties. He argues that in these romances, "Europe is often the place for American sexual awakening and self-discovery" (xiii). The repressed Kate, whom we see in Canada, the one Luc accuses of being sexually cold, undergoes a transformation. A change in her visual appearance emphasizes the change in her personality as well. An oversized white T-shirt hanging out of her jeans replaces the tucked-in shirts, belted trousers, and layers of clothes that previously cocooned her. The tightly wound image she presented gives way to carefree happiness and an embrace of all things French. The change in her appearance clearly underlines the sexual freedom France represents. Kate gives in to abandon as she gorges on cheese and then falls sick, perhaps realizing the limits to this freedom as well.

On the one hand, France seems to make her (an American woman) become more open and feminine; on the other, the film makes French women seem excessive in their sexuality. Kate summarizes the femininity represented by Juliette as "mysterious, sexy, and manipulative," as opposed to herself, whom she characterizes as someone who puts "the corresponding face to the corresponding emotion." Ryan's star text also plays a role here in establishing the polarities between the two characters. According to Evans, "Meg Ryan provides the safe-sex alternative to some of her rivals. For every siren out there, there is a Meg Ryan character . . . with a friendly grin" (193). Therefore, Kate's sexual liberation is accompanied by a childish innocence emphasized by the whiteness of the shirt and her pixyish appearance. Except for one scene, in which she looks beautiful in a dress, her clothes are jeans and loose shirts, contrasting with those of the "siren" Juliette, whose body is always on display, encased in tight, revealing clothes. Thus, while the French experience is liberating for the American girl, France itself is still exoticized and othered through the hypersexualized French woman. Moreover, the film makes a direct correlation between Juliette's threatening sexuality and her sexual availability. In comparison, Kate is the heroine of the romantic comedy, and therefore sex does not factor in until an emotional commitment has been established between Luc and her.[30]

Pyaar To Hona Hi Tha's Nisha is very similar to Juliette in her sexual availability and her objectification. She is the convention of westernized Indian woman against which is pitted the ideal femininity of Sanjana.[31] Technically, Juliette and Nisha should not be seen as evil simply because the two men fall in love with them. However, they are portrayed as having dangerous sexualities, and their relationships are seen as primarily sexual rather than loving. As melodramatic types, these women are rendered manipulative and evil as opposed to the heroines, who are virtuous. Nisha's life is comprised of parties and leisure activities. Her life of consumption is further underlined by selfishness, snobbery, and cattiness. Her character seems to be directly connected to her devouring sexuality because she is ultimately only self-serving. Sanjana seems naïve in comparison to Nisha, who is in control. Nisha is not just the sexualized object; she uses her sexuality to have control over Rahul and is therefore powerful as well as aligned with monstrous and castrating femininity.

Contradictory Interpellation and Gender

Early on in the film, *Pyaar To Hona Hi Tha* translates a scene from *French Kiss*. In *French Kiss*, Luc realizes that Kate is scared of flying and engages her in a verbal exchange that riles her up and makes her forget she is on a plane.

> Luc: Did you ever think that maybe it is not the airplane. Maybe it is something else that you're afraid of?
>
> Kate: What do you mean?
>
> Luc: It is not the plane you are afraid of. I know your type. You're afraid to live, to really live. You're afraid of life, you're afraid of love, you're afraid of sex.
>
> Kate: That is ridiculous.

Luc: I can tell that from looking at your face and the way you dress, with your little white buttons all the way to the top . . .

Luc continues to focus on her sexual conservativeness, and Kate responds by saying, "You don't know anything about me. And Charlie never complained." As she continues, the plane's takeoff is completed, and Luc draws her attention to the beautiful scenery visible below.

The scene functions very much like a meet cute. When Luc accuses Kate of sexual prudery, she hotly denies it and instead accuses him of fearing intimacy. The accusation fits within Ryan's star text as a girl next door and at the same time indicates potential for mutuality of desire because of the sexual tension the scene conveys. A slight addition to the scene in the remake adds layers of concerns about ideal femininity that are also connected with Kajol's stardom, particularly as tied to the genre of the family film. A similar conversation has a different connotation because of how it is contextualized and because of Shekhar's first response to Sanjana. The moment the airplane starts moving, Sanjana covers her ears with her hands and mutters her own lyrics to the music of another Bollywood song, "Duniya ri Duniya" ("Oh World, you are good"), from the film *Trimurti* (Mukul Anand 1995). The song's lyrics articulate how the world is good, but the people in it are not. She sings, "India ri India, very good very good; India waale, very bad very bad. Mera Rahul, very very good, Uski girlfriend very bad very bad" (India India very good very good; people from India very bad very bad. My Rahul, very good very good; his girlfriend, very bad very bad). Then she turns to Shekhar, who is watching her, and says, "Sorry, it's my first time on an airplane." She proceeds to explain that she is on the plane despite her fear because her fiancé, Rahul, is in the clutches of another woman, Nisha, and she is going to get him back.

Shekhar: Dekhne mein tum theek thak ho; to tumhara mangetar tumhein chhor kar kyun chala gaya? (You look okay, so why would your fiancé leave you for another woman?)

Shekhar: Aur koi wajah toh nahin . . . Mera Matlab hai shaadi se pahle . . . (Is there another reason . . . I mean . . . anything before you got married . . . ?) (The suggestion that

Sanjana might have had sex is conveyed via how Shekhar utters the words and trails off instead of completing the question).

SANJANA (*offended*): Ai mister—mangni ki hai who alag baat hai, lekin maine Rahul ko kabhi apne paas aane nahin diya hai! (Hey Mister, I might be engaged to him, but I have never let Rahul come close to me in that way!).

SHEKHAR (*nodding*): Main samajh gaya . . . Modern dress pahan rakha hai par khayalat bahot puraane hain . . . Woh bhi bechara insaan hai. (Now I understand . . . You are wearing a modern dress, but your thinking is very old fashioned and outdated . . . Poor thing . . . he is human too.)

SANJANA (*very angry*): Tum mujhe nahin jaante, Rahul ko nahin jaante; aur hamaare bare mein bake hi jaa rahe ho. (You don't know me, you don't know Rahul, but you keep on uttering nonsense about us).

Shekhar conjectures that Rahul is not interested in her because she slept with him already and that there is no reason for him to pursue her anymore. When she hotly denies it, he says that maybe Rahul left her because she hadn't been sexually available to him. Instead of denying her sexual coldness (like Kate does), Sanjana denies the presence of any sexual activity altogether. Angry at Shekhar's first insinuation that she would sleep with a man before getting married, she emphasizes, "Main koi aisi vaisi ladki nahin huun" (I am not that kind of a girl). Her response indicates that she understands the Indian values whereby virginity and chastity are important for a woman. Shekhar's reply to this assertion is borrowed from the source text: "Oh, Now I know. You are wearing a modern dress, but your thinking is very old fashioned and outdated." Here, he echoes Luc's perspective because it locates negativity in this kind of modesty and blames the woman's lack of sexual availability for the man's straying. By explicitly connecting Western clothes with being modern and therefore sexually liberated, Shekhar implicitly associates traditional values with being old fashioned. This exchange results in several (contradictory) interpretations. First, instead of making Sanjana seem like a prude, Shekhar's comment presents her as someone who can bridge the split between modernization and tradition: the twin values that now need to cohabit within the mobile Indian woman. This conversation between the couple asserts Sanjana's sexual innocence and purity (and therefore her Indian sensibility) despite the westernized life her clothes symbolize—something that had previously been established for Kajol in another family film, *DDLJ*. Second, it draws attention to the doubled and contradictory interpellation at work here. If Sanjana had sex with Rahul, then she's too modern; if she didn't, she is too conventional and backward. The impossibility of the two things being true simultaneously reveals the contradiction at the heart of this remake: she can't be modern and conventional, Western and Indian, at the same time. Finally, since the conversation is not meant to be taken too seriously, and since it is performative in how Shekhar engineers it to deflect Sanjana's attention from the reality of the airplane, it ultimately points to inherited ideologies about femininity that form the unconscious of the genre and the 1990s. In so doing, it makes obvious the double bind and the impossibility of a fusion of the Western and the Indian, the global and the local, even though the resolution of the film's plot promises a happy coexistence of the two: Sanjana cannot be both virginal and sexually experienced, but she can have modesty and be a modern woman. The local is made possible by the global, and a negotiation with what is Western is required to create an idea of the Indian.

The utopia this melodrama promises, the (false) happy ending of the Bollywood family film, portrays an easy coexistence of the local and the global. Bollywood family films are one example of the industry's response to globalization and the liberalization of the economy in the 1990s; remakes are another. The family films validate the Indianness of the diaspora and thus indicate that Indianness is mobile and can exist in the West; the Indianization in this remake does so, too, but by moving the diasporic woman within the physical bounded space of the nation instead of having her return to the West. Because *Pyaar To Hona Hi Tha* translates the female protagonist of *French Kiss* and retains her active centrality to the plot, it creates a product that is similar to and yet different from the family film, and this difference disturbs, or at least exposes, the family film genre's ideological imperatives. Specifically, *Pyaar To Hona Hi Tha* reveals some of the assumptions of the family film: the affluent male NRI as the hero;

the role and function of women, the heroine in particular, to define Indian values; and, the representation of patriarchy and patriarchs. Bollywood family films validate the diaspora as Indian and NRI men as desirable grooms for Indian daughters. In order to do that, the films often depend on essentialist conceptions of nation and Indian culture and end up raising the issue of national borders (Mankekar 750). Indianness can therefore be carried outside of the physical nation, and the national borders can be metaphorically expanded to include the diaspora who live outside of the geographically bounded nation. In so doing, these films also complicate the industrial codes and conventions that underwrite popular Hindi cinema because the West cannot be so easily "othered." Through the woman, these films try to suture the gap created by the diasporic Indian residing in the West.

In the Bollywood family films, patriarchy is assured via gender roles as connected to the idea of the nation. While it is important that men display their respect for Indian traditions, women are also pivotal to the production of Indianness. Their controlled sexuality and respect for familial hierarchies assign their roles as being dependent on their future husbands, who contribute to the liberalized Indian economy and are part of a Western capitalist workforce. The NRI in *DDLJ* complicates the Indian/Western binary of good and evil; the Indian suitor is rejected in favor of the NRI Raj, who displays his Indianness by showing respect for the patriarch, father of the heroine, Simran. In *Pardes*, the conflict is between two male NRIs: one who is presented as westernized and one who understands and respects Indian values and traditions. The women in these two films are brides who travel—in *DDLJ*, Simran travels from London to India and then comes back to England to be with Raj; in *Pardes*, Kusum travels to the United States from India—yet display their understanding of and respect for Indian culture.

Pyaar To Hona Hi Tha challenges the gender dynamics of the family film. Instead of the male NRI being the character who is elite and affluent, here Sanjana, the female NRI, has built a nest egg for herself. Only Shekhar's masculinity is reaffirmed—he is the hope for the entire family. The film uses and changes the portrayal of two important male figures of the family films—the father and the NRI groom. The patriarch, a very important figure in the family films, is rendered powerless; the NRI groom, Rahul, is humiliated. In *DDLJ*, Raj understands the importance of the father and refuses to run away with Simran. Instead, he stays and earns his respect and then asks for Simran's hand in marriage. Parental permission and happiness are paramount. Amrish Puri's star text (he plays the father in both, *DDLJ* and *Pardes*) also plays a role in representing the father as the ultimate patriarch. In contrast, Shekhar's father in *Pyaar To Hona Hi Tha* is old and powerless. He is an object of pathos when he tells Sanjana about the problems the family is going through. He is not able to provide for his family, and they will lose their land unless Shekhar can find some way to raise enough money. Shah Rukh Khan, who played the role of the NRI hero in many family films, labels the new hero as the yuppie: "If the 1970s hero was anti-establishment, as a yuppie I promised a better world . . . [T]he yuppie believes in capitalism, not communism" (qtd. in Deshpande 186). Interestingly enough, the yuppie is also physically located in the West instead of India. *Pyaar To Hona Hi Tha* has only one such yuppie—Rahul—who is rejected along with all that he stands for, namely capitalism and westernization as they are associated with individualist aggrandization.

Sanjana is made the site of "Indianness," but she is both similar to and different from the heroines in the family films, the brides who travel.[32] While female desire is articulated in *DDLJ*, the way in which female agency functions in *Pyaar To Hona Hi Tha* is different. Simran, in *DDLJ*, falls in love with Raj and rejects the Indian suitor her parents want her to marry, but her transgressive love still needs the sanction of her father. Sanjana, on the other hand, does not have a family. She is a single woman who is financially independent and not subject to the hierarchical unit of the family, through which a patriarchal head would have dictated her future via an arranged marriage. She pursues her NRI fiancé and later rejects him when she realizes he does not deserve her. Although she fits the image of the feminine ideal because she sacrifices all her savings for Shekhar and his family, she is also powerful because she becomes the provider that Shekhar could not become. She saves his family from financial ruin.

The contradiction of Sanjana being Indian and modern is thus intimately connected with the film's negotiation of the local with the global. The seeming disavowal of Westernness in Sanjana and Shekhar takes place through the film's portrayal of Nisha (the westernized Indian) and Rahul (the NRI) as undesirable westernized people and by the film's generation of certain Indian values in line with the family films. *Pyaar to Hona Hi Tha*'s ending resolves this contradiction and ensures the Indianization of Sanjana by placing her in a rural space that is seemingly removed from the effects of globalization. It becomes a microcosm of the nation as produced by the film. The village that *Pyaar To Hona Hi Tha* imagines represents the fantasy of the nation uncorrupted by Western influence and is in line with the remake's attempt to exorcise all signs of westernization by Indianizing the Hollywood film and by transforming the family film. This utopian regression into a romantic France (in *French Kiss*) or a nostalgic fantasy of the Indian village, however, is excessive and false because its very existence depends on capitalist or NRI money. In both cases, the utopia is threatened because of a lack of money, which is then made available, respectively, through Kate's income, which is a product of Western capitalism, or through Sanjana's income, which is NRI money.

Conclusion

The happy endings in both films are in many ways fantasies that the genre of the romantic comedy or the resolution of melodrama imposes on to the story. The convention of the love triangle is used in both films to weed out the unwanted. In the romantic comedy, argues Shandley, the person at the apex must choose, and the choice is often an ideological one (48). Kate chooses Luc over Charlie and therefore rejects capitalism. In the family film, the melodramatic mode seeks to resolve all contradictions, which, in *Pyaar To Hona Hi Tha*, are between the local and the global. The film not only defines Indianness within the nation space but also rejects urban cosmopolitan centers in favor of a local village. Cities are no longer viable spaces because they, too, have been corrupted by globalization, and Nisha epitomizes that corruption. Further still, by making Sanjana "find" her way home to rural India, the film advocates a local identity over a transnational one.

The idea of home gets connected with that of the nation in both films and presents another critique of capitalism and globalization by rejecting the spaces where the ideologies of individualism and consumption are rampant. The difference is that this is only implicitly there in *French Kiss*, while the remake makes it very explicit. Kate's move from the United States to Canada to France shows her quest for this home, and she rejects the United States and Canada in favor of France. *French Kiss* is unlike other runaway romances (mostly during the postwar period) in which the heroine of the romantic comedy goes to Europe, has an affair, and then returns home.[33] Kate never returns to the United States; she actively tries to undo her connections with the country. The film therefore constantly rejects the idea of America as home—in fact, the United States is symptomatic of values she is running away from. Her (assumed) lonely existence is contrasted with the happiness she finds with Luc and his family; her career, however unambitious it might have been, is traded for domestic bliss; and corporate America is rejected in favor of the rural pastoral.

In *Pyaar To Hona Hi Tha*, this connection between nation and home gets played out differently. Sanjana moves from France to India, and the journey is framed in terms of going home. Despite Sanjana's presumed French citizenship, the film actively tries to depict her as someone who is finding her roots. Her realization that her dream house in France is not a home is corroborated by the song "Ajnabi Mujhko Itna Bata," played in a dream sequence in which she imagines her blissful life in her French house with Rahul. Shekhar replaces Rahul as the song progresses, and gradually the French hills and valleys give way to the mustard farm of Shekhar's village. The song is doing more than just presenting a section on foreign locales as spectacles for the audience's viewing pleasure. It is replicating what the diegesis is doing—recontextualizing the idea of home as the place where love is and depicting it as India instead of France.

The utopia that romance imagines or that melodramatic resolution promises functions in both films to offer a critique of capitalism and globalization. Talking primarily about musicals but offering the argument for entertainment in general, Richard Dyer mentions the feeling of utopia that entertainment presents through feelings of abundance, energy, intensity, transparency, and community ("Entertainment" 20). The village as representative of the nation is an older trope in Hindi cinema that the film harks back to; the abundance of the mustard crop in the dream sequence discussed above adds to the feeling of lushness and vitality of the space of the village. An intertextual nod to another song from *DDLJ*—"Tujhe Dekha Toh Yeh Jaana Sanam" ("When I Saw You, O Beloved"), which is set in mustard fields—also builds on the family film's production of rural spaces as the heart of India. In "Ajnabi Mujhko Itna Bataa," the crop is also a fantasy, as the song imagines a future in which the farm will be able to provide the family with enough profits instead of resulting in losses that will make them take on further loans, probably from corporate banks. The crop here serves only as a backdrop, a seeming preference for the earthy reality of the farm instead of the romantic French hills. Further, the dream sequence presents an equivalent of "happily ever after" that obfuscates the reality after the wedding. In rejecting France for rural India, Sanjana is likely trading her job and financial independence for a life structured by patriarchy. It will be a life of domesticity like that of the rest of the women in Shekhar's family. In imagining this resolution, the film is associating female financial independence with westernization and therefore with loss of Indian traditions: the stigma that is often attached to feminism in India. Instead, the song celebrates the couple's love and their future together, papering over any inconsistencies that may result from such an alliance.

Dyer indicates that the problem of this utopia is that "it implies wants that capitalism itself promises to meet" ("Entertainment" 27). Thus "abundance," argues Dyer, "becomes consumerism" ("Entertainment" 27). The France *French Kiss* presents is very touristy; in line with other runaway romances, the film is selling a French fantasy as well as the idea of love encapsulated in the romantic-comedy genre. *Pyaar To Hona Hi Tha* resists the celebration of diaspora in the manner of other family films. However, its critique remains at the level of content. Family films such as *DDLJ* openly embrace globalization and try to harmonize it with Indian traditions, usually through the woman, however problematic the effort might be. Dissanayake argues that in these Bollywood films there is "an uneasy union among globalization, tradition and capitalist modernity" ("Globalization" 144). Despite its rejection of the global via preference for the rural, the ending reestablishes gender roles with the male protagonist as the provider. The local has been asserted over the global even as global capital makes that assertion possible, and patriarchy is asserted over subversive gender roles even if the subversion made this patriarchal family unit possible.

The double bind that the remake reveals at several levels—of bringing together tradition and modernity, of resolving the Western and Indian values, and of seamlessly transforming Hollywood generic characteristics into Bollywood conventions—tends to make the melodramatic oppositions impossible to bring together. Yet, the remake simultaneously marks the inevitability of the coexistence of the local and the global, of national and transnational identities, as the two always produce each other. The very promiscuous form of the remake—as an Indian copy of a US film—betrays the presence of the West within the Indian film, and of Hollywood within Bollywood, especially via the same attempts that are meant to exorcize the West. The process of Indianization, of grappling with the foreignness of a text and adapting it to conventions that produce a cultural identity aligned with Bollywood generic conventions, coproduces the two texts as representatives of their respective cultures at certain historical points. My analysis of Indianization in this context has questioned the idea of complete cultural transformation in the remake. Therefore, if "Bollywoodization" as argued by Rajadhyaksha, implies transnationalization of the industry, then the Indianization that is remaking by the Hindi film industry also participates in that "Bollywoodization" (29). *Pyaar To Hona Hi Tha* indulges in these practices that have ensured its appeal in India and the overseas market. As a remake, *Pyaar To Hona Hi Tha* integrates the Western story with the cultural and industrial conventions of Hindi cinema at the level of both form and content. The remake thus cannot have been Indianized fully, although it may follow certain codes. Instead, it serves as an in-between product that is not a hybrid like the family film. This split that *Pyaar To Hona Hi Tha* displays represents the unresolved tension between the so-called Indian culture and Western culture and between Indianization and Bollywoodization. And this tension that the process of remaking reveals is ripe for analysis in terms of ideologies of gender and nation. Post-2000 remakes tend to be splintered as far as ideologies are concerned because of changes in the industry. The next chapter extends this discussion to defamiliarized femininities within the genre of noir.

2

The Vamp and the Femme Fatale

Defamiliarized Femininities in the Bollywood Remake

*B*ODY HEAT (LAWRENCE KASDAN 1981) is a loose remake of Billy Wilder's film noir, *Double Indemnity* (1944), and the Bollywood film *Jism* (*Body*) (Amit Saxena 2003) borrows from both films. *Jism* intertextually hails both of its Hollywood sources and creates a triangulated relationship with them. This triangulation, however, is not the same as that discussed by Thomas Leitch, in which a remake disavows the more recent adaptation of a past text or property (39); the transnational aspect and the temporal distance between the three films disallow this kind of approach. Instead of competing economically with the previous iterations of the story, *Jism* establishes an intertextual relationship with them that foregrounds the transnational movement of ideas, particularly those relating to the figure of the femme fatale, within the context of industrial changes in the new millennium. The film is both a continuation of and a radical departure from the various femininities populating past Hindi films.

Murder (Anurag Basu 2004), released within a year of *Jism*'s release, does something similar by remaking *Unfaithful* (Adrian Lyne 2002), which itself is a Hollywood remake of a French New Wave film—*La Femme infidèle* (*The Unfaithful Wife*) (1969)—by Claude Chabrol). *Murder* retains the connection between the suggestion of

Figure 2.1. Phyllis hiding behind Walter's apartment door to avoid being seen by Keyes. *Source: Double Indemnity* (Billy Wilder 1942).

Figure 2.2. Sonia hiding behind Kabir's apartment door to avoid being seen by Vishal and Siddharth. *Source: Jism* (Amit Saxena 2003).

uncontrolled female sexuality and male death that are central to its previous two sources, and it continues in the vein of *Jism* by presenting a female protagonist who departs from the Bollywood heroines of the 1990s. Both *Jism* and *Murder* hint at the postmillennial changes that come to define New Bollywood in the arena of gender and sexuality. Thus, I focus on the triangulation in these two films, not to disavow the more recent adaptation of the earlier film, but to explore how this triangulation reveals the layers of intertextual conversations in these remakes—conversations that are spatial as well as temporal, both across and within the industries. These intertextual overlaps, especially in terms of femininity, simultaneously create convergence as well as dissonance, resulting in an affective and intellectual engagement, and a domestic and transnational one, with the femininities expressed in these films. The pleasures of familiar tropes wrought through mainstream conventions that invite an immersive experience of these films coexist with the pleasure of recognizing the tropes that are defamiliarized. I borrow from Andrew Horton and Stuart McDougal here to argue that the resultant femininities of the intertextual composite that we see encourage this interpretation because they render the familiar unfamiliar, thus defamiliarizing what has been naturalized via repetition of tropes (2). The femme fatale and the vamp, deviant femininities that exist in Hollywood and in popular Hindi cinema, respectively, combine and make apparent the ideological stakes of what has become acceptable and normalized. Thus, while repetitions of formulae within each industry and genre have conventionalized these character types and their associated gender dynamics, their repetition in a remake as it crosses culture, industry, and genre undoes their conventional moorings and draws attention to their construction.

Jism's central protagonist is Sonia (Bipasha Basu), who is a combination of the femme fatales, Phyllis Dietrichson (Barbara Stanwyck, *Double Indemnity*) and Matty Walker (Kathleen Turner, *Body Heat*).[1] *Body Heat* is arguably a remake of *Double Indemnity*, its primary plot centering on a femme fatale who persuades the noir protagonist to help her illegally acquire her husband's money after his death and subsequently to kill him. In *Double Indemnity*, insurance salesman Walter Neff tells the story of his doom at the hands of a femme fatale in a flashback sequence of events. In his voice-over, he blames Phyllis, who had convinced him to commit fraud by secretly taking out a life insurance policy on her husband naming her the sole beneficiary. Despite his fears about getting caught, the two of them implemented a plan in which Neff killed her husband. His fears about the scheme were realized when Barton Keyes, his friend and boss, suspected something was off. Neff and Phyllis grew suspicious of each other as the investigation continued, and Neff killed Phyllis with a gun that she had brought to the scene. She then shot him as well. *Body Heat* broadly follows a premise similar to that of *Double Indemnity* and other noir films like *The Postman Always Rings Twice* (Tay Garnett 1946). It is more sexually explicit and provides a different ending for the femme fatale. In it, Matty, the young wife of a much older tycoon, tells Ned, an incompetent lawyer, a story of being unhappy in her marriage and wanting a divorce. Ned decides to kill her husband, Edmund, so that she will be free of him. In the meantime, Matty forges a new will naming Ned as the attorney; however, she deliberately prepares it improperly so that this new document will be considered null and void, and the entire fortune revert to her as his widow.[2] The film ends with Ned in prison, while Matty escapes all suspicion and gets away with the money as well.

Jism weaves the two films together and makes their intertextuality more explicit as a result. Kabir (John Abraham) is a young lawyer who falls in love with Sonia, a beautiful woman married to a millionaire, Rohit (Gulshan Grover). Like *Body Heat*, the film abandons the voice-over that's there in *Double Indemnity* and instead tells the story from a third-person perspective. The main plot resembles both films in that Sonia manipulates Kabir into altering her husband's will and subsequently killing him. Kabir cannot seem to resist the temptation Sonia offers, and she uses his desire for her to make him alter Rohit's will to remove his niece so that Sonia is the sole beneficiary. In the same way that Lola, Edmund Dietrichson's daughter in *Double Indemnity*, suspects that Phyllis killed her mother in order to marry her father, here too it is suggested that Sonia is responsible for the death of Rohit's first wife. Her vampiric femininity is thus established in the film and becomes complete once it is clear that she later tries to get Kabir killed as well.

In *Jism*, Sonia dominates as the central protagonist; her character updates the vamps of earlier Hindi cinema by combining them with the energies of the noir femme fatale. Like the vamps, Bipasha Basu's character, Sonia, is highly sexualized; like Phyllis (Stanwyck) and Matty (Turner), she wields a gun and kills. This representation of deviant femininity as the thrilling subject of the film was so popular that it resulted in a spate of films that tried to follow its formula.

Anurag Basu's *Murder*, while a remake of Lyne's *Unfaithful*, is the next film to use a version of marital infidelity to express deviant femininity. As I mentioned earlier, here again we see a triangulated relationship as Lyne's film is itself a remake of Chabrol's *La Femme infidèle/The Unfaithful Wife*. In *Murder*, we see another iteration of the other woman, the dancing vamp or moll. The film stars Mallika Sherawat, an actor known as an "item girl," in the role of Simran. Since item girls are known for their cabaret-like erotic dance numbers, this casting choice already indicates to the audience that they can expect visual pleasures in the line of *Jism*. Sonia and Simran are integral to the diegeses of the two films, and their frank embrace of their sexuality and ambition is given a central platform. These powerful representations of alternate femininities, drawn from the Hindi cinema vamp and the Hollywood femme fatale, however, ultimately prove too powerful; still, their resonance is not mitigated by the films' endings, which seek closure in killing or reinscribing these dangerous women in marriage.

Jism scandalized its audiences with a hybrid femininity that threatened the codes and conventions of popular Hindi cinema by collapsing the binaries of good and evil via a single female protagonist.[3] In this chapter, I argue that because the time was ripe for the filmmakers to experiment with new subject matter, the remake ushered in this kind of threatening femininity that had previously often been othered and contained. By creating a blend of the vamp of Hindi cinema and the Hollywood femme fatale, *Jism* and *Murder* present a defamiliarized femininity that is both feminist for depicting female agency and desire and exploitative in its objectification of the female body. By providing majority of the cinematic space and time to the female protagonist, these films also offered strong roles to female stars, who have often been secondary to male stars in the industry. The remakes, especially *Jism*, revert to the singular dominance that female stars had in the 1980s as they combine the transgressiveness of the femme fatale with that of the vamp. I contend therefore that as a remake, *Jism*—and later remakes like *Murder*—makes obvious the importation of Western ways of mainstream representation, encapsulated by Hollywood, in Hindi cinema through this hybrid figure. The ambivalence of this paradoxical figure that represents male fantasy as well as female power then needs a feminist theoretical approach that takes into account the cultural and industrial contexts of both Bollywood and Hollywood cinemas.

National Anxiety and Deviant Femininity: The Cultural Travels of the Vamp

The vamp is a figure that has been part of Western mythology for a long time but assumes different forms in Hollywood and Hindi cinema. The idea of the vamp changes historically in both industries even as it draws from the same roots in nineteenth-century British literature. The vampiric femininity of the Victorian era evolves into the vamp of Hollywood silent cinema and then the femme fatale of the 1940s film noir. In Hindi cinema, the vamp develops as a westernized woman known for her sexual looseness and association with villains. The binary femininity of good girl/vamp continues in Hindi cinema across various genres, except that it is aligned with a selective ideology of Indianness that conveniently elides the westernization that was a part of "good femininity" too.

In Hindi cinema, the vamp is one expression of the deviant and desiring women that populate its screens. Even though both industries, Hollywood and Hindi cinema, draw from the same nineteenth-century European source, the resultant images of vampiric femininity in the two contexts—while they share similarities—are representative of opposite kinds of othering. The commonality comes from the shared anxiety about the woman who threatens patriarchy because she is intelligent and aware of the power of her sexuality. She is also a loner without a past or a family. And it is her desire for money and for sex that contributes to her representation as a blood-sucking vampire. The opposition comes from the intersection of racism and sexism that is part of both cultures. The East/West binary operates in the representation of the vamp in Hindi cinema as well as in its Western representations.

Nineteenth-century representations of the vamp often use orientalized sexuality to connote the threat this woman presents. Victorian anxieties about sexuality and race get projected onto this figure, who becomes the foil to cultural representations of the "angel in the house." In the Victorian vamp, then, the gendered other reinforces the raced other, thus exposing Western patriarchy's deep anxieties about both. The oriental connotations are carried into Hollywood silent cinema, where the binary takes the form of the dark lady and her innocent sister. Theda Bara, the famous vamp of silent cinema, said, "I think most vampires are dark women, though some have blood-red hair and green snake-like eyes" (Staiger 160). Mary Ann Doane, too, comments on the orientalized vamp, arguing that these representations are a constant return to the figures of Salome and Cleopatra in the nineteenth-century femme fatale (1). The studio's publicity on Theda Bara promoted seamlessness between her persona as the vamp and her personal life. Even her name is supposed to be an anagram of *Arab death*, which further contributes to distancing her from white—in this case American—womanhood. To manage a female sexuality that refuses to be contained within patriarchy, race is used to other the female and deem her monstrous. White womanhood therefore gets preserved as innocent, and any deviance from ideal femininity becomes proof of racial impurity.

In the case of the Hindi film industry, the vamp gets defined against a portrayal of the ideal Indian femininity that can be traced back to pre-independence cinema.[4] Due to the film industry's close ties with Nehruvian nationalism, after independence, Indian women were idealized as the upholders of tradition and culture, and anxiety about the West was projected on to the vamp in Hindi films. The conception of ideal Indian womanhood formed during colonization arose from a combination of British Victorian ideals and Indian traditions. The concept of *bhadramahila* (respectable woman) was borrowed from Victorian ideals of domesticity and had much in common with the angel of the house.[5] It is this ideal woman that populates postindependence films and is celebrated as an icon of Indian tradition. Ira Bhaskar, while discussing the disappearance of the women's education and the "woman's question" from reform agendas in India in the late nineteenth and early twentieth centuries, cites Partha Chatterjee to argue that the issue was resolved by locating this reform within the national ideological project: "Not only did nationalist modernity demand that women be educated, but also that their education must serve a modern patriarchal vision of nationalism such that educated modern women embody the authentic spirituality of the nation" (Chatterjee qtd. in Bhaskar 29). In fact, Bhaskar argues that the expression of female deviancy in pre- and postindependence Hindi films—*Achhut Kanya* (Franz Osten 1936), *Tarana* (Ram Daryani 1951), *Dillagi* (a.r. Kardar 1949), and *Heer* (Hameed Butt 1956)—is a result of the nature of this anxiety about the modern woman. While the women in these films are forced into situations from which they can only escape via death, "their deviancy highlights the anxieties around women's passions, sexualities, articulations and the challenges they pose to patriarchy" (Bhaskar 43). Such a formulation also creates a binary in which the undomesticated, mobile woman gets marked as Western and evil, and a sacrificing femininity forms the opposite as good. For example, films such as *Shree 420* (Raj Kapoor 1955) split the anxiety provoking women into those representing good and bad femininity: Maya, the woman who leads Raj astray with her allure and promise of riches, is the vamp, and Vidya, who is an educated woman (her name literally means knowledge, and she is a schoolteacher) is the heroine who enables the development of the male protagonist representing the new modernized nation.

This figuration of the vamp was not new in the late 1970s. In Hindi cinema of the 1950s and 1960s, the vamp often lived openly with the villain. The antithesis of the heroine, the vamp was characterized by habits that were used to other her: "smoking, drinking, dressing skimpily and having no interest in marriage or children" are examples of some of these undesirable aspects (Nasreen Munni Kabir 95). These attributes of the vamp involving sexual promiscuity, dress, or lifestyle were associated with westernization. The most famous vamp of Hindi cinema, Helen Richardson (often known simply as Helen), was considered non-Indian because she was biracial. Her Spanish and Burmese parentage intensifies the westernization Helen projects because of her comparative whiteness as opposed to other stars. Jyotika Virdi argues that "perceived as part of the Anglo-Indian community . . . Helen plays with the pleasure and anxiety the othered Westerners' lifestyle elicits" (168). Her roles were often limited to being a cabaret dancer. The East/West binary gets flipped insofar as, instead of being orientalized as is the case in Hollywood, the vamp becomes associated with a certain conception of Western values, with her westernization serving as an indication of her evil. The attributes characterizing the vamp in both industries are otherwise similar: she is alone, manipulative, greedy, and promiscuous. As a result, she stands for a self-aggrandizing selfishness as opposed to the innocent and selfless woman who is often contained within a network of relations as a wife, mother, and daughter. But whereas her unbridled sexuality was seen as oriental in the West, here it is seen as Western. In both cases, racialization of the vamp is used to malign the powerful woman as evil.

The vamp's lineage, in Hindi cinema, is also mixed. Mukul Kesavan points to her hybrid roots located in both Hollywood and

Hindi cinema. In addition to the Hollywood vamp and moll, he argues that "her Indian bloodlines lead directly to the *tawaif*" (253). The *tawaif* inhabits the Islamicate films or the courtesan genre, which is littered across Hindi cinema's history, including films such as *Mughal-e-Azam* ("The Great Mughal") (K. Asif 1960), *Pakeezah* ("The Pure One") (Kamal Amrohi 1972), and *Umrao Jaan* (Muzaffar Ali 1981), but she can also be found in films from other genres; Roy's *Devdas* and Bhansali's remake both centralize the *tawaif* as an important character. The *tawaif* dances seductively across the screen in these films and is the main protagonist of the courtesan films, but she is often salvaged through a rhetoric of victimization. For example, the *tawaif* in *Pakeezah*, Sahibjaan, is the daughter of a *tawaif* and a *nawab*. While her mother, unwed and pregnant, lives in a cemetery and dies after giving birth to her daughter, Sahibjaan falls in love and gets married. The name of the film, *Pakeezah*, suggests her pureness. Umrao in *Umrao Jaan* is kidnapped as a child. She too falls in love, but that love remains unrequited. The Islamicate genre tends to sublimate the sexual aspects on to the *mujra*, a Kathak dance performance that highlights the aesthetic aspects and adds a layer of romance to the song and dance, which is all about desire. While an example of deviant and powerful femininity, the *tawaif* is rarely evil. Kesavan argues that "when the *tawaif* turns malevolent, she begins to shade into the Hollywood seductress to produce the vamp of Hindi films" (254). Her othered status as vamp is thus again secured in her sexual availability to patrons and in her Westernness. The vamp also partially borrows the *tawaif*'s persona in the song-and-dance number, where she is both a desiring and desired person. The vamp's cabaret "is founded on the suggestive movements and mannerisms of the mujra," which is combined with dance steps from other traditions such as the flamenco (Kesavan 254). Shades of the *tawaif* and the vamp continue to be visible in the Bollywood item number—a sexually suggestive song-and-dance number that often objectifies the female—of contemporary Hindi cinema, in which the woman uses similar gestures as the *tawaif*. I'll return to the item girl when I discuss the 1990s.

The rise of Amitabh Bachchan as a star in the 1970s ushered in genres like the angry-young-man films, which were more focused on the male protagonist than previous Hindi films had been. The films of this genre often blurred the boundaries between the hero and the antihero and concentrated more on the as-yet-marginalized world of villains. This period, then, also saw a larger role for the vampish foil to the ideal woman, making her an important and complicated character instead of a stereotype. The change in the vamp character was considerable enough that Virdi and Nasreen Munni Kabir note the disappearance of the vamp in Hindi cinema from 1970s onward. They argue that with the modern heroines played by Zeenat Aman and Parveen Babi, the vamp transformed into the gangster's moll but with fewer scenes until she disappeared from the Hindi screen altogether.

The characters played by Babi and Aman, however, were particularly transgressive since they retained some characteristics of the vamp while they adopted those of the moll. The moll is ambiguously located between the heroine and the vamp as on the one hand, she is often "given the chance to claim the desire for a 'normal' life of marriage" and she is more essential to the plot than the cabaret dancer; on the other hand, she does not get the centrality that the heroine gets and she still represents an out-of-control female sexuality since her sexuality exists outside of the bounds of marriage (Neha Yadav 155–56). Babi and Aman's characters were unlike contemporary heroines because they were known for exhibiting physical desire. For example, in Yash Chopra's *Deewaar (The Wall)* (1975), Anita (Parveen Babi) smokes, drinks, approaches Vijay (Amitabh Bachchan) in a bar, and proceeds to have a sexual relationship with him without getting married. Even though Vijay is on the other side of the law, he is the hero of the film. The representation of his relationship with Anita and of this kind of femininity were groundbreaking. The earlier vamps played by Helen were punished with death for being bad, undomesticated women (Virdi 168). Anita dies, too, but she is affectively central to the diegesis as Vijay's partner.

The 1980s saw the emergence of revenge films, which "stage the aggressive and contradictory contours of sexual identity and pleasure that in turn throw up aggressive strands of feminism" (Lalitha Gopalan 51). These films truly blur the characteristics associated with deviant and ideal femininities and create a narrative that is completely driven by the female protagonist; it often includes a horrific rape of a woman followed by an equally horrific revenge enacted on the perpetrator (Gopalan 48). Virdi and Lalitha Gopalan emphasize the complicated politics of female agency in these films "where the film truly centers on women's narrative" (Virdi 162), but "the genre demands that a violent assertion of masculine power in the form of rape is the price that has to be exacted for such power" (Gopalan 49). The scopophilic pleasures of violent sex inflicted on the female body are met with violent acts, including castration and death, done to the male bodies by the female avenger.[6] Virdi sees a simultaneous masculinization and eroticization of these women who can wield guns (159), and Gopalan adds that these transgressive women "incite[s] masculine anxiety about the phallic female" (49). These women's actions are in line with the feminist outcry against the Mathura rape case.[7] Located in the on-the-ground reality of feminist work, these films portray female characters who diverge from the vamp and yet are a continuation of that figure, as these women are also sexualized and ultimately contained by narrative closures.

The family film of the 1990s, however, effectively did away with such aggressive roles for women as anxiety about globalization created a return of "good femininity." As I have argued in "Behind Her Laughter," the domestic abuse film cycle of the early 1990s is, in a way, a continuation of the avenging women films. The cycle is short-lived, giving way to family films which resurrect the "ideal" Indian woman again, in line with ideologies of the nation.[8] In these family films, the female protagonist would be modernized in her inhabiting of non-domestic spaces, in how she dresses, and in how she loves and desires, but she remains respectful of traditions. Nevertheless, some films maintain a sexualized, decadent "other" as the vamp, as is the case of Nisha in *Pyaar to Hona Hi Tha* (as I discussed in chapter 1), or in "item numbers," which became the song-and-dance units for safely containing deviant femininities in the 1990s.[9] They are subjected to a voyeuristic gaze in the fetishized item number. The item girl shares affinity with previous deviant femininities; like the *tawaif*, she uses similar gestures that Kesavan mentions: "the underlip caught between the teeth or the coyly wrinkled nose" (254); and like the vamp, she dances suggestively to a song that is quite explicit about desire. The item girl, however, also borrows from dancing women who have a life outside of A-circuit films.[10] Silpa Mukherjee's work on item numbers and item girls uncovers the association between these dance numbers and sleazy B movies in India, which cater to a largely urban, male, working-class crowd and are characterized by low production quality, violence, and pornographic bits.[11] She argues that in the item number, "we see elements associated with dances in B grade films of the 1990s transformed into fashionable music video like dances within 'A circuit films.' Squatting on haunches, gyrating torsos, vigorous pelvic thrusts, and heaving breasts—these iconic markers of item numbers are mostly borrowed from B films" (Mukherjee, "Behind the Green Door" 218). In this particular context, the B movie, with its association with sleaze, is the product of the B circuit, but aspects of it move into the mainstream, high-production-quality, A-circuit multiplex film via the item number.[12] The item girl may seem very far from the vamp, but she is the 1990s version of the vamp in how she is sexualized. Despite the ways in which her frontal address and self-conscious awareness of her sexual appeal empower her, her restriction to the item number seems to render her declawed and defanged as compared to the vamp.

Popular culture always throws up contradictory ideological positions, as is the case with representations of femininities across the 1990s, but this particular amalgam is an expression of the historical moment. The heroine is someone whose desires are conveyed in these films, and a softer, more vulnerable, masculinity is presented as an alternative to an aggressively misogynist one. Yet, this idealized heroine replaces the avenging-women roles that were performed by big female stars like Hema Malini. The remarginalization of deviant femininities from the 1980s is an effect of the cultural and industrial context of the 1990s, which I mentioned earlier. Tejaswani Ganti's observations of discussions by filmmakers about possibly remaking *Fatal Attraction* (Adrian Lyne 1987) reveal not just how filmmakers imagine what their audiences would like but also how the filmmakers themselves are constructing these audience desires that are subject to their own whims, which are bound to be affected by the cultural moment and how it defines a successful film. The filmmakers decide not to remake the Hollywood film in part because "Glenn Close's character of a lustful, obsessive other woman" was considered difficult for adaptation in an Indian context (Ganti, "And Yet My Heart" 141). Thus, Lyne's *Fatal Attraction* was considered unremakeable not because its representation of femininity could not exist on the Indian screen—the presence of the vamps, molls, and avenging women in Hindi film history disprove such thinking—but because the film was not amenable to remaking in the 1990s. Given that *Fatal Attraction* was remade in 2001 as *Pyaar Tune Kya Kiya* (*Love . . . What Have You Done?*) (Ram Gopal Varma), one can extrapolate from the filmmakers' discussion in 1996 that it is the regressive turn in the decade regarding gender—one that is exhibited by the family films—that makes that kind of femininity unviable, or at least unprofitable, for the filmmakers. Ganti rightly argues that the filmmakers are the "cultural mediators, evaluating the appropriateness of their audiences of stories, characterizations, and themes from certain Hollywood films" ("And Yet My Heart" 141). To this, I would add the importance of considering the ideological pulse of the historical moment. It is because of the preference for a certain kind of ideal femininity that anchors the anxiety about the nation, resulting from the regressive turn in the 1990s, that the film could not be remade with a deviant femininity as its protagonist.

A decade later, Mahesh Bhatt transgresses these 1990s codes by remaking films in which the vamps occupy the center, and the virtuous heroines are written out. Changes in the industry in the 1990s are partly responsible for such treatment of the subject matter and for the transformation in the codes and conventions of Hindi cinema that these remakes announce. The increasing address of films to urban middle-class and diasporic audiences, and the beginning of the multiplex crowds in the early 2000s, allows for a film to make profits even if it is not a mass success in India. The success of this kind of film depends on niche marketing, the profit potential of a film certified as A (adults only), and its popularity with audiences familiar with Hollywood films. *Jism* and *Murder* consequently indicate a changing relationship between Bollywood and Hollywood in which Bollywood can remake films that refuse to be Indianized the way they were in the 1990s. The remake translates plots and stories that are already popular in the West and presents characters that appeal to audiences at home and abroad as well.

The Transnational Femme Fatale

By remaking the femme fatale, a specific articulation of the vamp in the Hollywood films of 1940s and later, *Jism* reintroduces the element of danger and power emanating from female sexuality that had been made obsolete in the previous decade. The Hollywood femme fatale of classic film noir is a product of censorship under the Production Code Administration (PCA) and American anxiety about women's sexual roles during and immediately after World War II. Doane argues that the femme fatale emerged as a central figure in the nineteenth century, whereas other scholars differentiate between the vamp of the nineteenth century and the femme fatale of the twentieth. Julie Grossman uses the description of Cora from the publicity image of *The Postman Always Rings Twice* to argue that "the culmination of the late-Victorian vampire, who became the vamp of silent cinema, is film noir's femme fatale" (*Rethinking the Femme Fatale* 129). Parasitic images of excess, blood-sucking, and contamination are used to express contemporary anxieties about female power and transgression, Grossman contends (*Rethinking the Femme Fatale* 129). This femme fatale, then, is a specific invocation of the earlier vamp. She is the expression of anxieties regarding female mobility, sexual freedom, and economic independence during the Second World War. Unlike the vamp of silent cinema, this femme fatale was always punished because her immorality could not be rewarded under the PCA.[13] She could be Phyllis in *Double Indemnity*, who is manipulative and cunning, carries a gun, and is sexually promiscuous as she spins her web around the noir hero. Alternatively, she could be Laura (in Otto Preminger's *Laura* [1944]) or Gilda (in Charles Vidor's *Gilda* [1946]), who attract men and drive them to their doom simply because they are women. The femme fatale of early noir was always threatening and anxiety producing for the noir hero. Chris Straayer argues that the classic femme fatale's lust was overwhelmingly for money rather than sexual pleasure: "Despite her sexualized image, economic ambition supplanted her libido and violence displaced sexual pleasure" (152). The sexual pleasure, then, is for the man, whereas the classic femme fatale uses it to manipulate the man. On the other hand, claims Straayer, the neo-noir femme fatale—a recognizable character in films from the 1970s onward—wants sexual pleasure as well as economic power (153). In all cases, these women's sexual availability and sexual magnetism are what Doane calls the "secret" or "enigma" of the femme fatale that threatens men, the source of her power over and control of her male victims.

What comes across in each inflection of the vamp (including the femme fatale) is her strength and intelligence, even if she is damned. Theda Bara was very aware of the expression of female power through the vamp: "The vampire that I play is the vengeance of my sex upon its exploiters. You see . . . I have the face of a vampire, perhaps, but the heart of a 'feministe'" (qtd. in Staiger 160). Grossman argues that the *femme moderne*, the feminist New Woman of the nineteenth century, is the precursor of the vamp.[14] Viewed like this, the femme fatale's desire is for empowerment, and she is a feminist representation. This kind of interpretation of the femme fatale has roots in 1970s feminist film scholarship (in the United States), in which scholars were trying to recover this figure from the deep misogyny to which it had been traditionally subjected. Helen Hanson sees this work as important in forming an image of the femme fatale "as sexually, and generically, transgressive: a female figure refusing to be defined by the socio-cultural norms of femininity, or contained by the male-addressed, generic operations of film noir narratives in which her fatality resulted in her ultimate destruction" (xv). The neo-noir femme fatales have been influenced by much of this feminist theory. Fredric Jameson may have a point about *Body Heat*'s pastiching of noir, which empties it of history, but the film is a product of its time if viewed through the femme fatale Matty.[15] The character of Matty would not have been possible in the 1940s noirs or even in the 1930s, the era in which it is set. She is very much a post-PCA and post-1970s-feminism femme fatale.

The femme fatales under discussion in this chapter are from different moments in this historical spectrum of the evolving femme fatale. In Billy Wilder's *Double Indemnity*, Phyllis is the classic femme fatale: she seduces Walter Neff, an insurance agent, and manipulates him to murder her husband and collect the insurance money. They kill each other at the end of the film. The plotline of *Body Heat* is very similar to that of *Double Indemnity*; here too a frustrated wife manipulates the noir hero to kill her husband so that she can inherit all his property. As a neo-noir, *Body Heat* pays homage to the classic noir but at the same time updates it. At one level, Matty Walker is a combination of all noir femme fatales—and she seems more dangerous, more manipulative, and therefore more destructive than any of them. At another level, she is a continuation and extension of them.[16] Kasdan retains the destructive power and agency of the femme fatale but changes the ending; instead of punishment or death, Matty Walker gets all the money, and the last shot of the film depicts her lazing on a beach on an exotic island.

Hélène in Chabrol's *La Femme infidèle*, the source of Lyne's *Unfaithful*, is not a classic femme fatale, but she shares a few traits with them: her sexual availability to a man who is not her husband, and her ability to drive men to their doom.[17] Her lover is killed by her husband in a jealous rage, and the film's ending suggests he is convicted for the murder. *Unfaithful* remakes Chabrol's film but shifts the focus a little by adding the story of the affair between its characters Connie and Paul. Connie is a close copy of Hélène, except that she is portrayed as helpless in controlling the events of her life, whereas Hélène seems to choose to pursue the affair. Both women betray their husbands because of their sexual desire. But where Hélène's story has no past and aligns her more with the femme fatales who are represented as having a devouring sexuality, Connie is portrayed more sympathetically. The affairs ironically heal the relationship between the couples in both films, but the conclusions in both nevertheless remain ambiguous, refusing to grant happy endings.

Given the various incarnations of the vamp in Hollywood and Bollywood, it is easy to see why this figure has cultural valence and makes perfect sense as a subject of cross-cultural remakes. At the same time, the particular inflections the Hollywood femme fatale and the Bollywood vamp have taken on collide to present hybrids of these in remakes, their transgressiveness even more pronounced because of their newness. In all the Hindi variations, the vamp remains a diegetically marginal figure. Even when she plays the modern heroine in the films of the 1970s, her role is minimal because the angry-young-man genre is very male oriented, and the vamp/heroine is not the central character. *Jism* and *Murder* translate the femme fatale from Hollywood films noir for the Bollywood audience into what seems like an updated vamp of early Hindi cinema, the Bollywood vamp. As a result, the contained item girl and the marginalized vamp inherited from earlier cinema are made to occupy center stage. The vamp becomes the central female character. While *Jism*'s Sonia is a combination of *Double Indemnity*'s Phyllis and the early Hindi vamp, *Murder*'s Simran (played by Mallika Sherawat) is an update along the lines of Parveen Babi. *Jism* is more transgressive in refusing to let Sonia's personality change into that of a "nice" woman unlike Simran's. Sonia almost gets away with everything, too, until she dies. On the other hand, given Sherawat's image, which overwrites the ending, even *Murder* remains ambiguous about Simran's conversion to ideal femininity. Sherawat becomes famous in Bollywood as an item girl after *Murder*, but the associations of sexuality and promiscuity accompany her image because of the on-screen kisses she shared with Himanshu Malik in *Khwahish* and the music videos she had done before the film.[18] These undercut the role of chaste wife that her character promises at the end of the film. Her notoriety affects the interpretation of her character and eclipses the diegetic happy ending.

Therefore, when the remake Indianizes the Hollywood film, the femme fatale is both translated from Hollywood noir and transformed into an updated vamp of Bollywood, thus registering the cross-cultural exchange at this historical moment. Synthesizing the deviant sexuality that threatens the patriarchy and bourgeois normativity that is common to both the vamp of Hindi cinema and the Hollywood femme fatale, these films express the complicated binary of Indian/Western in Hindi film in the twenty-first century.

Defamiliarizing Femininities: Transference and Transformation in the Remake

Sonia and Simran, in *Jism* and *Murder*, respectively, are composites of the Hollywood femme fatale and the Hindi vamp. They transfer and transform—terms used by Carolyn Durham to convey how a remake is involved in the dual activity of transference and transformation where it transfers the cultural and ideological aspects of the source text or how it transforms into the cultural context of the remake's culture—from the femme fatale to the vamp (Carolyn Durham 2). As incarnations of femme fatales, these women possess dangerous sexualities and precipitate events that lead to the death of the men in their lives. Like Phyllis and Matty, Sonia is intelligent and manipulates the men around her for her sexual and economic desires. Simran's agency, like Connie's, on the other hand, is located in her body and not in her consciousness.[19] That is, unlike Sonia, she does not intend consciously to act on her desires. In her voice-over, she admits to her transgression of giving in to her desire at the time but also suggests that she had no control over her actions. As Bollywood vamps, Sonia and Simran can be separated into two kinds: Sonia resembles the early vamps such as Helen, who associated with the villains and were killed at the end; Simran, on the other hand, seems to be a version of the vamps of the 1980s films played by the likes of Aman and Babi, whose sexualities were often contained through their transformation into devoted, saree-wearing wives. The remakes position both Sonia and Simran as the central female characters who drive the narrative forward.

Through these transformations of the femme fatale into the updated vamp, *Jism* and *Murder* provide "defamiliarization" in the remake.[20] Talking about the intertextual relationship between remakes and the texts they draw on, Horton and McDougal argue that remakes provide the pleasures of defamiliarization and "invite the viewer to enjoy the differences that have been reworked, consciously and sometimes unconsciously" (2). The remake, therefore, constantly involves the viewer in the dual activities of watching and "reading" a text (2). This defamiliarization is also connected to the industrial and cultural transformation that happens in the remake because through this "reading" the viewer is able to make sense of history and ideologies that affect that transformation. The remake retains and therefore transfers the source text into new contexts; at the same time, it also gets rid of the temporal/historical, cultural/national, and industrial contexts of the Hollywood film.

In remaking *Double Indemnity*, *Body Heat* also reworks film noir into neo-noir and registers the changes from Old Hollywood to New Hollywood. Neo-noir's self-consciousness about the noir genre makes it an ideal vehicle for this defamiliarization. Classic film noir remains a contentious category for scholars who now accept (but still debate) the indeterminacy of film noir as genre, aesthetic style, or cycle. Each category seems to limit what noir really is. However, neo-noir is a genre that uses, pays homage to, and updates the noir characteristics. Neo-noir thus already invites audiences to immerse themselves in the story but also to distance themselves as they keep seeing how the genre is being reworked. As a neo-noir, *Body Heat* is already engaged in this reformulation. However, it also reworks a particular film and its characters. Matty Walker is not just a remade and updated femme fatale; she is Phyllis Dietrichson without the PCA's censorship. Whereas the earlier femme fatales were a product of anxiety about women during the Second World War, Matty is a product of the feminist movement of the 1970s, so she is not punished at the end and killed off like Phyllis.

The intertextual relationship between *Body Heat* and *Double Indemnity* is emphasized by *Jism*, which moves seamlessly from one story to the other as it weaves together another version of the same plot. However, *Jism* crosses generic *and* cultural boundaries, hailing audiences that are distinct from those of the Hollywood productions. Rosie Thomas argues that Hindi remakes undergo a process of Indianization where the film adheres to the codes and conventions that define verisimilitude in Hindi cinema ("Melodrama" 159–62). These codes, which Thomas argues are present in films from the 1970s and 80s, and which I argue are present later in the 1990s as well, are in flux, especially with regard to gender. In a remake like *Jism*, for example, this process is always in contention with the foreignness or Westernness of the source text because the Hollywood codes of representation are very different from those of Bollywood. Yet, the film also betrays Bhatt's refusal to Indianize the femininities, bucking the trend by staying close to the characters of the noir femme fatales. As a result, the text is not completely transformed and thus forces the viewer to engage with it at both levels—of watching and of reading.[21] Thus, the cross-cultural remake provides the pleasures of defamiliarization even for viewers who, not familiar with the Hollywood source texts, read it alongside other Bollywood films.

In Sonia's character, *Jism* borrows heavily from Matty in *Body Heat* but at crucial moments reverts to *Double Indemnity*'s Phyllis. This coupling allows the director to both depict the eroticized transgressive femininity of Matty and punish the femme fatale for enacting this transgressiveness. In film noir, the femme fatale is often placed in a position of power and knowledge, and both Phyllis and Matty have power and therefore control over the men in their lives (see figures 2.3, 2.4, 2.5, and 2.6). Similarly, in *Jism*, Sonia's femininity is transgressive because she is smarter than everyone else, because she is central to the narrative, and because she is driven by personal greed and sexual desire. Like Phyllis and early noir femme fatales, Sonia's lust is for money. Like Matty and the neo-noir femme fatales, her sexual desire also remains central. The very first time Kabir encounters Sonia is in the precredit sequence: Kabir, in a state of drunkenness at the

Figure 2.3. Sonia's control is suggested as her hands run over the crisscross pattern of a makeshift hut in the song "Jadoo Hai Nashaa Hai." *Source: Jism* (Amit Saxena 2003).

Figure 2.4. Theme of entrapment continues as Kabir kisses Sonia behind the crisscrossed wall. *Source: Jism* (Amit Saxena 2003).

Figure 2.5. Noir aesthetic as vertical blinds cast shadows behind Phyllis's head. *Source: Double Indemnity* (Billy Wilder 1942).

beach, imagines her emerging from the ocean. Her sexual allure and self-awareness of that allure are on display; she sensuously strokes her braid as a closeup of her face emphasizes her kohl-rimmed green eyes, reminding one of a serpent or *nagin*.[22] She walks right past Kabir,

Figure 2.6. Neo-noir aestheic of imprisonment is suggested by the patterns in the doorways. *Source: Body Heat* (Lawrence Kasdan 1981).

who follows her only to find that she has disappeared. Confused and befuddled, he looks around but does not find her. In the next scene, as he walks up to a restaurant, he sees her on the terrace and smiles confidently to himself. The camera then cuts to a medium shot of Sonia's bare back as she looks out and then turns around to face the camera (aligned with Kabir's gaze). In the conversation that follows, Kabir tries to woo her with *shayari* (poetry), but she doesn't respond in typical traditional ways of the heroine. Her direct gaze and her sharp responses to Kabir's bumbling poetry immediately set her apart from the shy, coy femininity of heroines in Hindi cinema. More importantly, her appearance and her behavior establish her as someone in control. Kabir might have approached her assuming that he could be in control but from the very beginning the film sets her up as a femme fatale—Kabir is caught in her web, and she constantly eludes him and maintains the upper hand. Sonia's devouring femininity is almost sociopathic in its rejection of human emotion. When confronted, she tells Kabir, "This body does not know love . . . All it knows is lust." It is not just an articulation of female sexual desire here but also a desire divorced from love and all other heteronormative rhetoric that includes the male. The destructive power of her femininity is clearly underlined because all the men she encounters die—her husband, her lover, and the noir hero, Kabir.

The endings of all three films are attempts to heterosexualize the narcissistic desire of the femme fatale. Since neither Sonia nor Phyllis can fire the second shot to kill their noir hero, in both films this inability can be interpreted as the femme fatale's realization that her desire is not purely sexual or personal but that she loves the noir hero. Even in *Body Heat*, Kasdan makes the ending deliberately ambiguous so that the audience wonders whether Matty is really happy without Ned in her life.[23] This seeming insight into the femme fatale's character indicates the promise of hope for her incorporation within a heteronormative order of desire. The sexual desire of the woman becomes secondary to this emotion of love for the man who has been under her sexual and intellectual control. The repeated admission of love by Sonia also introduces doubt about her earlier avowals of love for Kabir, which had then seemed forced and manipulative. It is this admission of love that makes her weak and leads to her death because it allows Kabir to take control, shoot her, and attempt to inscribe control over her agency through the voice-over.

This final indication of love in *Double Indemnity* and *Jism* might function as access to the true emotions of these women whose subjectivity is otherwise inaccessible except through the noir heroes. Within Bollywood codes of representation, the admission of Sonia's love and weakness along with her death add another dimension: it makes her readable as a heroine of the film and not just a vamp. As I have mentioned before, the inherited melodramatic codes in Hindi cinema were careful to maintain a split between Indianness and Westernness through the binary of central protagonists and villains or vamps. The narrative is supposed to resolve the contradictions that arise from the manipulation of certain characteristic moral oppositions in Hindi cinema: good and evil, country and city, Indian tradition and Western culture, purity and sexuality, duty and desire (Vasudevan 39). Like the vamps of early Hindi cinema, Sonia is evil, urban, and westernized, and she oozes sexual desire. But like the sexualized and westernized heroines of 1970s films, she is also the central affective female figure in the film. Bipasha Basu's star text also exerts an influence on her character as she is the protagonist despite her deviant femininity and is not marginalized in the narrative. Moreover, unlike the 1970s films, which are male centered, *Jism* is a film about Sonia, who I'd argue is its only protagonist. Finally, through her death and her admission of love for Kabir, she is somewhat redeemed. Sonia's character, then, collapses the boundaries between the Hindi vamp and heroine and announces the unviability of older melodramatic codes.

Despite Sonia's close similarity to the Hollywood femme fatale, just the translation of the femme fatale figure into Bollywood codes of representation provides a different context for reading the ending of *Jism*. For an audience who reads the film through these Bollywood conventions, Sonia's character resembles the updated vamp. The ending should be familiar to the Bollywood audience as the melodramatic romantic resolution that often characterizes the assertion of moral heteronormative order. For the Bollywood vamp not to be othered as too Western and to retain audience sympathy, the individualism that characterizes the Hollywood femme fatale has to give way to individual desire located in a larger structure, usually family, but connoted here through the romantic couple.

Murder, inspired by the success of *Jism*, remakes *Unfaithful* to create a slightly different vamp than Sonia. Part of the reason for this difference lies in its different trajectory. *Unfaithful* is a remake of Chabrol's *La Femme infidèle*, which is a crime thriller that shares only few characteristics with noir. While the femme fatale as a character is heterogeneous and inhabits different genres as versions of the vamp, it does not have the same inflection as it does in the noir films of the 1940s (Neale, *Genre and Hollywood* 162–63). Chabrol's Hélène and Lyne's Connie are not self-aware in the same way as Phyllis, Matty, or Sonia. In Chabrol's film, Charles suspects his wife, Hélène, of infidelity when he walks in on her talking on the phone to someone, and this becomes the catalyst for his actions and for the events in the narrative. Lyne's remake adds plot background that makes Connie more relatable—Connie's chance encounter with Paul (played by the French actor Oliver Martinez) on a street in New York as a gale blows everything everywhere belongs in a romantic comedy. The irresistible attraction between them (and particularly Connie's attraction to him, in no small part aided by Martinez's blue eyes and French accent) provides the causality that fills the gap in Chabrol's film regarding the wife's actions.[24] This attempt to present the beginning is an example of the ways in which *Unfaithful* conforms to the Hollywood style of filmmaking in which the viewer identifies and is emotionally involved with the characters. Chabrol is a French New Wave director. While his love for Hollywood's genre cinema is reflected in his work, his style distinguishes it from the mainstream: here he does so by creating ambiguity at the level of plot and through distanciation via camerawork. As a result, *La Femme infidèle* is a perfect film to be remade by Hollywood.[25] But Lyne also tries to import some of Chabrol's vision by retaining the ambiguity of the ending instead of providing closure. The difference between the French film and the remake, and therefore the defamiliarization the remake can engender, can be understood in terms of Lyne's auteurism in the manner in which he updates the film, the movement between French art cinema and Hollywood mainstream styles of filmmaking in the remake, and the related impact on the characterization of the adulterous wife as a femme fatale-vamp.

Unfaithful tries to be open-ended in the same way as Chabrol's film, but it provides the immersive Hollywood experience. In contrast, Chabrol's style often creates discomfort in the viewer. *La Femme infidèle* underlines the madness and irrationality behind bourgeois normativity.[26] It is impossible to empathize or sympathize with Chabrol's characters because he keeps the viewer at a distance from them. The camera moves slowly, resting on surfaces that are opaque like the walls in the house or the sickening pale blue and green that dominate the interior, or it zooms out and gives long shots that again add to that distancing effect. The characters' faces remain blank for the most part, canceling out the presence of any emotions that their words might be trying to otherwise convey. The camera work and the mise-en-scène contradict the façade of bliss that the couple's suburban house represents. The characters' actions therefore don't seem to be motivated by interpersonal relationships and arise more out of the conditions of bourgeois life. Hélène's adultery is a symbol of Charles's loss of control over his wife and therefore over the bourgeois household. Charles's actions, then, are not merely those of a man who realizes that his wife does not love him anymore but of a man losing his control over his stable life. The distancing effect that Chabrol brings to his treatment of the plot serves to undermine the narrative and articulate his view of bourgeois life as diseased by creating dis-ease in the viewers. In this case, then, Hélène's adultery might be an attempt to escape this oppressive condition, therefore making her resemble femme fatales of film noir, who similarly undermine bourgeois values.

Even though Chabrol is known for being heavily influenced by Hollywood and has expressed his love for genre films, which makes him side with mainstream cinema instead of art cinema, his vision remains influenced by the French New Wave. Lyne's remake transfers the French source but also transforms it into a more conventional Hollywood film; that is, it retains Chabrol's irony and critique of the bourgeois family but frames it within the ideological codes of representation that characterize Hollywood films, displacing attention from the institution onto the individual. Continuity editing and close-ups complement the suspense and drama in *Unfaithful*, making it into a story of a happy bourgeois family threatened by Connie's sexual desires. This is how the film invites audience immersion instead of enforcing critical objectivity. The opening shot of the film might be interpreted as an omen as the heavy winds knock things around inside the house and portend the tumult that will upset the household, but it is very different from the repulsion that the calm image of unruffled happy domesticity engenders in Chabrol's opening scene.

Unlike Lyne, who tried to transfer some of Chabrol's treatment of *La Femme infidèle* in *Murder*, Anurag Basu Indianizes *Unfaithful* by changing the plot to achieve greater verisimilitude for Bollywood audiences. Chabrol's film provides no diegetic explanation for how the affair begins. Lyne's version shows sparks flying at the first encounter of the cheating couple, thus adding some kind of rationale for Connie's desires and inability to resist the sexual attraction. Anurag Basu adds several plot points to make Simran a sympathetic character, despite her suspected infidelity. Her lover, Sunny, turns out to be a previous boyfriend who is still obsessively in love with her. But that alone does not sufficiently explain to an Indian audience why a woman who is a wife and mother would start an affair. Therefore, the narrative reveals that her husband, Sudhir, is her dead sister's husband and that Simran married him out of a sense of obligation to her sister's memory and her child. Simran's frustration is not located in a bourgeois life but in the absence of a relationship with her husband. The film's ending is not similar to the endings of the other two films, in which there is actual or suggested apprehension of the husband by the police for the murder of the lover. Unlike the bland lover in *La Femme infidèle* or the irresistible one in *Unfaithful*, here Sunny emerges as the villain of the film because of his obsession with Simran and his mistreatment of his previous girlfriend, Radhika. Both Sudhir and Simran confess to the murder of Sunny; Sudhir actually believes he has killed Sunny, while Simran takes the blame out of a sense of guilt for starting the affair. However, both are exonerated at the end because it turns out that Sunny is still alive.

Hélène, Connie, and Simran do not fit neatly into the category of the vamp–femme fatale. Their trajectories start with an assertion of sexual desire through infidelity but are then followed by reincorporation of that sexual desire within marriage. Unlike Connie and Simran, Hélène does not regret her actions, nor does she decide to end the affair. Still, the affair and the subsequent events have made her and Charles realize their love for each other, and Hélène's last words in the film express her love to Charles just before he leaves her to talk to the police. Both Connie and Simran feel bad about their affairs and regret their actions. Simran even goes so far as to confess to the murder. In all three films, the adultery serves to bring the initial (married) couple closer together and reinfuses life into their relationship. The women are thus not punished, although the endings suggest that their transgressive desires are now contained within marriage. Another detail that almost makes them unrecognizable as femme fatales is that they are mothers.[27] Chabrol shows repeated scenes of Hélène with her son, Michel—the only relationship in the film that seems to be affective. Connie decides to end the affair when she realizes that as a result of it, she forgot to pick up her son from school. While Simran is not a biological mother, she married Sudhir for the sake of her motherless nephew, Kabir, and she stays home to care for him when he is sick.

At the same time, the three women share characteristics with the femme fatale and vamp. They are women deriving their power from their sexuality. As with the spider woman, their lovers are enmeshed in their web and are doomed; their desires disrupt the bourgeois family and patriarchy. All these factors combine in the femme fatale to create anxiety about this femininity. Unlike Phyllis or her reincarnations discussed above, these women are not deliberately manipulative. They are not aware of the power of their sexuality and are therefore similar to femme fatales like Gilda. Doane argues that this femme fatale, whose power is not subject to her own consciousness, is an ambivalent figure because she is not the subject of power but rather its *carrier* (2). Hélène, Connie, and Simran resemble this kind of femme fatale. Their lack of awareness of their sexuality and power allows them to be interpreted as innocent as opposed to the femme fatales who are sexually self-aware.

The combination of innocence with an anxiety-producing sexuality not only allows Simran to be read as Connie's Indian avatar, but also as one who shares a history with sexualized heroines of Hindi cinema such as Parveen Babi. Meenakshi Durham views Sonia as more transgressive than Simran because she deliberately disrupts the institution of family and is aware of her sexuality and power over men. While that is true, I see Sonia and Simran as both transferences of different kinds of femme fatales and alternate transformations into Bollywood codes. Both Sonia and Simran are readable as defamiliarized femininities, and the feminist politics lie in the ways in which their characters question and transform contemporary understandings of female sexuality. But they also present two different models of these femininities, a distinction having to do with the genres they are remaking. If *Jism* centers a heroine who exists outside of patriarchal constructs like the family, it also punishes her through death and translates the misogyny of film noir into terms more familiar for Hindi cinema. *Murder*, on the other hand, deriving from domestic melodrama, presents Simran as someone who may not be as cunning and smart as Sonia but is clearly a subject who opts out of a relationship that does not satisfy her emotionally or sexually.

Further, the ex-wives of Victor in *La Femme infidèle* and of Paul in *Unfaithful* (both extremely minor characters) are replaced by Sunny's ex-girlfriend, Radhika. Radhika's sexuality is more outwardly vampish because it is not contained within a marital unit. Her association with Sunny and the plot they hatch together to blackmail Sudhir further associate her with evil, thereby making Simran seem innocent in comparison. As a result, Simran also resembles the *femme attrapée*, the innocent sister of the femme fatale.[28] Thus, Simran is both the femme fatale and the *femme attrapée*, the vamp and the heroine. Reading her against these polarities serves to break down the binaries of active/passive and whore/virgin that have been utilized in Hindi cinema to play out the melodramas of vice and virtue. Sonia's transgression lies in rejecting institutions such as marriage because they are ultimately exploitative of women. Simran, on the other hand, is working from within the system to change it. She articulates a desire for change, transgresses the boundaries dictated by Hindu marriage when her needs are not met, and as a result of her transgressions is able to satisfy her needs. Therefore, even if she is reinscribed within family, her husband and their life together must change.

"This Body Only Knows Lust": Male Gaze, Female Desire, and Feminism

The femme fatale and the vamp have been complicated figures in relation to feminism. They articulate complex femininities: they can be simultaneously passive and active, fetishized objects and sexually desiring subjects, innocent and cunning. Their fetishization and portrayal as devouring monsters make explicit the misogyny behind such representations. The films representing these women often function as attempts to nullify and contain their monstrous sexuality diegetically (e.g., by punishing them) or extradiegetically (through their voyeuristic portrayal). This kind of representation reinforces the angel/whore binary by presenting the passive, domesticated woman as the angel and the active, desiring woman as evil; the unmarried women who occupy public spaces and enact their individual economic, sexual, and emotional desires are consequently othered as bad women. At the same time, these women, even if they are punished, articulate aggressive deviance that exceeds the control of the men around them. These women are in charge, whether they are conscious of it or not; the very anxiety that they create is the source of their power. And whether their portrayal is read against the grain as an expression of misogynist male projection or as one that represents actually powerful femininities, it carries within it resistance to patriarchal interpretations of the figure.

It is hardly surprising therefore that this transgressive femininity has been subject to censorship within mainstream cinema that caters to dominant ideologies of heteronormativity, which are further sanctioned and maintained by capitalism or by concerns of national culture. During the studio era in Hollywood, films were regulated by the PCA. Not only did the PCA tamp down on revealing displays of bodies and suggestions of illicit sex, but it also listed that the sympathies of the viewer should never be thrown to the side of crime and evil. Thus, femme fatales were always punished or reformed. In India, film censorship is governed by the state's Central Board of Film Certification (CBFC). The charge of obscenity is often used to warrant cuts to a film. Ganti's interviews and conversations with various Bombay film industry people reveal the subjective and arbitrary nature of the CBFC's response to films ("The Limits of Decency"). Unlike other actors and directors, Shabana Azmi, a veteran actor known for her work in art and mainstream films, points to the need for censorship but in ways different from others. She doesn't care about explicit nudity but about representation of women: "If I was on the Censor Board, I would hack a lot of things that have to do with the subservience of women, or in dialogue suggesting that women need to be put in subservient positions" (Interview qtd. in Ganti, "The Limits of Decency" 100). Alankrita Shrivastava's film *Lipstick Under My Burkha* (2016) was also flagged by the censor board for being "too lady oriented."[29]

The Bhatt family, who produced these films, is well known for challenging the censor board. Mahesh Bhatt, producer of *Murder*, coproduced *Jism* along with his daughter Pooja Bhatt. *Jism* was shocking; its representations of sexual desire and the female body did not conform to Bollywood codes, and it addressed the subject of sexuality directly and frankly. *Murder* was released a year later and pushed the boundaries even further. The two films were followed by sequels that continued these kinds of representations, thus establishing a new kind of femininity that was alternately called feminist and/or reviled as exploitative because of its closeness to the B-circuit sleaze-film depictions of female bodies. This femininity, highly sexual and sexualized and embroiled in questions of censorship and feminist politics, is now codified into the DNA of Bollywood A-circuit films. Ideological contradictions abound in this figure, as they do in previous femininities populating Hindi cinema, but the matrix, as I have argued so far, has changed because of the intersection of the vamp and the femme fatale, the Hollywood and Bollywood conventions, and the transitional cultural and economic context of the Hindi film industry. In this section, I discuss the divergent nature of this kind of transgressive femininity and its function in the industrial apparatus of Bollywood by looking at the representation of the female protagonist, at its association with the B-circuit films, and at the paratexts that construct audience expectations and desire around *Jism* and subsequent films. I suggest that a feminist approach that crosses industrial and national borders is needed to deal with such transnational representations of gender.

What is common between the vamp of Hindi cinema and the Hollywood femme fatale is that their fetishized bodies are inseparable from their sexual agency. The same body simultaneously suggests exploitation and expresses power. In *Jism*, in a scene that can be seen as both foreplay and as suggestive of the sexual act, Kabir blindfolds Sonia, opens her shirt, and plays with ice cubes on her mouth and body. The ice cube becomes sexually charged as it drips on Sonia's lips, trails across her body and her navel, and is then eaten by Kabir.[30] The camera zooms in on her navel, a habitually fetishized body part in Hindi cinema, and then alternates between close-ups of her navel, Kabir's face, and her face. It eroticizes and displays her body but simultaneously flaunts the very same body being pleasured. While the close-up of the navel resembles displays of objectified fragments of female bodies in both A-circuit and B-circuit films in India, the scene simultaneously foregrounds female sexual pleasure along with male objectification. John Abraham's chiseled body, his past work as a model, and the vulnerability that his character often expresses not only serve as an alternative to inherited models of masculinity but also queer it.[31] Here, they add to the narrative and visual aspects of the scene as well, which displace Kabir's pleasure in favor of Sonia's.

This scene in *Jism* replaces the scene of the sex act in *Body Heat*. By not showing the act, the film bows down to censorship regulations just as *Double Indemnity* does. In *Double Indemnity*, because of PCA restrictions, sexual desire is implied through clothing and editing. The first time we see Phyllis, she is wearing nothing but a towel. Suggestive dialogue between Phyllis and Neff litters the entire script, and the fact that the two have had sex is insinuated via a cut and ellipsis.[32] *Body Heat*, as already indicated, is a product of the post-PCA era and influenced by the feminist movement in film studies as well.[33] As a result, the film has nudity and sex scenes, but it also showcases in Matty the femme fatale who escapes punishment because she is more intelligent than everyone else, including the noir hero and the law.

Jism flouts censorship conventions by following the impulse of *Body Heat* in showing exposed, almost naked, bodies, and it includes the beginning of the lovemaking; however, like *Double Indemnity*, it still censors the actual act. Nevertheless, this curious play with censorship and with what to represent and what to obfuscate results in the sexual act being displayed as one of female pleasure rather than male; the male pleasure in turn gets suggested and delayed but never performed or satisfied. In *Murder*, Anurag Basu copies the intimate scene from *Unfaithful*, but since *Unfaithful* is not as explicit as *Body Heat*, the actual act is left to audience imagination. And yet the close-up of Sherawat's quivering stomach as Emraan Hashmi takes off her clothes again focuses on the navel as a fetish object, even as the quiver resembles the orgasming body. In both remakes, *Jism* and *Murder*, the male gaze is even more operative in the defiance of censorship regulations, but because of simultaneous acquiescence to the CBFC by refraining from pushing the envelope too much, the films end up privileging female pleasure over male. Sonia and Simran, as Bollywood remakes of noir and neo-noir femme fatales are thus both fetishized objects of desire and active subjects articulating desire.

The erotic display, which is transgressive in its representation of the desiring and sexualized woman on the Bollywood screen, is part of Bhatt's anticensorship stance.[34] That this is also a feminist stance, however, is questionable, especially when one looks at the extratextual material that surrounds these films. Like the item number, the sexualized song-and-dance number that became very popular in the 1990s, these films share aspects of a particular kind of B-circuit film, the sleaze-sex film. Discussing the way sleaze films skirt concerns of censorship (pornography is illegal in India), Amit Kumar argues that they manage to "advertise the forbidden spectacle of sex to the spectators" and emphasizes that the actual depiction of sex is no more found in sleaze films than in mainstream films (28). However, "the CBFC laws are flouted in innumerable cases as pornographic 'bits' find space in the sleaze-sex films" (28).[35] In both *Jism* and *Murder*, suggestive scenes, usually relegated to item numbers, are a spectacle in themselves. These scenes often get inserted as bits in sleaze films. *Murder* is one of those films that had a second life in the sleaze theaters (Amit Kumar 30). In fact, Vibhushan Subba's interview of B-circuit filmmaker Kishan Shah is quite revealing of the connections between B- and A-circuit films, especially those of his own films with the A-circuit ones made by Mahesh Bhatt: "Whatever we did earlier is now being done by Mahest [*sic*] Bhatt. The only difference is that he does it in JW Mariott and our girls are poor" (Subba 225). An A-circuit film such as *Murder*, distinguished from the B circuit by its production quality and stars, is received differently by a B-circuit audience that expects a sex film.

The promos and interviews for *Jism* and *Murder* make it clear that it was the eroticism and the sexualized bodies of Bipasha Basu and Mallika Sherawat that were being sold as new pleasures for viewers. Sherawat's history was similar to that of an item girl; this star text adds an extratextual sexualization to her as well, even if her character in *Murder* hews closer to that of the heroine than Bipasha Basu's does in *Jism*. *Jism*'s promos marketed it as sensational with the promise of erotic scenes. The name of the film, *Jism* (meaning the physical body), indicates the bodies of the good-looking model-turned-actors, but the promos focus more on the female body.[36] The way in which the word *jism* is pronounced in promos as well as by Bipasha Basu in the film—in which her husky voice drops low, creating a breathy suggestiveness about the word—draws attention to the display of the almost-naked female body. The publicity of *Jism* also borrows from another aspect of sleaze films: the film's title suggests nudity and sex. Here, the Western slang associations of the word for jizz or semen are also part of the sensory evocation of sex the title arouses.[37] The poster further presents the promise of Bipasha Basu's body on display by depicting costar John Abraham bending over her as her strap is slipping halfway off her shoulder, suggesting that if the camera had lingered a little while, she would have been fully unclothed. The songs that were prereleased and functioned as promotional materials for the films replicate the same theme.

In an interview, Abraham admits to the steaminess of the promos of the film that the music industry came out with. For instance, in the song "Jadoo Hai Nasha Hai," a shot of Bipasha Basu's bare legs gives way to Abraham's hand running across them as he drives. While Bipasha Basu and Abraham recognize the shocking nature of the promos, like Pooja Bhatt, they keep disavowing the eroticization in favor of the serious work the film is doing. Bipasha Basu claims, "It is not a pornographic film. . . . I did feel the promos were steamy . . . but the film is about a mature love story which believes that attraction draws two people together" (Chhibber). Her words point toward the transgressiveness of the theme of desire indicated by the posters and promos and frame it within a context of mature love. But then in another interview, conducted a few years after the film's release, Bipasha Basu wonders if *Jism* was a skin flick in the same way as many later films, through which actresses become overnight successes by stripping off most of their clothes and doing erotically charged scenes.[38] She wonders at the appeal of these films and says, "For some reason even the multiplex audiences who have seen enough skin in Hollywood films want to see these Bollywood skin flicks" (qtd. in S. Jha, "I Can't Do Another *Jism*"). Bipasha Basu here inadvertently admits to the cultural borrowing in the film as she indicates Hollywood as the source for the explicit sexualization and eroticization of the woman in *Jism* but fails to see connections to the sleaze-sex film or why this would appeal to the audience who has already seen it in the Hollywood films.

Murder belongs to the category of skin flicks produced by the same Bhatt family. The film was promoted in the same way as *Jism*, and the promos promise a long kissing scene between Sherawat and Emraan Hashmi, who has since been named "the serial-kisser" in Bollywood. Finally, realizing the success of these formulae for the Bollywood audience, the Bhatts decided to make sequels for both films, which were released in 2011. While Sherawat was slated to be in *Jism 2* according to the promos, Sunny Leone, an adult film industry star who joined Bollywood, played the lead role; Jacqueline Fernandez (Miss Universe, Sri Lanka 2006) played the role of a men's magazine centerspread model in *Murder 2*. The promos of the sequels on Zoom TV invoked the previous two films by using phrases such as "bare legs," "Jacqueline bares it all," "steamier and more intense love scenes," and "sexy poses and smooch-a-lot." Not only are these films selling sex, but the buzz surrounds female nudity. The scenes kept showing Sherawat and Fernandez in various states of undress, and the voice-overs repeatedly emphasized their bodies.

Bipasha Basu's earlier and later interviews express the feminist politics of *Jism* and their incorporation into the capitalist machine, respectively: the push and pull common to popular culture as it questions dominant ideologies before getting co-opted by them. The transgressive femininity gets commodified, its newness giving way by being conventionalized. Mahesh and Pooja Bhatt simultaneously reveal the workings of the market even as their interviews seek to provide a preferred interpretation of anticensorship and feminist impulses. In an interview about *Jism*, Pooja Bhatt emphasizes its newness and its feminist politics. Denying the accusation of sleaziness, she claims, "*Jism* is a very audacious film. . . . It's so refreshing to see a heroine who's so comfortable with her sexuality in a way that's generally considered unacceptable" (qtd. in S. Jha, "*Jism*"). Bhatt's remarks point toward the performance of this transgressive femininity embodied by Sonia as the heroine. The newness of the film—which, according to Bhatt, makes it feminist—is in the depiction of female sexual desire and the representation of the sexually desiring woman. Bhatt pushes against the censor guidelines without crossing them but manages to have Sonia articulate her sexual desire, something that hadn't yet been done as explicitly in Bollywood.

Mahesh Bhatt, while denying the claim of westernization, argued that his films reclaim a premodern sensuality that is Indian (qtd. in M. Durham 47). Referring, perhaps, to the now-popularized ancient texts like the *Kamasutra*, the ancient erotic art in the Khajuraho temples, and the inherited myths of gods and goddesses, Bhatt is collapsing them all to suggest that his films are invoking their sensuality. In doing so, Bhatt denies the binary by which any expression of female sexual desire is automatically othered as Western within Indian cultural conventions, particularly as expressed by inherited codes from the 1990s films. But the profit motive that underlies his intention serves to underscore the irony of the cultural fervor, especially considering that the sensual scenes are directly lifted from the Hollywood films and reproduce the conditions of the fetishized gaze. Bhatt's choice of films to remake and the way they are remade, however, also moves the vampish deviant femininity from the item numbers back to the narrative, and it goes one step further by making the vamp occupy the position of the heroine in these films.

Jism and *Murder*, their promos, and the interviews surrounding them express the workings of market forces, the functioning of censorship, and the meanings accruing around the representation of female bodies, thus heightening the existing contradictions attendant on any female body displayed in visual art because of the weight of history in dominant representations of women. Just as the remake brings in newer stories that can compete with Hollywood films on Star TV, the vampish femininity of the femme fatale and other vamps, and the sexiness of the sleaze films, compete with MTV and other channels with Western music videos by using eroticized song-and-dance numbers.[39] Viewed this way, the politics of anticensorship and feminism get sidelined, or at the very least become contradictory, because the Bhatts have combined the two to commodify this transgressive femininity. In the case of Sonia and Simran, these femininities are not only a result of cross-cultural and cross-industrial remaking, but also of changes stemming from the globalization and economic liberalization of the 1990s. All these contexts pertain to the question of how to interpret and theorize these femininities.

If the misogyny of 1940s film noir was a result of the anxiety regarding women during World War II, *Jism* is one of the first films that displays the anxiety about the changing role of women in the urban landscape of India. The economic restructuring due to post-globalization and the feminist movements since the 1970s resulted in increased numbers of women working in nontraditional professions (such as engineering, software, and management), moving to different cities to work, and delaying marriage.[40] More women have been traveling outside the country for better work and education opportunities as well. The anxiety about women living alone without a husband or parents and women in control of their own lives takes a monstrous form as it is projected onto representations like Sonia and Simran. The regressive turn in the 1990s is sustained by the Hindutva politics that were in ascendancy then and have kept growing since. The extreme right-wing RSS organization has berated women who, like these two female characters, wear Western clothes and go to pubs and dance clubs. The RSS claims that these activities defile Indian culture and are examples of Western ideas infecting it.[41] Women in Western clothes are another sign of this westernization; on the other hand, this standard has not been applied to men, who have been wearing pants and shirts in Hindi cinema without being marked as Western and therefore, other. In February 2009, the Pink Chaddi (panties) Campaign was launched against the RSS leader by a group that calls itself the "Consortium of Pub-Going, Loose and Forward Women." This campaign has been denigrated by conservatives as an example of more westernization. It has also been denounced by postcolonial feminists who see it as problematic because it belittles the domestic violence and rape of women, especially working-class women. What the campaign does draw attention to, however, is the anxiety surrounding female sexuality and its expression. The RSS arguments fall back into the kind of binaries put in place fifty years ago that demonize the sexualized woman through the trope of her westernization, thus refusing sexual freedom for women within a construction of Indianness.

Jism and *Murder* certainly bring into focus these concerns about Indian values, femininity, and feminism in the twenty-first century. Meenakshi Durham uses these two films to talk about a change in which women come to represent the nation in the postliberalization era. She even goes so far as to claim that in this period, women become the ambassadors of the nation quite literally by, for example, competing in and winning beauty pageants (53). These women are global hybrids representing points of contact between India and the

West.[42] The characters of Sonia and Simran present something new in the ways in which they bring together Indian and Western values. They may sport Western clothing, or they may be saree-wearing sex sirens and present a modern femininity by combining the Bollywood vamp, the Bollywood heroine, and the Hollywood femme fatale. Instead of denying their power by seeing them only as examples of cultural imperialism or conversely by celebrating their empowerment uncritically, I'd argue that they represent complex expressions of an Indian globalized femininity and feminism. If they become symbols of national progress instead of guardians of national culture, furthermore, their problematic representation needs a new approach as well.

While it is liberating to see the reversal of this gender dynamic vis-à-vis the nation, as the analysis of these two remakes has shown, the new representation of the feminine is both empowering and debilitating for women. It can be empowering because women are allowed to modernize themselves and are allowed freedom from the ideologies of Indianness. And there is proof that many women are working and have the freedom to choose the kind of clothes they want to wear. At the same time, this is true only for a small section of urban and middle- or upper-class women. While the idea of a national culture is losing its hold, religious ideologies have become stronger and seek to control women's lives in the same way that national ideologies did in the postindependence period.[43] Further, the binary of Indian and Western is detrimental to an understanding of the feminist potential of these films. This binary may also disallow certain Western theoretical approaches that are very relevant here. The beauty queens share with the femme fatales their fetishization borrowed from Western ideologies. The beauty pageants where these women represent the nation are Western, and the eroticization of the femme fatale is a Western import as well. These remade vamps and femme fatales thus demand both a theoretical approach that takes into account Western feminist theory and a theoretical approach based in Bollywood's ways of representation and looking.

Scholars have sometimes applied Western feminist theory to Hindi films. For example, the Mulveyan conception of the gaze has often been used to analyze the fetishistic display of bodies in item numbers that are often similar to cabaret performances. While scholars tend to mention it, many (such as Ravi Vasudevan, Rachel Dwyer, and Philip Lutgendorf) have also indicated the inadequacy of using Western theory for mainstream Hindi cinema because its codes of representation and formal features are significantly different. Certainly, the visual spectacle of the item number, the affect of the performance, and the usual presence of audiences within the diegesis call for a different method. However, these approaches need not negate the presence of the simultaneous structuring of the gaze in these numbers as well. The intertextuality between the two cinemas, Hollywood and Bollywood, and the ways in which the camera splinters, cuts across, and ogles female bodies, often from the perspective of male characters, is common as a part of the production process. In fact, in an interview, the feminist filmmaker Alankrita Shrivastava mentions the frustration of teaching cameramen to not automatically fall into these patterns of filming for her shoots, thus indicating the insidious nature of this kind of filming that has become part of the mainstream.[44]

Lutgendorf talks about *darsán* to approach the gaze in Hindi films. He differentiates this gaze from the one at work in Hollywood films: "*Darsán* is a two-way street; a visual interaction between players who, though not equal, are certainly both in the same theater of activity" (234). *Darsán*, for him, is reciprocal between characters or between character and audience. This certainly applies to the item girls, who often perform to the audience within the film and to the audiences in the theater and at home. I mentioned earlier how the vamp mostly disappeared from the Bollywood screen in the 1990s, and the sexualized female body instead appeared and was contained within the item number, the word *item* literally reducing the woman to an object. At the same time, the songs sung by the character, the *item*, are very self-reflexive in the ways in which she draws attention to her body and its pleasures. She is thus a woman acknowledging the gaze directed at her and returning it by taking control of her body. Often placed as a woman dancing at a bar or at a performance, the item girl also addresses her viewers as customers, unequivocally exposing the prostitution-like purchase of bodies that is at the heart of voyeurism in cinematic viewing. This returned gaze is also evident in both Sonia and Simran, who embrace their sexuality and revel in its display. While they are objects of scopophilia, their agency also makes them identificatory subjects. Parallels can certainly be drawn between the concept of *darsán* and a kind of returned gaze in Hollywood films, but the cultural context ascribes different meanings to it. Another aspect of *darsán* is the hierarchy in which the star becomes the equivalent of the deity: god or goddess. The stardom of Bipasha Basu and Sherawat thus also creates a simultaneous inclusion of awe that accompanies the scopophilic gaze. The power dynamic between viewer and viewed is therefore in constant negotiation.

The different contexts of viewing films in the United States and India provide an additional approach to how these films are viewed and interpreted. Hamid Naficy's argument about accented cinema is applicable to certain kinds of viewing practices in India. Naficy argues that third-world film spectatorship can be very different from spectatorship in a US theater. Audiences may interrupt the viewing experience by talking among themselves and talking back to the screen,[45] instead of watching in silence and darkness—the latter essential to a Mulveyan understanding of the gaze that functions through immersion and identification with the male character, which is in turn dependent on the forgetting of cinematic apparatus and of other viewers in the theater. While audiences in an Indian theater may indulge in similar activities, even the form of Hindi films disallows immersive viewing practice. The constant interruption of immersion in a Hindi film through the actual ten-minute intermission, as well as the action sequences, song-and-dance sequences, and other visual spectacles, makes Lalitha Gopalan call Hindi cinema "a cinema of interruptions" (10). However, she also points to the movement between audience awareness of the film as a film and immersion in the diegesis. The interruptions may break immersion, but viewers are also used to their convention and still can identify with the world of the film. Recently, with the rise of multiplex cinemas, viewing practices are also changing, and often the multiplex audience behaves in ways similar to Hollywood audiences, the multiplex generating an etiquette amenable to conditions of voyeuristic viewing. Both *Jism* and *Murder* combine codes of representation from Hollywood and popular Hindi cinema. The camera angles and shots of Simran's half-clad body reference Western cinema's conventionally soft-pornographic and voyeuristic codes of representation (M. Durham 51). The song-and-dance numbers serve more like music videos, with the song playing in the background as characters are immersed in each other. These codes invite a passive audience as well.

While the industrial and sociocultural context is important for interpreting these films, some of these differences also exist in Hollywood cinema. For example, the returned gaze is also in evidence in the femme fatales, and spectacles often rupture diegetic continuity.

Recent phenomenological work opens up new ways of approaching the cinematic apparatus in which the camera does not merely become a conduit for the gaze. Instead, we are embedded in a constant mutual experience of the film (Barker 19). Other scholars use Deleuze to talk about spectatorial participation in film because of the affect that the performing body creates in the viewer.[46] The visceral effect of the item numbers and even the other musical numbers in *Jism* and *Murder* allow for alternative bodily ways of engaging with the films. The movement of the camera and the movement of the bodies on screen can create an affect that is further heightened by the sound and music. The camera revels in these women's excessive sexual display and indicates a progressive potential in the performance of sexual femininities as opposed to representation of fetishized bodies. In fact, the movement of the camera may heighten the aspect of *darsán* in these films because it often uses a lower angle, which gives these women looming presence.

To conclude, I want to return to the concept of cross-cultural defamiliarization engendered by the remake in the postliberalization era. The hybrid femininities represented by Sonia and Simran, and the potential for defamiliarization, are an effect of the changing nature of remaking by Bollywood. The remake, arguably a conservative form in the 1990s, does not have to completely transform the Hollywood film into one that fits within inherited codes. Rather, the experimentation made possible by a host of reasons—new filmmakers on the scene, multiplex cinema allowing for films for niche audiences, and changing cultural context—now allows filmmakers to both transfer foreign themes that were previously considered anathema and transform certain other characteristics within Bollywood conventions.[47] The resultant femininity, which is both similar to and different from the Hollywood femme fatale and the Hindi vamp, is then unconventional for audiences. Therefore, it creates a space for viewers to become aware of the changes from conventions, which here include a protagonist, who is an unapologetic, sexually desiring woman, and one who rejects the patterns of the ideal wife that are otherwise celebrated by Hindi cinema. This defamiliarization simultaneously enforces the viewer's implication in gazing at the fetishized female body, too. For viewers familiar with Hollywood noir, these characters invite a self-reflexive gaze by making explicit the characteristics of the femme fatale and the Hindi vamp that compose the new Bollywood vamp. And, given the different cultural contexts of representation and interpretation of the displayed female body, these two remakes also defamiliarize accepted notions of interpretation and allow for a combination of feminist approaches. This political potential ushered in by *Jism*, however, seems to be short-lived, as these patterns of representation soon become conventionalized and conservative, and the sequels of the two films promise more sensational bodies on display but without the individuality and power of the Bollywood vamp.

3

From Remake to Pastiche

Bollywood, Hollywood, and Noir Masculinity

S RIRAM RAGHAVAN'S *Johnny Gaddaar* (*Johnny the Traitor*) (2007) is bookended by a scene that is shown in gray scale at the beginning of the film and in color at the end. The black-and-white precredit scene evokes the atmosphere of classic noir: the night and rain create a claustrophobic effect as a police van patrols the area (see fig. 3.1). A car hurtles through the empty streets and screeches to a halt in front of a gated house; a man runs out to the garage door; very slowly, a hand holding a gun materializes in the lower right-hand corner of the frame and fires several shots; the man's body convulses against the half-opened garage door and falls to the ground moments before it comes crashing down. The frame is then suffused with blood-red color that streams down the garage door, and the name of the film is emblazoned across the screen, now saturated in a red haze. This scene's monochromatic color scheme gives way to a contrasting burst of color in the credit sequence that immediately follows. The neo-noirish red filters and the tint that gives the images a gritty illustrative look are combined with the music and style of credits reminiscent of 1970s Hindi films. The music recalls the kind of score that accompanied chase sequences in the action-laced masala films of the past and complements the montage containing shots from Vijay Anand's *Johny Mera Naam* (*My Name Is Johny*) (1970) and Jyoti

Figure 3.1. Opening scene of *Johnny Gaddaar* that pays homage to classic film noir. *Source: Johnny Gaddaar* (Sriram Raghavan 2007).

Swaroop's *Parwana (Moth)* (1971). The fonts and the languages (for example, the Urdu titles) likewise serve as reminders of pre-1990s films. The visual style also resembles the transnational neo-noir discernible in Quentin Tarantino's and Guy Ritchie's films and draws attention to the filmmaker's craft. The first few noir shots of this black and white sequence are reproduced in color at the end of the film thus showing how neo-noir does noir in color as well. Stylistically as well as textually, *Johnny Gaddaar* revels in announcing its intertextuality with international noir, including Hollywood and past Hindi cinema.

Raghavan's cinephilia and affection for noir and neo-noir genres and auteurs are obvious in the visual style of the film. *Johnny Gaddaar* also begins with a dedication to "crime thriller maestros, Vijay Anand and James Hadley Chase" (Bonus Materials on DVD). Much as the remaking of noir involves an immediate linkage with issues of masculinity, the auteurist neo-noir and heist films confirm that intentionality. Bollywood's love for noir as remake material finds expression in gendered ways. In this chapter, I focus on changing ideas of masculinity in Abbas-Mustan's *Baazigar (Gambler)* (1993), Sanjay Gupta's *Kaante (Thorns)* (2002), Navdeep Singh's *Manorama Six Feet Under* (2007), and Raghavan's *Johnny Gaddaar*. This particular charting from the 1990s and the 2000s allows me to pay attention to shifts in the industry that affect the ways in which the films represent their worlds. Further, all four films are influenced by noir, a genre known for its promiscuous intertextuality and traveling across international industries. Therefore, these films, while acknowledging their Hollywood influence, also complicate any hierarchy between Hollywood and Bollywood by foregrounding the transnational borrowing that is part of any global industry, including that of Hollywood.[1]

While these films exhibit noir characteristics, including its gender dimensions, they each present a new articulation of and anxiety around masculinity. The films are also different in the ways in which they each register the influence of their source texts, which I argue are representative of the industrial context within which they were produced. *Baazigar* is closer to Sheila Nayar's theorizations of Indian remakes as adaptations since it borrows the general plot, common to all versions of *A Kiss Before Dying*, but changes significant details and adds a whole new subplot. *Kaante* follows the plot of Tarantino's *Reservoir Dogs* (1992) but still Indianizes the characters by providing personal and familial motivations that justify their actions. Neither of these films overtly acknowledges its Hollywood influences.[2] On the other hand, *Manorama Six Feet Under* and *Johnny Gaddaar* each offer intertextual acknowledgements of the texts that influence them. *Manorama Six Feet Under* largely remakes Roman Polanski's *Chinatown* (1974) but includes some scenes that remind the viewer of Robert Aldrich's *Kiss Me Deadly* (1955). *Johnny Gaddaar* self-reflexively pastiches older Hindi cinema and Hollywood noir. The cinephilic imaginations of the two directors here and the nod to the source texts set these films apart from previous remakes and present pastiche as a form of meta remaking that simultaneously reflects on Hindi cinema's remaking practice and distinguishes itself from it. Instead of seeing these films as evidence of a change in Bollywood forms, however, I see them as examples of *hatke* cinema—a sort of auteurist alternative to Bollywood mainstream, which, at the same time, is made possible by and profits from the corporatized changes within Bollywood. *Manorama Six Feet Under* and *Johnny Gaddaar* both bear the stamp of the director, or auteur, and serve as reminders of earlier noir cinephiles like the French New Wave directors. The self-reflexivity about the borrowing puts these films in the realm of pastiche.

Film noir has close ties with cinephilia and auteurism, as well as with masculinity. The genre was recognized as such by French critics, and New Wave auteurs were already remaking noir. Jean-Luc Godard's *À bout de souffle* (*Breathless*) (1966) is one such example that serves to blur the boundaries between notions of originality and copying by presenting, through pastiche, a form of remaking that is quite original. Similarly neo-noir (particularly Tarantino's films) further undermines any claims to authorship based on the concept of originality because it borrows and reshapes a genre but paradoxically resurrects the auteur at the same time. Both Godard's *À bout de souffle* and Tarantino's neo-noir films use pastiche as their remaking practice. While it is a form of remaking, pastiche differs from other kinds of remaking because it "imitates other art in such a way as to make consciousness of this fact central to its meaning and affect" (Dyer, *Pastiche* 4). While *Baazigar*, and even *Kaante* to an extent, lends itself to discussions of the remake as a copy, the pastiches that Raghavan's and Singh's films present problematize such conceptions. Their films revel in intertextual invocations from both Hollywood and Bollywood sources, thus undoing any hierarchical understandings of the two industries as superior or inferior.

Like film noir, French New Wave, and neo-noir, Bollywood remakes and pastiches of noir are connected with concerns of masculinity at various levels. David Desser uses the term *global noir* for neo-noir to indicate its transnational movement and claims that these films tend to follow different aspects of noir. For instance, many neo-noir films abandon the trope of the femme fatale altogether; others might follow the formula of the couple on the run. Šarūnas Paunksnis discerns noir aesthetic in Hindi cinema of the 1950s but argues that noir becomes a much more common feature in postliberalization Bollywood films starting in the 1990s (91). Paunksnis also notices a stress on masculinity in these films and situates them as being connected to male anxiety and the development of identity. However, the cinephilic engagement with genre and style, which is also a facet of neo-noir, can be very masculinist and often misogynist. While some Western neo-noir films have complicated the role of the femme fatale, films such as Tarantino's *Reservoir Dogs* and Ritchie's *Lock, Stock, and Two Smoking Barrels* erase women from the diegesis. Even the extra features on the *Lock, Stock, and Two Smoking Barrels* special edition DVD present the actors and director as a sort of masculine club of buddies and the set as a comfortable male space where men can be men. The special edition of the DVD thus expands the all-male world to its audience and consumer, the fanboy. Instead of discussing all the noir films that Paunksnis mentions, I'm looking at Bollywood remakes or deliberate pastiches of noir, which then negotiate across these kinds of masculinities.

Kaante and *Johnny Gaddaar* function very similarly as masculine spaces because they borrow from the noir heist film as well as from Hindi cinema. Therefore, women exist in these films, but the films themselves are more concerned with masculinity. The central couple of contemporary Hindi cinema gets replaced by all-male relationships, which form the main affective unit. Furthermore, given that Bollywood's codes of verisimilitude have close ties with representation of gender, masculinity becomes pivotal in understanding the change in Bollywood's remaking processes through these films as being affected by changes in the industry. But while *Kaante* remakes *Reservoir Dogs*, it does not reach the stage of pastiche because the film does not reveal any self-consciousness about its imitation. *Johnny Gaddaar* on the other hand presents a pastiche of neo-noir and Hindi cinema through its aesthetics and its array of masculinities, recognizable to other cinephiles of noir and Hindi cinema.

From Antiheroes to Gangsters: Translating Noir Masculinity

In chapter 1, I discussed how Bollywood remakes of Hollywood films display the industry's anxieties about retaining its identity in the 1990s. While I focused on the family film and the concept of ideal femininity in that chapter, here I address the issue of masculinity in the remake. Several scholars, including Ravi Vasudevan and Rosie Thomas, have argued that in popular Hindi cinema (of the 1950s through the 1980s), women were often represented as upholders of Indian culture, whereas men were allowed some freedom to borrow from what were understood to be Western codes—therefore men could wear Western clothes as opposed to women, who had to wear saris, especially after they were married; men had more sexual freedom than women; and men could even be on the wrong side of the law as long as they adhered to the code of dharma in a way that explained or justified their actions within the melodramatic moral universe of the film. But hero and heroine remained as Hindi cinema's core templates in which "masculinity is the flip side of femininity" (Virdi 87).

Heroes and villains in post-1950s cinema are commonly aligned according to their relationship with the nation. In one of these popular East/West oppositions, the hero is often the one on the side of the masses, while the villain is a personification of evil, represented as surrounded with mise-en-scène that is a visual reminder of his foreignness (he typically wears Western, almost flamboyant, attire, including a suit and hat, and chains and rings, while employing an exaggerated and fake westernized accent). The hero figure is used to critique systemic inequalities, which can take the shape of caste or class differences in these films. In the films of the 1970s and 1980s, the hero struggles against threats to the nation, which are often represented by underworld dons, organized crime, and independent smugglers. Anxiety about the West is resurrected in the 1990s because of globalization and the movement of Indians to cities such as London and New York; many family films of this decade deal with the problematic diasporic hero whose home exists literally outside the nation's space. This anxiety regarding the national imaginary is manifest in films with names like *Pardes* (*Foreign Land*) (Subhash Ghai 1997) and *Phir Bhi Dil Hai Hindustani* (*And Yet the Heart Is Indian*) (Aziz Mirza 2000), the latter deliberately taking its cue from a 1950s film song that assures the listener of the hero's Indian heart despite his global travels and international commodities. *Pardes* resolves this problem by valorizing the diasporic hero, Arjun (Shah Rukh Khan), and contrasting him against the "bad diasporic hero," Rajiv (Apurva Agnihotri). Arjun respects Indian traditions and patriarchy, and he believes in Indian women's honor, whereas Rajiv, who has become westernized, ridicules his own fiancée's belief in virtue and even tries to rape her.

The antihero of 1990s films, however, proves that a larger range of expressions was made possible for heroes than for heroines. While the "yuppy diasporic hero" image of Shah Rukh Khan dominates the 1990s, it is preceded by a psychopathic and obsessive antihero image of him in thriller films, released earlier. *Baazigar*, the 1993 neo-noir remake of *A Kiss Before Dying* introduces this persona for Shah Rukh Khan that is quite the ideological opposite of his family film persona. Instead of presenting an upper-class, cosmopolitan hero, *Baazigar* and similar films present a vengeful and evil hero. The antihero in Hindi film is not new: several pre-1990s films were about male protagonists, not always heroic ones, who had gone bad but were recovered morally via the operation of an alternative moral code, dharma, that showed their anger as being rooted in systemic oppression and in the failure of the state to secure protection and rights for the most vulnerable. In antihero films of the 1990s, however, that code does not operate as the antihero's anger is very individualistic, likely a result of the translation of Hollywood film as well as of the privileging of capitalist and bourgeois ideologies over those of kinship, family, and class, ideologies that are symptomatic of neo-liberalism.

The figure of the mother, however, remains central in both kinds of films about the antihero in creating an affective and sympathetic relationship between the viewers and the protagonists. Thomas has talked about the centrality of the mother in Hindi films as one of the cornerstones of the melodramatic mode as it operated in pre-1990s Hindi cinema. Sudhir Kakar argues that India's hegemonic narrative centers around the *devi*, the mother goddess, instead of being an oedipal narrative (131–32).[3] As a result, the erotic desire between mother and son is disavowed by making the mother into an object of worship and adoration. In fact, Thomas mentions that one of the unwritten codes of popular Hindi cinema concerns the mother's sexuality—even the threat of rape is never admitted when it comes to this ideal figure ("Melodrama" 167). It is not surprising, then, that the mother becomes one of the central figures around whom masculine codes develop in the melodramatic mode. In fact, this mother-son bond assures the viewer of the hero's "Indianness" despite his participation in modernization.[4] Moreover, since many of these films deal with absent fathers, the son graduates to the role of the patriarch by becoming the protector of the mother, and by extension of all the other women in his family, the nation.[5]

For example, the connections of the mother and the nation, in the quintessential film *Mother India* (Mehboob Khan 1957), which emphasizes the mother-son bond, further connects the son with Indian codes of masculinity. In *Mother India*, Birju (Sunil Dutt) keeps trying to exact revenge against Sukhilala (Kanhaiyalal Chaturvedi), a moneylender who has harassed his mother, Radha (Nargis). As part of this revenge, Birju abducts Sukhilala's daughter on her wedding day. Radha is presented as the idealized mother of all (as Mother India), and to protect the village's daughter, she shoots her son, who then dies on her lap. This trope of the son avenging his mother has become iconic and one of the central codes of the hero's *dharma* due to its repetition over several films.[6]

Deewaar (Yash Chopra 1975) almost reenacts the scene of Birju's death from *Mother India*. Amitabh Bachchan plays the role of Vijay, who, along with his mother and brother, has been harassed and mistreated because his father had betrayed the workers in his own union. While serving as his union's leader, Vijay's father stopped the protests when he was blackmailed and his family was threatened; unable to take the shame, he abandoned his family. Some of the angry workers tattoo the young Vijay's arm with the words *My father is a thief*; subsequently, the mother takes Vijay and Ravi and goes to Bombay to work as a laborer. The kids grow up in poverty, and the two sons end up taking divergent paths. Ravi studies and becomes an upholder of the law as a policeman. Vijay, after working as a boot polisher, first fights against the underworld don Iftekhar and then eventually joins him. Vijay becomes rich and wants to help his mother, but she refuses. He says to her, "Whatever I did, I did for you," but his mother, much like Radha in *Mother India*, holds the moral center, and it is because of her that Vijay never becomes completely evil. The film ends with the two brothers pitted against each other as the police chase Vijay. Like in *Mother India*, the film ends as the son succumbs to his injuries in his mother's arms.

Deewaar introduced Amitabh Bachchan's star text as the angry young man, and many of his films in the 1970s have him reprise this role as a critique of systemic oppression. His characters' anger often rests in their working-class roots and they challenge the system by being on the wrong side of the law. While this angry-young-man character pushed at the boundaries of accepted masculinity, he was often killed off because there was no place for a self-appointed vigilante or revolutionary figure. Still, the villain in these films was always represented as an extremely westernized, lascivious, and evil goon who served as a clear contrast to the hero, or in this case, also the antihero. Therefore, when Shah Rukh Khan's character tested the limits of masculinity in *Baazigar*, it was radical—especially for the 1990s when the mainstream heroes were playing cute nextdoor neighbors or diasporic yuppies—but it was not rejected by audiences as unfeasible. Khan problematized the clear hero/villain binary by recovering the strain of the antihero from pre-1990s films as the central affective figure; in this character's translation from the Hollywood film, it brings with it differences that disallow its redemption.

Nayar argues that *Baazigar* is proof that Hindi remakes of Western scripts are adapted versions because they borrow broad plotlines (74). Certainly, it is hard to ascertain which version of *A Kiss Before Dying* it remakes because it borrows loosely from the main story. The film then adds significant plot in order to provide a rationale for the revisionist hero figure, who is a murderer. However, while the codes of popular Hindi cinema still exerted a force on how the film was remade, the violent, sadistic masculinity that *Baazigar* ushered in shocked and thrilled its audiences. Like many remakes in the 1990s, *Baazigar*'s remaking process still occurred within the cultural codes of Indian masculinity. The antihero introduced by the remake is the misogynist male of neo-noir, but his translation needed significant alteration for audiences to have sympathy for him. Nayar discusses *Baazigar* as an adaptation while discussing Hindi remakes of foreign texts because she argues, "Even given the filmmakers' borrowing, stealing and blatant plagiarism, these finished products are *indisputably* Indian. American plots and themes cannot be diaphanously disguised in Indian clothing; duplication is impossible" (75). At the same time, she sets the remakes she discusses apart from others that flop at the box office because "they are cheap imitations of an earlier film" (74). In the latter case, she is referencing Bollywood remakes of previous Hindi films because they don't have to go through the cultural and industrial transformation necessary in a cross-cultural remake. *Baazigar* fits her description because it borrows the plotline from *A Kiss Before Dying*—the borrowing is blatant enough to qualify *Baazigar* as a remake, but at the same time, it is not a close copy, and therefore it is impossible to know whether it is an adaptation from the book or a remake from one of the film versions of the book. Nevertheless, the triangulated relationship that arguably exists between the book, the 1956 film version, and the 1991 film version of *A Kiss Before Dying* does not really extend to *Baazigar* since the remake is not competing in the same market with the other two.

The bare-bones plot of *A Kiss Before Dying* contains an obsessive psychopathic man, Bud/Jonathan Corliss, who lives with his mother near the railway tracks. He kills his rich girlfriend, Dorothy, when she tells him that she is pregnant and that her father will disinherit her when he finds out. Then he starts wooing Dorothy's sister Ellen in order to get access to her father's fortune and business. But Ellen investigates her sister's death and inadvertently finds out that he is her murderer. In the book, he kills Ellen and pursues a third sister, Marion, who is nonexistent in the films. In each film version, a confrontation occurs between Corliss and Ellen, and he dies. There are differences between the versions: in the 1956 adaptation, a former police officer helps Ellen investigate the crime; and in the 1991 version, Ellen investigates on her own.

Baazigar changes some aspects, which are instead reminiscent of *Mother India* and *Deewaar* in how the past shapes the hero's present psyche. *Baazigar* starts with a flashback to Ajay's childhood (Ajay, played by Shah Rukh Khan, is the Bud/Jonathan character), and the rest of the film is interspersed with scenes from Ajay's childhood that show his family's sharp decline into poverty. Ajay's father, Vishwanath Sharma (Anant Mahadevan), is a rich businessman who owns his own company. Madan Chopra (Dalip Tahil), one of his trusted employees, cheats Vishwanath and usurps his business, and Vishwanath is forced to live on the streets with his family. Unlike *A Kiss Before Dying*, in which the protagonist's resentment has roots in poverty, here the poverty itself is a result of evil carried out in the film; this extra plot is added to create sympathy for Ajay and an understanding of his desire for revenge. Anjum Rajabali, writer for *Ghulam*, talks about how plain ambition of *A Kiss Before Dying*'s protagonist wouldn't have worked in *Baazigar*: "Guy killing for ambition? No sympathy for him at all. But, if the guy has a back-story, wherein his father was cheated by his company *wallah* (guy) and now wants the company back as revenge and retribution for that . . . I can consider forgiving him all those killings. Not entirely of course, killing is killing, so he has to die himself in the end, but he will carry my sympathy with him" (qtd. in Ganti, "And Yet My Heart" 145). The filmmakers' additions to the film show how emotion and sympathy are constructed to appeal to viewers. Unable to take the blow of treachery, and unable to provide food and safety to his family, Ajay's father gives up and dies. Soon Ajay's baby sister succumbs to illness and dies too. These deaths unhinge Ajay's mother to the extent that she suffers from memory loss. Therefore, even before Ajay plots his vengeance, he has been portrayed as a victim and an object of pathos. Moreover, a justification for his psychopathic personality is also set in place by the remake because a murdering hero who kills just because he is poor would not jibe with the parameters of masculine heroism on the Bollywood screen in the 1990s.

In another twist, Ajay assumes a double identity like Jonathan does in the 1991 version. Unlike Bud/Jonathan, who first gets rid of one sister and then moves to the next, Ajay dates both sisters at the same time. As Ajay, he dates and kills Seema (Shilpa Shetty); as Vicky, an assumed name, he wears brown-colored contact lenses and dates Priya (Kajol), who is living in a hostel in Madras. Ajay/Vicky is able to get into Madan Chopra's good graces and eventually reenacts the exact same scenario with Chopra that Chopra had done to his father—take over the business and make him leave. Meanwhile, Priya's investigation into her sister's death leads her to Ajay's home, where his mother is still living. A fight sequence follows as Ajay arrives, and then Chopra arrives with his men. Ajay is able to kill Chopra, but mortally wounded, he approaches his mother, who is now suddenly cured, and he dies on her lap.[7]

Baazigar adapts the story for a Bollywood audience in terms that are familiar. As I mentioned earlier, it has multiple resonances with *Mother India* and *Deewaar*, particularly in the fact that the son's resentment stems from a horrible childhood that is rooted in systemic injustice and poverty. Vijay, in *Deewaar*, dies on his mother's lap, but he never plots the murder of innocent people like Ajay does in *Baazigar*. The additions and changes to the plot humanize the otherwise psychopathic Ajay, and Priya's compassion and love for him align the audience's sympathies with him. Furthermore, his vengeance strikes a chord with audience members, who are persuaded via melodramatic tropes into identifying with the little boy who is trying to find medicine for his dying sister, is feeding a mentally ill mother, and is attempting to earn some money by doing small menial jobs. Still, although we are blatantly manipulated by the film into sympathizing with Ajay, none of these details is ultimately enough to offset the shock at seeing him indulge in the carefully planned, cold-blooded murder of innocent people such as Seema, which is why he cannot survive at the end of the film.

This role of the hero-villain marked a break from the portrayal of masculinities in Bollywood films especially when seen in the context of other roles Shah Rukh Khan performed in his films around that time. *Baazigar*, followed shortly by *Darr* (*Fear*) (Yash Chopra 1993), introduced this new persona for Shah Rukh Khan, who was not yet very famous in the industry. Ultimately, through this new, transferred role of the antihero, Bollywood shocked audiences by going against its codes for the hero. Nevertheless, Khan's image with this film and later on was, and continues to be, heroic, and it therefore already exerts an interpretive force over his reception in conjunction with that film. It still retains enough continuity—for example, through the mother-son bond and familial loyalty—for *Baazigar* to be a popular hit. Nayar asserts, "The psychopathic snapping is not without 'cause'—unlike in the original, where the murderer's motive is sheer greed: a desire for power and entry into an otherwise impenetrable world of business moguls" (80). While it is true that *Baazigar* provides enough reasons to sway audience sympathies into accepting this new character, the film is simultaneously very problematic. The familial connections here remain at the level of personal vengeance, and the film offers no critique of society, which again differentiates it from the angry-young-man films of the 1970s.[8]

I also disagree with Nayar about the character of Bud/Jonathan Corliss in *A Kiss Before Dying*. The lack of familial motivation in his case does not automatically signal the individualism that is often seen to characterize Hollywood film noir, neo or otherwise. The juxtaposition of the dilapidated house with the railway tracks right next to it, where trains branded "Carlsson Copper" (in the 1991 film) constantly run transporting metal, allows us to see how his obsession to own the company has its roots in his class position. His attempts to wrest power and money through unethical means are undoubtedly a critique of the capitalism and class divisions that enforce terrible conditions for the poor and working class and that allow the rich to keep getting richer. Linda Williams, while writing about body genres, applies the idea of the originary fantasy to the noir protagonist, his desire for this fantasy being rooted in a preoedipal past. This past, "which exists at the juncture of an irrecoverable real and an imaginary event that never took place" is always out of reach because it never fully existed and cannot exist (Williams, "Film Bodies" 154). While there is a literal mother present in *A Kiss Before Dying*, the protagonist's attempts to secure a future is rooted in this fantasy of an idyllic past in which poverty doesn't exist, and the class-based trauma would never occur.

Baazigar, on the other hand, presents that preoedipal past as real. It gets rid of the critique of class divisions that had been integral to

Hindi films from the 1970s and 1980s. We are made to sympathize with and take pity on Ajay and his family, but this pity is targeted at a family that is not used to poverty and has been forced into this deplorable condition. Because Ajay lacks a connection with a larger collectivity that exists in earlier Hindi films, his story is not a depiction of poor people but of a once rich family that loses everything. This past then is not one of idyllic fantasy but of a neoliberal fantasy resulting from capitalism and patriarchy. The melodramatic moral order of the film therefore tends toward a sense of rightness that is about the rich regaining what they consider theirs instead of being about a working-class revolution. It is the means that Ajay takes to achieve this that are shocking and that therefore make us believe the individual character is in the wrong. Nevertheless, the film sympathizes with Ajay's plight by presenting a story arc in which moral order is restored through his destruction of the Chopras. The erasure of working-class context in the film—whether we see it in the difference from the source texts or from the previous Hindi films—is actually a symptom of industrial changes. Bollywood in the 1990s increasingly targets the middle classes and the diaspora as desired audiences, and therefore the films of that time represent an ideological shift to validate a bourgeois value system.[9]

As much as *Baazigar* violates Bollywood conventions in presenting this psychopathic murderer as hero, it also retains continuity with some of these conventions so that this new figure is not completely rejected by the audience. The film became very popular partly because of the way Shah Rukh Khan broke the mold of the hero. This character retains audience sympathy, moreover, because he carries within him the ambiguity and sense of doom that usually characterize the noir hero. Ajay sets out to take revenge on Chopra and get hold of his father's business. Despite his careful manipulation and planning, however, he increasingly loses control. The events he sets into motion exceed his plans, so he seems caught in a web where the only option available to him is to keep on murdering people to prevent the truth from coming out. Having been unable to save his family from ruin when he was a child, and later unable to take care of his mother, Ajay exemplifies failed masculinity. The only way he can regain it is by taking over the business from the man who unmanned his father. The concept of family honor, for Ajay, is tied to the performance of masculinity as the patriarch who protects and provides for his family and that constantly evades him until the very end. The ending restores to him his family honor and his fantasy (complete with the cured mother), even though he has to die for it. Unlike the lone protagonist of classical Hollywood noir who is defined against the family, Ajay is reinscribed into the family through the mother and through his death. Thus, the Hindi film translates the noir hero but makes him into Bollywood's hero by emphasizing his valuation of family, one of the tenets of 1990s family films. While he shares similarities with the earlier male heroes of Hindi cinema, the difference here is in the interiority the character is allowed to display.

As I mentioned earlier, one of the ways 1990s Bollywood deals with the threats of globalization and westernization is through family films that constantly present family values as ideals that reassure in the face of the movement of Indians into the West. The bourgeois Hindu family becomes the epitome of Indianness in these films, and often sons and daughters are willing to sacrifice personal and individual desires for the sake of the family.[10] While it is clear that the emphasis on Indianness through family values is a more conservative adaptation of pre-1990s codes of Bollywood, the masculine hero becomes reduced to the wealthy male diasporic Indian.[11] The articulation of an alternate masculinity that emerged through the translation of the noir hero in *Baazigar* disappears for almost a decade and then resurfaces in the twenty-first century when Sanjay Gupta remakes Tarantino's *Reservoir Dogs*. However, by the time *Kaante* hit the market in 2002, there had also been a shift in the way that Bollywood's product was changing, thus opening up space for more experimentation with codes of gender.[12] The mid-1990s concern with a cultural identity ceased to hold sway in the same way, although films continue to be marketed to bourgeois and diasporic audiences.

Since the remake tends to translate its source into the codes of an industry, the way that Gupta reimagines Tarantino's film is interesting because of its differences from previous remakes of noir and Hollywood films. The entire film revolves around an Indian gang operating in Los Angeles, the quintessential Hollywood noir city. The men are given backstories that explain and justify their involvement in the gang. As a step further from the antihero of *Baazigar*, the film introduces the idea of a Hollywood-style Bollywood gangster film for its globalized Indian audience.[13] Instead of one antihero, *Kaante* is concerned with an entire gang, and all of its members are antiheroes.

In *Reservoir Dogs*, a gang of men decides to commit a jewelry heist, which goes horribly wrong. As a result, the gang members are mutually suspicious of each other, and the film ends with all but one dead on the floor.[14] In *Kaante*, the story gets expanded to include the personal lives of these members. While ostensibly these men meet each other in jail and decide on the heist because they are angry about the racism of the Los Angeles Police Department (LAPD), their individual needs for money also play a role in the decision. The wife of Major (Amitabh Bachchan) is dying, and he wants to take her back to India as that is her last wish. He is trying to fulfill it through honest means and is almost successful in getting a client to consider his business proposal, but the LAPD picks him up as a suspect, thus wrecking his chances. Marc (Sunil Shetty) wants the money so he can "rescue" his girlfriend from a life of stripping at the bar where he used to work as a bouncer. Andy (Kumar Gaurav) needs to be able to provide for his son, or he will lose parental rights to see him. Ajju (Sanjay Dutt) had to lease his club, and he wants to recover it, but his reasons are tied up with hatred of the LAPD as well. Bali (Mahesh Manjrekar) is a drug peddler who, perhaps, has the least sympathy from the audience because he comes dangerously close to being amoral. He is the one who is willing to leave his friend Mak (Lucky Ali) to die, his sadistic mistreatment of the cop is very cruel, and he suggests to Major that they should take the money and run. It is only through his death, caused by Mak (who turns out to be a traitor), and his defense by Ajju and Marc that his character is reclaimed from the depths of evil.[15] Similar to *Reservoir Dogs*, the film ends with a standoff—three of them pulling guns on each other—and melodramatic music plays as the camera keeps intercutting between the dead bodies and scenes from the past, evoking affect for these characters. While many of these flashback scenes are about their bonding as a gang, there is also a scene of Bali and a disabled girl in a hospital. She is probably his sister, and we see him humoring her as she makes him eat her food. Mak, the traitor, retains our sympathy through his own stance of honor and duty for which he gives up his own life. Further, the film starts and ends with his voice-over, thereby aligning us with his point of view.

The intentions of most of these characters are tied to something honorable that they need to do. But all of these things are framed within a context of familial masculinity inherited from earlier codes of Hindi cinema. The heist would restore their masculinity to them by completing them as husbands, lovers, and fathers. The lack that they try to overcome, however, gets further emphasized by the time the film ends. None of them is able to be a successful male figure. Neelam Sidhar Wright discusses this film to claim that "contemporary Bollywood produces an altogether confused and inconsistent form of masculinity because the Western modes of gender representation it chooses to pastiche fundamentally clash with or counteract its own cinematic language" (166). As much as their incomplete masculinity is about their failure to satisfy Bollywood codes of masculinity, it is also a product of the remake's inability to Indianize the original film within inherited conventions of masculinity. The characters often seem like collages of Hollywood and Bollywood conventions: violent, amoral gangsters on the one hand, and weeping, dialogue-delivering male heroes of older Hindi cinema on the other. The film's inability to translate the noir hero while retaining anxiety regarding masculinity, however, is a product of the film's remaking practice that clings to older Bollywood codes even as it seeks to introduce the Western style for its audiences. Moreover, the split in the film betrays the historical moment when the industry itself is in a transitional period; *Kaante* straddles the old and the new somewhat unsuccessfully as a result.

Hollywoodizing Bollywood in *Kaante*

Kaante is an example of remaking in a cross-cultural context in which the remake tries to profit from the newness of foreign storylines. By employing both Bollywood and Hollywood to maximize its attractions, *Kaante* attempts to introduce something different that, therefore, will appeal to various audience demographics.[16] At the same time, remaking Tarantino's film was a risk for *Kaante*'s filmmakers because of how inconsistent *Reservoir Dogs*, and consequently *Kaante*, is with Bollywood films; however, this inconsistency is not just a product of the very different subject matter. It is also a product of the filmmakers' decisions in trying to make the film have the look and feel of Hollywood productions. Most remakes until *Kaante* had gone through what Carolyn Durham calls "transformation" into the new culture by stripping the film of its host culture (5). Contrarily, *Kaante* uses the remake to bring in foreignness as a selling point. In interviews before the film's release, the principal actors repeatedly mention its newness and its difference from usual Bollywood productions. Mahesh Manjrekar, who plays Bali, refers to the audiences' changing tastes: "It is difficult to predict whether this film will do well. Who knows? People might like it. It is not a typical hero/heroine film; it is not what people are used to. But then people have been rejecting films they are used to, so it might succeed" (qtd. in Khubchandani). Sanjay Dutt, who plays Ajju and is also a producer of the film, talks about the slump in the industry that, he argues, is occurring because of lack of change in the product. "Let us not forget every Hollywood film is now dubbed and shown in Tamil, Telugu and other regional languages. So Indian audiences know what international standards are all about," he says (qtd. in "I Am Too Old to Be Wild"). He then situates *Kaante*'s production within this context: "We made *Kaante* because we believed the audience was ready for a Hollywood kind of action thriller" (qtd. in "I Am Too Old to Be Wild"). The film's story and visual style try to mimic international or Hollywood genres because of the "audience imaginaries"—how filmmakers imagine their audiences' tastes and desires—created by the producers (Ganti, "No Longer" 344). The idea of remaking as Indianization therefore loses meaning in the film's connection to any idea of Indianness, as it also includes a simultaneous Hollywoodization, but it retains that cultural connection in order to appeal to the filmmakers' understanding of the audiences' changing desires. This approach to the audiences and to the remaking (although neither the director nor the actors ever acknowledge that *Kaante* is a remake) explains the resultant schism in the film.

The characters in *Kaante* are given stories in order to make them palatable to the Indian audiences at home and abroad. Stars such as Amitabh Bachchan, Sanjay Dutt, and Sunil Shetty are included to attract audiences as well. Dutt's understanding of what a Hollywood action thriller is and his choice of Tarantino's film for a source, however, also have to do with how the film can appeal visually. The gangster genre allows for the depiction of stunts and fights that function as attractions. However, the film also revels in the mimicry of Hollywoodesque deployment of technology and spectacle. It uses a lot of pans, slow-motion shots, jump cuts, brief black-and-white snapshots, and CGI effects that become excessive. In addition to serving as cool tricks, these effects draw attention to the melodramatic construction of the film's characters. The camera does several close-ups of their faces in which they express joy or a sense of shared bonding with other characters. But the excess is so marked that it breaks the codes of verisimilitude of both industries.

Multiple scenes demonstrate how the filmmakers understand the Hollywood style. In the manner of other Hindi films trying to appeal to diasporic and urban audiences through a globalized look, *Kaante*'s characters often speak in English (and indeed, the diegesis often requires them to); the film uses American actors for roles that aren't major ones; it is a remake but models the heist after Hollywood films instead of choosing to transform it into the type of heist typical of Hindi films; and even the gang's attire, complete with sunglasses and black clothes, can be interpreted as code for Hollywood-through-Bollywood. But *Kaante* does not really try to follow the look of neo-noir that *Reservoir Dogs* has. Instead, the film is littered with stunts and visual effects, reminiscent of the action genre, that often interrupt the viewing experience.

The scene after the heist is one such example. When the gang walks out of the bank, they are all laughing and completely lost in the euphoria of success. However, the scene is shot in a haze of yellow and employs slow motion. The camera keeps moving from one character to the other, often showing close-ups of their faces as they laugh and share in that laughter, exhibiting their homosocial bonding as well as their joy. Then, as the camera keeps panning across their faces again and again, their expressions start changing, and they take out their guns (still in slow motion), indicating to the audience that something bad is happening. We don't get a reverse shot even though their expressions lead us to assume that they are probably surrounded by police. Because of the excess involved in depicting the scene—and this includes its length especially because of the slow motion—audience suspension of disbelief is already interrupted. The absence of a reverse shot further encourages deliberation on what the slow motion is achieving. However, a further disjunction is created by intertitles that splash across the screen: "AND THEN . . ." In the theaters, this is when a formal interruption in the form of intermission occurs, when audience members go and get popcorn. On the DVD, there is a pause after the intertitles. In both cases, the immersion is broken as the scene is broken midway and repeated after the interruption. When the film restarts, the scene is replayed with additional reverse shots and diegetic sounds of police cars screeching to a halt as they surround the bank. What follows is the action scene—the gang members throw grenades at the police cars, start shooting, and then run. The frame shows a slew of shots that resemble those of a Hollywood action film as bombs explode; fires start; Marc flees on a cop's motorcycle, driving it down a staircase; Ajju slides down a hill headfirst as he keeps shooting at the cops who chase him, though he never gets hit; and the chase continues.

This particular translation of Hollywood into Bollywood through the remake is based on the number of spectacles the film can have. Already working within a genre that is excessive in its portrayal of stunts and masculinity, these visual additions become jarring because of the special effects. Not only does this kind of combination serve to indicate an incommensurability of Hollywood codes with Bollywood codes, but it does so by creating an effect of unreality that Wright claims creates a "distancing-like effect between spectator and text" (178). She also notes that in *Kaante*, "the Indian film industry's fantasy of 'being Hollywood' is realized in order to eliminate its Western superior. This form of mimicry is thus a symptom of the remake's ambivalent feelings of adoration and abhorrence towards its predecessor—its intimacy and distanciation, valorisation and denial, and ultimately, its *disavowal* of its counterpart" (180–81; original emphasis). Considering that the filmmakers never acknowledge that the film is a remake, disavowal of the source text is certainly part of the remaking process here. The film's plot—the Indian gangsters taking over the Los Angeles (LA) underworld—can be seen as a metaphor for what the film is blatantly doing: remaking a Hollywood film, setting it in LA (the home of Hollywood), and doing so without acknowledging its influence.

While I agree with Wright's analysis of *Kaante*, the film goes beyond mimicry in its translation of Hollywood-like effects for a Bollywood film. The Hollywoodizing attempt is very clearly there to attract audiences fed up with the usual way Bollywood tries to hail transnational audiences, hence the effort to make the film transnational not only in its diegesis, but also in its production. *Kaante*'s failure to successfully transfer Hollywood style into Bollywood is also a result of its historical moment. It is a film that actively tries to separate itself from most Bollywood productions that deal with diaspora and transnational subject matter. Unlike previous Bollywood films dealing with foreign settings (for which some scenes would be shot on foreign soil and the rest in the studios), the entire film was shot in LA. The promos of the film mentioned shooting in this foreign location as part of its transnational production. Furthermore, instead of flying the entire crew from India, the producers used technicians and production assistants from LA. However, the unreal effect of the film's action sequences is a product of not knowing how to realize its vision of successfully integrating the Hollywood and Bollywood codes in a new way.

This transnationalization is a symptom of changes within the industry, the filmmaker's understanding of changing audience desires, and changes in the target audiences that allow filmmakers to take these kinds of risks. In that way, *Kaante* is " 'seared' by its immediate context" and "foregrounds a crisis of representation" between Indian and Western and between Bollywood and Hollywood (Wang 11). Yiman Wang borrows the idea of "searing" from Walter Benjamin and expands on it to argue that a film is imprinted by its geopolitical ambiguities and contradictions in an allegorical manner (11). *Kaante* is similarly imprinted by the conflict between older and newer cinematic forms in the transitional period during which Bollywood is becoming corporatized and globalized.

Intertextuality and Pastiche in *Hatke* Cinema

Tarantino's response to *Kaante* is central to understanding this cross-industrial negotiation. In an interview at the Indian Film Festival of Los Angeles, Tarantino responded to the film: "Here I am watching a film that I've directed, and then it goes into each character's background. And I am like WHOA! That's something." Earlier in the interview, he said, "I LOVED IT. I think it was fabulous. Of the two rip-offs I loved are Hong Kong's *Too many ways to be number one* and this one—'*KAANTE*.' "[17] Tarantino's response is an acknowledgment of *Kaante* as a remake, but at the same time, it is crucial here as an alternative interpretation of the unacknowledged Hindi remake, which has often been seen as an example of plagiarism. As I have mentioned in the previous section, in addition to its music and dance numbers, *Kaante*'s inclusion of backstories for each character shows that its industrial transformation exceeds a process of simply remaking. Tarantino's pleasure at the remaking of his film can also be attributed to the fact that his own films are cinematic homages to films that influenced him. *Reservoir Dogs* is a pastiche of at least twenty-three known sources that Tarantino admires; David Desser argues that one of these, Ringo Lam's *City on Fire* (1987), is the immediate and direct precursor to *Reservoir Dogs* (524). A master at the genre of neo-noir, which is known for borrowing and pastiching, Tarantino celebrates the borrowing that is a widespread cinematic practice and that even underwrites economic categories in all mainstream film industries, whether the borrowing takes place through genres, sequels, or adaptations.

Tarantino's position here needs further analysis for its location in a cross-cultural circulation from Hong Kong cinema to Hollywood when he remakes *City on Fire* and then from Hollywood to Bollywood when his film is remade by Gupta. In both cases, he presents himself as the auteur. While discussing Tarantino's Asiaphilia in his films such as *Kill Bill*, Leon Hunt argues that his cinephilic re-creations are both reverent and aggressively territorial and thus bear the mark of the colonizing oppressor (233). *Kill Bill* is highly citational and nods toward its sources even if they become an undifferentiated collage of different cultural influences and end up showing his love for Asian cinemas as orientalist cinephilia. As problematic as his cultural appropriation might be, Tarantino has acknowledged his love for Asian cinemas in his later films. Still, despite close similarities in plot and even certain shots in the films, he initially rejected the claim that *Reservoir Dogs* was a remake of *City on Fire*. Instead, he and his fans emphasized the originality of his film. His refusal to acknowledge *City on Fire*'s influence reflects an issue of power where Hollywood productions are viewed as superior and original compared to cinema from non-Western countries. *Kaante* borrows the plot of *Reservoir Dogs* (which is also the plot of *City on Fire*) but then embellishes it with more subplots; it is therefore an adaptation. Tarantino's benevolent attitude toward this remake, then, is double edged. At one level, it indicates his awareness of intertextuality and borrowings across cinematic borders. At the same time though, his response to the film is extremely problematic because he considers *Kaante* a film that he himself has directed. His refusal to admit to the influence of *City on Fire* on *Reservoir Dogs* but then claiming *Kaante* as his own reproduces the hierarchies of cultural imperialism that are at the center of remaking in a transnational context.

Manorama Six Feet Under and *Johnny Gaddaar* have very different relationships to their Hollywood sources than *Kaante* does, and therefore they reveal different political responses to the transnational negotiations of power that remakes articulate. Both films are marked by cinephilic appropriations of noir and neo-noir aesthetics, although in distinctly different ways. They translate the visual style of noir instead of adhering to the story. Further, both films self-reflexively invoke their influences. While *Manorama Six Feet Under* strongly bears the influence of Polanski's *Chinatown* and borrows a little from *Kiss Me Deadly*, *Johnny Gaddaar* displays the combined influences of the genre of the neo-noir heist or caper film and the crime thrillers of past Hindi cinema. Both films are short, have a tight and linear storyline, and do not include any song-and-dance numbers. While these characteristics make them more appealing to a Western audience, and these films can be argued to be following a Hollywood style in their refusal to follow the Bollywood formula, they are quite different from the spectacle-ridden Hollywood style that Gupta tried to accomplish in *Kaante*. Moreover, both films foreground a relationship between the local and the global that have extra-diegetic implications.

Manorama Six Feet Under eschews the Bollywood glitz and glamour of urban or diasporic life in favor of representing issues of abuse and corruption in rural India. A review of Singh's film on *Rediff.com* ends by celebrating it as a remake: "Forget originality Jake, this *is Chinatown*. This is a *noir* tribute where fans of the original will have seen it all before yet sit through this freshly developed retelling with a smirk on their faces, the kind of smirk that understands why a Chivas and soda could work with *daal-baati churma*" (Raja Sen). The smirk on the fans' faces can only be possible if they are familiar with Polanski's film and with the way that *Manorama Six Feet Under* borrows from Hollywood and Bollywood. The fact that Chivas whisky and soda, which are Western, can work with *daal-bati churma*, a local dish from Rajasthan, indicates the hybridic seamlessness the film creates between the local and the global and between Bollywood and Hollywood.

The website for *Manorama Six Feet Under* characterizes the film as "an homage to the noir genre," and the film strongly bears the influence of Polanski's *Chinatown*, in particular. The adaptations to the plot, the translation of Polanski's visual daylight-noir, and the intertextual invocations establish the film as a loose remake and, more importantly as a pastiche of noir. Multiple instances in *Manorama Six*

Feet Under remind the viewer of *Chinatown* and *Kiss Me Deadly*, thus establishing Singh's self-reflexive evocations of the genre. Unlike *Kaante*, in which the interruptions in the film result from the disjunctions created by bringing the Hollywood style to bear on the Bollywood style, *Manorama Six Feet Under* is marked by cinephilia through self-reflexive intertextuality. The film is also a direct homage to Polanski. In it, Singh inserts a scene that indicates his love for and his debt to Polanski's film: *Chinatown* plays on a TV in the background in the home of Satyaveer (Abhay Deol), specifically, the nose-slitting scene in which Polanski plays a cameo role. The scene functions at multiple levels. In the remake, the plot detail is different—Satyaveer gets his fingers broken instead of getting his nose slit—but the insertion of this scene from *Chinatown* clinches his similarity to Polanski's hero, Jake Gittes. Moreover, while it is an intertextual homage to Polanski's film, this scene betrays Singh's debt to Polanski himself. By showing these levels of intertextuality within the film, director Singh uses the presence of the auteur Polanski in his film in order to point his finger at what is not seen—himself as an auteur.

Johnny Gaddaar revels in cross-cultural cinephilia as well. The opening shot of the film, discussed at the beginning of this chapter, establishes Raghavan's love for classic Hollywood noir and neo-noir. Raghavan, along with other well-known *hatke* cinema directors such as Anurag Kashyap, worked under Ram Gopal Varma, who is known for making films in the Bombay noir genre. *Johnny Gaddaar*, however,

Figure 3.2. Scene from *Chinatown* (with Polanski's cameo) plays on the TV in Satyaveer's home. *Source: Manorama Six Feet Under* (Navdeep Singh 2007).

evokes Hollywood noir through its visual style and combines that with the style of older Hindi cinema. While Gupta used his cinephilia for neo-noir and Polanski to tell a story about a village in India, Raghavan's cinephilia extends to Hollywood as well as to past Hindi cinema. *Johnny Gaddaar* constantly announces its intertextuality with numerous sources from both industries. Monika Mehta questions the hegemony of Western cinema (Hollywood in particular) and suggests alternative transnational exchanges between India and other non-Western countries like Israel through cinephilia, which she traces back to France ("Reading Cinephilia" 149).[18] These factors are relevant to the remaking and pastiche in which *Manorama Six Feet Under* and *Johnny Gaddaar* are involved. Noir, as a genre, was belatedly recognized as such because of the French love for particular Hollywood films of the 1940s, which already bore influences of German expressionism and Italian neorealism. Furthermore, French films like Godard's *À bout de souffle* (*Breathless*) are a pastiche of and homage to the genre. Therefore, noir is a genre that from its beginnings does not categorically belong to any one industry and is instead quite transnational. The cinephilia connected with noir in particular also gets associated with auteurism. *Manorama Six Feet Under* and *Johnny Gaddaar*'s use of noir and neo-noir thus problematizes neocolonial hierarchies because they indicate Hollywood as just one user of an international and intertextual genre. Moreover, since noir privileges the director as auteur, these films grant their filmmakers positions of authority over the genre even if they pay homage to their Western influences. Finally, both films emphasize the importance of the non-Western local in terms of context, setting, and the past of Hindi cinema.

As homages to noir, Polanski's film and Singh's version are marked by the sickness and decay of the system. Their heroes, Jake Gittes and Satyaveer Singh Randhawa, themselves flawed, try to fight the system but end up failing. Gittes is dogged by his own failures. He tells Evelyn Mulwray (Faye Dunaway) that he had once endeavored to protect someone and in the process ended up bringing harm her way. In trying to protect Evelyn, he repeats his past failures: Evelyn gets killed, and her daughter/sister is taken by her abusive father, Noah Cross (John Huston). Satyaveer is a failed writer able to produce only one pulpy novel, reminding viewers of the pulp-fiction roots of classic noir. His wife constantly nags him about his inability to provide her with everything she wants and keeps complaining about his refusal to take commissions, unlike other junior engineers whose salaries are not enough. But Satyaveer is no morally upright person. He has been fired for taking bribes with which, it is suggested, he bought his shiny new motorcycle. When his wife Nimmi, (Gul Panag), leaves town to celebrate Diwali with her parents, another woman, Sheetal (Raima Sen), moves in after she convinces Satyaveer that she is Manorama's friend, and her life is being threatened. This woman, however, is Neetu, who has been sleeping with P. P. Rathore (Kulbhushan Kharbanda) and has been sent to spy on Satyaveer. It seems that he is constantly taken in by the lies women tell him, whether from Manorama pretending to be Mrs. P.P. Rathore or Neetu pretending to be Sheetal. Here, the film uses the figure of the failed detective and includes three women—Nimmi, Manorama, and Neetu—as references to the figure of the femme fatale who populates noir and drives the noir protagonist to his doom. Guided by his desire to play the detective and get justice for Manorama, who died before being able to tell him why she needed his help, he is able to reveal that Rathore is a pedophile, but he discovers as well that Manorama and her brother were also trying to use Rathore's daughter to get all of his money before letting him die. Therefore, by the time the film ends, the only fool is Satyaveer, who has been played by all these other characters; he is nothing more than the character of a failed noir hero in a pulpy story, and the women are no femmes fatale, but rather victims.

Manorama Six Feet Under can actually be seen as both a traditional remake and a pastiche. It differs from Indianized remakes such as *Baazigar* and *Kaante* because it does not try to make the noir hero into a Bollywood hero. Diegetically, the film adapts within Bollywood sensibilities, but only barely: a small town in Rajasthan replaces LA, Satyaveer is given a family, the water crisis gets transformed into issues of drought and corruption in Rajasthan, and P. P. Rathore (Bollywood's Noah Cross character) is a pedophile, who sponsors an orphanage that houses the products of his illicit affairs. Because of the setting, the characters don't converse in English, another departure from many Bollywood multiplexers. Stylistically, however, the film translates the aura of Polanski's noir. The muted colors and haze that permeate every scene convey the sickness at the heart of this world. The voice-over of the noir hero, and the intertextuality in scenes that remind one of Polanski's film or of Aldrich's *Kiss Me Deadly*, establish Singh's self-reflexive evocations of the genre. The film also eschews certain codes of mainstream Bollywood cinema regarding gender or the use of song-and-dance sequences. Satyaveer does not resemble any hero from mainstream Hindi cinema. Like Gittes and other noir heroes, he is almost pathetic in his ordinariness. His incapability to achieve a stature similar to that of a Bollywood hero or antihero is an effect both of *hatke* cinema's rejection of mainstream Bollywood and of Singh's remaking of noir. Satyaveer is the failed noir hero who thinks he is in charge of his life but remains largely unaware of the events around him.

The glamour that marks films such as *Kaante* through the item numbers, lavish mise-en-scène, and special effects is also absent in *Manorama Six Feet Under*. The blend of Hollywood and Bollywood is more integrated than in *Kaante*, but the intertextuality constantly draws attention to Singh's cinephilia and his homages to both the genre and Polanski. Unlike a remake that seeks to both honor and eclipse its source, as a pastiche, *Manorama Six Feet Under* remembers and celebrates the original through intertextual invocations instead of copying it.

Considering that mainstream Bollywood has also turned its energies inward in self-reflexively recycling the remains of past Hindi cinema, the choice of pastiche in *hatke* cinema bears some discussion here. Such recycling is not new and is part of the intertextual as well as transnational nature of many films. Even Vijay Anand's films in the 1960s borrowed from Hollywood films—including Hitchcock's films and 007 capers, and also from Hong Kong cinema—and can be arguably seen as pastiches. The tremendous success of *Om Shanti Om* (*OSO*), released a few months after *Johnny Gaddaar* in 2007, has resulted in a spate of films trying to use nostalgia for older Hindi cinema and pastiche as new global commodities. However, the potential appeal of *hatke* cinema's style in the international market is only increased through its references to Hollywood. Therefore, pastiche here also functions as a commodity since it references and borrows from both Hollywood and Bollywood. Certainly, *Johnny Gaddaar* seems to be eminently cross-overable as a heist film in the international market.

That said, the pastiches presented by *Johnny Gaddaar* and *Manorama Six Feet Under* also articulate a different relationship between Hollywood and Bollywood by demonstrating how difficult it becomes to separate a film's influences into neat categories of Hollywood genre or Indian cinema. The use of the novel written by Satyaveer in *Manorama Six Feet Under* and the homage to the popular British writer James Hadley Chase in *Johnny Gaddaar* are winking nods to the audience familiar with the pulpy roots of film noir.[19] The works of Tarantino and Ritchie complicate any industrial or national affiliation of neo-noir since they reflect multiple transnational influences also; for example, Tarantino's work invokes Hollywood B movies and classic noir but also Hong Kong cinema.

Many recent Bollywood films have been engaged in self-reflective nostalgia regarding past popular Hindi cinema, whether campy pastiching in the manner of *OSO* or the updating and adapting of classics like Bhansali's *Devdas* does. *Johnny Gaddaar* is similar in its celebration of Hindi crime films, especially ones made by the likes of Vijay Anand. However, it also emphasizes the influence of international cinema on past and present Hindi cinema. Scholars of Hindi cinema such as Creekmur have discussed Hindi films like *C.I.D.* (Raj Khosla 1946), which, he argues, "exhibit many of the stylistic devices that French critics would identify through the evocative term noir" ("*C.I.D.*"). Creekmur suggests the use of the term *historical noir* for these films ("*C.I.D.*"). *Johnny Gaddaar* thus inadvertently includes this past even as it marks the influence of Hollywood crime films and classic noir on the Hindi crime films of the 1960s and 1970s.

Johnny Gaddaar invokes a generalized remembrance of older Hindi cinema through its visual aesthetic full of saturated color and the repurposed older fashion styles such as the shirts worn by Shardul (Zakir Hussain). In doing so, it resembles the neo-noir style of Tarantino's films because it bears the weight of the cinemas that have left an impact on Raghavan: it is a film overloaded with TV screens that play Hindi and Hollywood films; the characters keep referencing and discussing other films; and the central action of the film is borrowed from *Parwana*, an older Hindi film. *Johnny Gaddaar* is also similar to Tarantino's films because its visual style exceeds the narrative motivation and adds a comedic strain to the corrupt and bleak world. For example, the expressionist use of red to indicate the cynical violence and the theme of betrayal often becomes ironic or parodic. But it is also a reminder of Tarantino films, in which color and tint serve as signifiers. For example, the use of green haze in *Reservoir Dogs* that conveys a perpetual sickness about the world appears in *Johnny Gaddaar* in the back rooms of the gambling joint where Vikram (Neil Nitin Mukesh) paces after killing Shardul. Similarly, the now-obsolete conventions of wipe cuts, split screens, and numerous low-angled shots that Tarantino uses as nostalgic devices are used by Raghavan too. In Raghavan's case, they announce a deliberate invocation of Tarantino and draw attention to the craft instead of adding to the impact of particular scenes. *Johnny Gaddaar* presents a pastiche of all its sources.

For Richard Dyer, pastiche "imitates its idea of that which it imitates" and is critical because it makes obvious its imitation (*Pastiche* 124). *Johnny Gaddaar* imitates its idea of past Hindi cinema but inflects it through neo-noir, thus creating pleasures of familiarity and difference. The potential for self-reflexivity in pastiche lies in the ironic play with conventions. Certainly, in addition to the defamiliarized style, the self-conscious intertextuality in *Johnny Gaddaar*, creates a critical distance that facilitates a cerebral instead of immersive viewing experience. However, it is not just a distanced position that is critical; instead, it is affective. *Johnny Gaddaar* revels in love for all of its sources, and its pleasures lie in the visceral experiences that these references invoke in the viewer. The affect it invokes through these references indicates that the film is simultaneously about reading/interpreting and feeling. The reading is central to experience, and thus the film positions the viewer in simultaneous intellectual/reading and sensory/feeling positions. The film is therefore a cinephilic montage of quotations that, borrowing from Greg Singh, can be said to articulate affectively the subtleties and complexities of cinematic encounter between the viewer and the viewed (Singh, *Feeling Film* 12). Singh has discussed elsewhere the connection between cinephilia and affect: "The aspect of experience through memory and pleasure raises some interesting questions concerning the role of nostalgia in the mediation of affective responses" ("Kitch Affect" 193). The pleasures of repetition that *Johnny Gaddaar* provides to its audiences are mediated through nostalgia. Dyer emphasizes in his book *Pastiche* that "pastiche makes it possible to feel the historicity of our feelings" (130). *Johnny Gaddaar* invokes deep affect for the films it pastiches. Therefore, Dyer's approach allows me to ground the film in the industrial moment when current Bollywood is transitioning to newer forms of expression in the global marketplace but is still trying to maintain a relationship to its past.

Johnny Gaddaar is a simultaneous disavowal and embrace of Hindi cinema—the affinity of its form with international standards indicates its transnational leanings and involves the rejection of the older Bollywood form; at the same time, through intertextual invocations and homage, it celebrates popular Hindi cinema. Therefore, the film comes close to Hollywood conventions and is similar to newer films produced by Bollywood—for example, it is only two hours long, the continuity style is tighter, and the song-and-dance numbers are diegetically motivated and exist mostly in the background. In other words, the film exhibits the features of New Bollywood, which is corporatized and digestible for the international market. Since New Bollywood has erased many of the markers that made Bollywood stand apart from Hollywood, as much as it allows *hatke* auteurs freedom from the burden of culture, it is also accompanied by deep anxiety about losing its distinctiveness. Furthermore, it is dogged by concerns similar to those associated with India's parallel cinema, which was often critiqued as elitist and produced for the Western and film festival circuits.

As I mentioned earlier, unlike mainstream remakes that tried to Indianize the foreign text within the codes of Bollywood, *hatke* cinema films exercised more freedom in remaking, and thus these films are often auteurist pastiches. But as much as it ruptures connections with hegemonic Indianness and allows for exploration of diverse characters, stories, and filmmaking styles, this kind of borrowing has been made possible by New Bollywood with its transnational production mergers and increasingly westernized styles of filmmaking. And while these fears of losing Hindi cinema's distinctiveness from Hollywood continue to be raised and allayed by scholars, Bollywood's *hatke* cinema also grapples with it.

This is where pastiche is made political by Raghavan. He foregrounds the borrowing of noir conventions instead of just following international standards. And in both content and style, he draws on older Hindi cinema so that the past is placed securely within the present. The pleasures of the intertextuality of *Johnny Gaddaar* are not merely for the cosmopolitan and urban viewer, but also for audiences whose love for the golden age of Hindi cinema is presented in the film. Vikram decides to use the name Johnny as an alias at the hotel because *Johny Mera Naam* is playing on the hotel TV—thus directly connecting *Johnny Gaddaar* with Anand's film. Similarly, at multiple points, characters are watching *Parwana*. In fact, the TV screen playing *Parwana* provides the bridge from one scene to the other. Pakiya (Vinay Pathak) and his wife discuss the stars in *Parwana*—Amitabh

Bachchan and Navin Nishchol—as they watch it, their cinephilia obvious for audiences to see and participate in. The camera zooms in on their TV screen and then zooms out to show Vikram watching the same scene. This time, the camera keeps going back to the TV as Amitabh's voice-over explains his character's plan—the same plan that Vikram will follow to steal the money from the gang. These references serve as more than self-reflexive interruptions. They demonstrate a deep love and nostalgia for these crime thrillers but at the same time point to their continued popularity through the characters' enjoyment.

Raghavan's authorial intentionality (and Navdeep Singh's as well) is explicit in his cinephilic engagements with local and global texts of noir and crime films, and therefore the pastiche he presents is a complex articulation of transnational cinematic flows and the position of Hindi cinema within it—this pastiche is a playful celebration of intertextual influences; it is anxious about the form of emergent Bollywood that is seemingly moving closer to westernized forms; it is a solid acknowledgment of Hindi cinema's distinction from, instead of incorporation within, the genre of globalized international noir; and it advances an argument that past Hindi cinema is presented as being just as valid as Western films, as aesthetic and cinematic texts.

Masculinity, Bollywood, and Neo-Noir

Johnny Gaddaar also evokes the older codes of masculinity through its references to three big male stars of popular Hindi cinema: Amitabh Bachchan, Dev Anand, and Dharmendra. Further, because the earlier films these actors are in are cited instead of just being referenced through a style, they retain their integrity and identity within Raghavan's neo-noir. In this, *Johnny Gaddaar* is different from Bollywood's nostalgic love and parody of the past in films such as *Dil Chahta Hai*, *OSO*, and others in which, argues Usha Iyer, Bollywood visually quotes past Hindi cinema by reshooting them, thus "creating different investments in the present" ("Looking for the Past in Pastiche" 220). *Parwana* remains distinct from the present film in which it is quoted. In the scene from *Parwana* that Pakiya and his wife watch, Amitabh Bachchan's character is markedly different from the characters who inhabit Raghavan's film. It is here that pastiche functions as more than mere postmodern nostalgia. Even as *Johnny*

Gaddaar imitates its idea of the crime thriller, it is not obliterating the past in its imitation and reformulation. In fact, it seems to represent the contemporary impossibility of masculine heroism as represented by the three alpha males of older Hindi cinema: Dev Anand was a Casanova-like figure whom women couldn't resist, Dharmendra was known for his strength and for his roles as hero in action films, and Amitabh Bachchan's star text includes the angry-young-man character as well as the characters of the sensitive lover and that of the best friend. Vikram, while he takes the name Johnny like Dev Anand in *Johny Mera Naam* or tries to follow Bachchan's plan from *Parwana*, only proves himself insufficient to fill those shoes.

Masculinity in *Johnny Gaddaar*, therefore, is split between older ideals and present representations. The past that *Johnny Gaddaar* remembers presents past Hindi cinema as one inhabited only by male stars. Dev Anand, Dharmendra, and Amitabh Bachchan dominated the screen, and very few female stars got the same billing or rating in the industry from 1970 to the late 1980s. Still, the selective gendered memory of the past connects with the masculinist strain of *Johnny Gaddaar* in general. It is a noir-inflected heist film and as such is concerned with masculinity and male bonding. Unlike the noir-influenced Bollywood films, Raghavan's film comes closer to the faux style of caper films.[20] Raghavan, along with other well-known *hatke* cinema directors now, for instance Anurag Kashyap, worked under Ram Gopal Varma, who is known for making films in the Bombay noir genre.[21] But where Varma recreates noir to explore the psyche of his protagonist gangsters in films such as *Satya* (*Truth*) (1998) and *Company* (2002), *Johnny Gaddaar* is an irreverent pastiche of heroes and gangsters from mainstream Hindi films. Vikram and other Raghavan characters in the film demonstrate noir characteristics at times, but they remain playful recreations and lack interiority.

As Ranjani Mazumdar argues, even the shots of interior spaces in Varma's film *Satya* deploy the noir style and convey the claustrophobia of that film's world through camera angles, use of light, and the mise-en-scène. Varma attempts to render bare the actual Bombay underworld, and he used Gerard Hooper, a documentary filmmaker, as *Satya*'s primary cinematographer to record the urban sprawl as well as the congestion of Bombay, which Mazumdar calls the "urban detritus" of the city (174). *Johnny Gaddaar* keeps reminding the audience of the presence of the cities in it by zooming in on the signs that herald their names at airports or train stations, but the actual city of Bombay does not really figure in the film in the same way as in Bombay noir. The gambling joint, the apartments, and the offices of the gang members could be from anywhere. The interior shots present a world that is too bright and plastic. The exterior shots are murkier and more in line with the noir aesthetic, but even then, it seems like the characters are inhabiting a hermetically sealed, fake world. There is little connection between the world these characters inhabit and the larger world of the city, let alone between the diegetic world and the Bombay underworld.

The comedic strain and the "faux-ness" of this world brings *Johnny Gaddaar* closer to the style of Ritchie, whose films are an example of what Steve Chibnall calls "gangster light." As opposed to heavy films that require suspension of disbelief, argues Chibnall, "light" films, "encourage a more distanced viewing position and an awareness of the artifice of filmmaking. Characterizations may be thin or even consciously one-dimensional . . . and authenticity is replaced by pastiche" (376). So how do we think about the masculinities performed by these characters if the world they inhabit is so artificial? They all resemble caricatures—Shardul and Pakiya remain shy of two-dimensionality. Shardul with his bright shirts and his abuse of his wife fails to completely convince us of his evilness. Pakiya is a loving husband and father, but even his death fails to move us completely. Shiva is a towering hulk of a man who gets killed off and returns in Vikram's nightmares, able to beat him to a pulp even with a broken arm and bruises all over his body from being thrown off a train. Vikram, the central character, with whom we identify, possesses neither intelligence nor strength and is able to survive through sheer luck. The metaphor of gambling that forms a backdrop to the film serves as a commentary on his role. He bungles up the plan from the very beginning and continues to make mistakes. He is unable to overpower Shiva and knock him out—instead, Shiva finds out his identity by unmasking him in the struggle; it is a stroke of luck for Vikram that Shiva dies because his head hits the sink as he falls in the scuffle; Seshu/Sir finds out that Vikram is the one who double-crossed them because Vikram inadvertently lets it slip that he knew Seshu came to drop off Shiva at the station; and, finally, in making his plan based on a scene he watches from *Parwana*, Vikram seems ignorant of the presence of cameras and tracking at airports and train stations—information based on which Kalyan (Govind Namdeo) is able to figure out that he is the one who identified the murderers and stole the money.

Like the noir hero, Vikram is doomed and keeps killing more and more people until he himself is killed, ironically by Pakiya's wife, who mistakes him for Shardul. But his doom is largely an effect of his own stupidity. The name that he adopts, Johnny, further indicates that his character is also a combination of noir heroes from all the Johnny films.[22] Even the direct reference to Vijay Anand's film, *Johny Mera Naam* (*My Name Is Johny* or *Call Me Johny*) is crucial here since Dev Anand's character Sohan, a police officer, takes the name Johny in order to pretend to be a thief to infiltrate a gang.[23] Dharmendra, who serves as a bridge between references to older Hindi cinema and the represented masculinities in the film, is only a pastiche of his past performances. He often goes into his dialogue-delivery style from the older films, the song he keeps listening to is a song from one of his earlier films, and his character's past as a smuggler of watches is actually a role he played in an earlier film. The masculinities that *Johnny Gaddaar* represents are perhaps then emptied of any real substance and are merely pastiches of noir heroes and Bollywood stars.

Johnny Gaddaar's use of pastiche foregrounds the complex relationship between the newer emergent forms of contemporary Bollywood cinema and those of past popular Hindi cinema. Its attempts to hold on to the past articulate the anxiety about the changing form of Bollywood, and changing codes of masculinity, even as it participates in that change. The relationship to past Hindi cinema is no longer through the codes but through intertextuality, so masculinity is not accessible through the codes but rather through pastiche. This crisis might very well be a crisis of heterosexual masculinity in Bollywood. The failure of men to be adequate husbands, fathers, and sons in *Baazigar*, *Kaante*, and even *Manorama Six Feet Under* somewhat assures us of their heterosexuality. *Johnny Gaddaar* also shows the men involved in heterosexual relationships even if their affective relationships to each other are emphasized throughout the film. This constant addition of the female counterpart, irrespective of how little space the women are given in the diegesis, betrays the anxiety about the lone man or gang of men who populate the world of neo-noir—alternate masculinities that don't really have a space in the Bollywood heterosexual order of desire. In the next chapter, I analyze comedy as a vehicle for articulation of some of these anxieties.

4

"Lihaaf Maang Le" ("Ask for the Quilt")

Queerness in the Cross-Cultural Remake

ONE OF THE MOST distinctive differences between Dennis Dugan's *I Now Pronounce You Chuck and Larry* (2007) and its Bollywood remake, Tarun Mansukhani's *Dostana* (*Friendship*) (2008), is the kiss between the pretend-gay couple. Chuck (Adam Sandler) and Larry (Kevin James) do not kiss even when it is expected (such as at their wedding) or when they are asked to (in the courtroom during their trial). But in *Dostana*, Sameer (Abhishek Bachchan) and Kunal (John Abraham) lock lips for quite some time (eleven seconds), as if to complete the kiss that should have happened in the film's Hollywood source. The camera zooms in and rotates around the kissing couple in the dance club, the people around them keep cheering them on, and the kiss becomes a spectacle that overwrites any diegetic meanings that might seek to contain it. The kiss has the flimsiest of diegetic motivations and could have been avoided. Kunal and Sam kiss to prove to Neha how much they love her, even though by now everyone knows that they have been pretending to be gay just to be her roommates. It doesn't make sense extra-diegetically, either, at least not given the aversion of the Indian Censor Board of Film Certification (CBFC) to on-screen kisses and of the mainstream Hindi film industry to nonnormative sexuality. This kiss exemplifies both what the film borrows from the source text and how it exceeds it in transforming it for the Indian viewer. It does the latter by framing the kiss within a bubble of heterosexual desire and by updating the Hindi cinematic convention regarding a kiss's portrayal: the characters kiss; the actors do not. Hyperbolic and dizzying camera movement and reflective lights obscure the space where their lips would actually touch (see fig. 4.1). And yet, this drawn-out moment expresses the transgressive through its excessive interruption.

Dedh Ishqiya (Abhishek Chaubey 2014) presents a very different intertextual relationship with its sources, the short story "Lihaaf" (Ismat Chughtai) and the film *Fire* (Deepa Mehta 1996). *Dedh Ishqiya* does not follow the plot of "Lihaaf" or of *Fire*, but it includes scenes that engender a sense of déjà vu because of their closeness to certain scenes in both texts. It also directly references Chughtai's story in a moment that functions as both a citation and a homage. In doing so, it presents itself as a participant in an intertextual matrix of queer desire rather than in a relationship of power.

Harold Bloom's conceptualization of the anxiety of influence has often been applied in the context of remakes and adaptations. In such analyses, the remake or adaptation is viewed as being in an oedipal relationship of sorts with its source text, and therefore it is seen to both emulate (or desire) and annihilate its predecessor (Leitch 50). Fidelity to the preceding text and differences from it are therefore read in terms of this relationship. Scholars, like Neelam Sidhar Wright,

Figure 4.1. The kiss between Kunal and Sameer in *Dostana*. Source: *Dostana* (Tarun Mansukhani 2008).

who work on Indian remakes of Hollywood films have discussed the power dynamic in this relationship as a colonial one in which the remake's repetition does not stem from a need to emulate the source with more power, but rather serves as an example of mimicry that Wright argues may function as reverse colonialism (179–80). While borrowing from both approaches but not fully embracing either, I also look at other works on cross-cultural remakes that are useful in these contexts. In discussing American remakes of French films, Carolyn Durham qualifies her approach by defining two terms, *transference* and *transformation*. According to her definitions, transference occurs when a remake conveys the source's foreign culture as is, and transformation happens when the remake transforms certain aspects to align with the culture associated with its context (5). Here transference can be seen in terms of Bloom's conceptualization as the desire to copy and transformation as a "betrayal" of the original. Durham's understanding of transference, which she describes as the transfer of something essentially French about French films that their remakes are unable to eliminate, is expressed slightly differently by Yiman Wang, who uses the idea of "searing": something intrinsically cultural that is stamped onto the original, which somehow cannot be extricated during its remaking (10). Durham's understanding of transformation, on the other hand, is what most people working in Indian cinema are familiar with as Indianization due to the cultural codes and conventions that are part of the dominant order shaping the unconscious of mainstream Hindi cinema. However, instead of seeing remaking simply in terms of power play between two cultures, especially given how globalization and capitalism muddle how power flows geographically, I prefer to use these approaches, particularly Durham's—along with Kenneth Chan's understanding of the cross-cultural remake as a contact zone of competing cultural ideologies—to separate one type of transnational matrix from another (Chan 11).

Dostana and *Dedh Ishqiya* have different transnational trajectories. *Dostana* is a Bollywood remake of a Hollywood film. It, like other cross-cultural remakes, undergoes the process of transference and that of transformation: it serves as a vehicle of certain cultural ideologies and functions as an adapted text because it transforms its source material to reflect the culture of its intended audiences. Several scholars of Indian cinema have used the term Indianization to indicate not only cultural transformation but also industrial transformation. While it is perhaps obvious that any remake or adapted text will combine both transference and transformation to varying degrees, in this case the remake functions as a contact zone to privilege stereotypical representations of queerness.[1] *Dedh Ishqiya*, on the other hand, is a palimpsest of its previous iterations. There is something different in its articulation of queerness that defies globalized stereotypes that are imported in *Dostana*. I argue that the different transnational movement of these films and their forms influences their fractured and opposing intertextual relationships with their source texts, resulting in ideologically diametric articulations of queerness.

Dostana is an unacknowledged remake of *I Now Pronounce You Chuck and Larry*, a film about two straight firefighters (played by Adam Sandler and Kevin James) who pretend to be gay. Larry is a single dad. Concerned for his children's future if he dies, he asks Chuck to marry him so that his children will receive his life insurance and pension benefits. In remaking *I Now Pronounce You Chuck and Larry*, *Dostana* expands that film's very minor heterosexual love story and incorporates it into the main plot. Kunal (a fashion photographer) and Sameer (a nurse) want to rent an apartment in Miami. To allay the fears of the landlady, who won't rent the apartment to heterosexual men because her niece already lives there, they pretend to be gay. Soon, both Sameer and Kunal fall for the niece, Neha, and vie for her attention. She, however, is completely convinced of their love for each other and tells them to apply for immigration together as that will ensure that they get their resident permits faster. Just as Steve Buscemi's character does in *I Now Pronounce You Chuck and Larry*, a gay inspector visits their home; just as in the Hollywood film, the remake shows their friends and family accepting them as gay; and, just like its source, *Dostana* ultimately reminds its viewers that their gay relationship is an act. Beyond this, the remake transforms to follow codes and conventions associated with mainstream Bollywood in the manner of 1990s films. Like other cross-cultural remakes, then, *Dostana* both emulates its predecessor, *I Now Pronounce You Chuck and Larry*, by serving as a conduit for globalized ideologies about sexuality and betrays it by Indianizing it.

Dedh Ishqiya, on the other hand, functions as a palimpsest that registers each text as different but contains the faded remnants of a particular past. Both Deepa Mehta's *Fire* and *Dedh Ishqiya* are influenced by Chughtai's story, "Lihaaf" ("The Quilt"), which is told from the perspective of a little girl who goes to live with her aunt, Begum Jaan, for a few days (*begum* is an honorific for an upper-class woman, such as a noblewoman). In "Lihaaf," Chughtai depicts the patriarchal feudal setup attendant on the upper-class begum, who is ignored by her husband. She is isolated and lonely and begins to get sick. She starts to feel better when a maid, Rabbu, begins giving her massages. Mehta's film *Fire* attacks patriarchy too, as sisters-in-law Radha and Sita, unhappy because their husbands don't care about them, develop a close relationship with each other. *Dedh Ishqiya*, a sequel to *Ishqiya* (Abhishek Chaubey 2010) is about two goons, Khalujaan and Babban, who keep landing in trouble and are running for their lives. In *Ishqiya*, both of them fall in love with the same woman only to discover that she has been using them for her own ends. In *Dedh Ishqiya*, Khalujaan falls in love with Begum Para, and Babban falls in love with her maid, Munniya, but the *begum* and her maid are in love with each other (it is in this subplot that "Lihaaf" resonates). The articulation of queerness stemming from "Lihaaf" defies globalized stereotypes that are imported in *Dostana* and instead maps a different historical path of the expression of sexuality and desire.

This chapter, therefore, draws attention to how the differences across borders affect the representation of nonnormative desires. The transnational borders between Hollywood and Bollywood are networked into concerns of hegemony in *Dostana*, whereas the cross-border movement in *Dedh Ishqiya* normalizes a non-Western (or nonglobal but transnational) expression of same-sex desire.

Transferring Hollywood Stereotypes

As a remake of a Hollywood film, *Dostana* is placed at the nexus of Indian and Western ideologies that are manifest in the two industries. The particular expression of queerness in the remake is a result of this cross-cultural and cross-industrial negotiation between transference and transformation. The cultural context of same-sex marriage debates in the United States and the increasing work being done by queer activists in India affects the media landscape within which the two films articulate the paradoxical affirmation and denial of homosexuality. The comedic mode in the two films is also responsible for the doubled impact in both. Support for gay marriage in Dugan's film is accompanied by homophobic, racist, and misogynist jokes, and *Dostana* walks a tightrope between making queerness visible and reducing homosexuality to Western stereotypes of gayness.

The film *I Now Pronounce You Chuck and Larry* has been criticized for its misogyny and homophobia even though its narrative portrays transformation in the characters as they eventually come to accept and defend the rights of LGBTQ+ community. The ambivalence regarding the representation of homosexuality in the film is a result of several factors, the primary one being the cultural context within which the issue of homosexuality was being discussed at the time of the film's creation. In the United States, same-sex marriage was a hot topic for debate in areas including law, politics, morality, and religion in the years preceding the film's release. The film's diegesis that deals with issues of gay marriage indicates its awareness of the Defense of Marriage Act (DOMA) context.

The controversy surrounding same-sex marriage in the United States started in the 1990s. In September 1996, President Bill Clinton signed DOMA, which declared that no state was required to recognize same-sex marriage performed in another state. Then, in December 1999, Vermont held that same-sex couples must be granted the same rights and protections as heterosexual couples; civil unions were established there shortly thereafter. In November 2003, the Supreme Judicial Court of Massachusetts ruled that the state could not deny the rights of civil marriage to same-sex couples, and in May 2004, Massachusetts became the first state to recognize same-sex marriage. The years from 2004 onward saw a frenzy regarding same-sex marriage in the legal arena, particularly in New York.

Large-scale, voter-approved, homophobic bans on civil unions and same-sex marriages became common across many states. New York allowed for domestic partnerships but in most cases did not provide many benefits. *I Now Pronounce You Chuck and Larry* is placed in this context even though it only superficially alludes to the debates that were raging. Larry could have made Chuck his children's legal guardian, but after reading the news—the headline "New York Upholds Benefits for Domestic Partners" is clearly visible to the viewers—he proposes the idea of entering into a domestic partnership with the only person he can trust, his best friend, Chuck.

The film does not go into detail about what benefits Chuck would have received as a domestic partner, given that many New York state agencies still refused to extend health and retirement benefits to people in domestic partnerships in 2006. Right next to the headline Larry reads is a picture of people protesting with banners asking to legalize same-sex marriage because domestic partnerships didn't extend the same benefits to same-sex couples as marriage did to opposite-sex couples. While it's impossible to figure out if the newspaper Larry holds is real or not, the film's attention to the contemporary climate regarding gay marriage is on point. Since 2003, there had been intense debates about same-sex marriage in New York. In July 2006, the New York Court of Appeals refused to grant same-sex couples equal access to the rights and privileges of marriage (Peterson). However, since 2004, New York State's retirement system had recognized out-of-state same-sex marriages for purposes of benefits and pension. This is why, when Chuck and Larry's domestic partnership is being investigated in New York, their lawyer tells them to go and get married in Canada, where same-sex marriage was legalized in 2005. This out-of-state marriage would ensure that Chuck get the benefits in case of Larry's death.

This narrative premise seems to be there solely to create humor through irony. Nevertheless, Chuck and Larry's efforts to try to get married and their performance of a gay relationship queers the idea of family and directs attention to other aspects of the same-sex marriage debate. The alternative family is in place even if it is a family of two straight best friends responsible for the children of one of them. There is no provision in the state's law to recognize nonnormative understandings of family. They can be recognized as long as they perform normative understanding of gayness and enter marriage, which is a patriarchal institution that allows entry to certain queer people as long as they follow the rules. Scholars arguing against same-sex marriage cite alternative family units that the state will still not recognize. For example, Paula Ettelbrick understands the desire for gay and lesbian people to achieve the right to marriage but considers the institution of marriage itself unfair. She argues that legalization of same-sex marriage will not result in the fixing of social inequalities that LGBTQ+ people have been fighting against. It will only allow certain kinds of gay people to enjoy the benefits reserved for heterosexual married couples while maintaining borders that keep out a significant portion of already marginalized people who don't accept monogamous marriage or the nuclear family unit; who have alternative understandings of family; or who are too poor to ever enjoy the benefits of health insurance, which is reserved for the bourgeoisie (24).

I Now Pronounce You Chuck and Larry maintains a distance from these debates through a disavowal at the same time—it presents a story of two straight men pretending to be gay and does not seriously engage with the issue of homosexual desire. Its comic mode further reduces the expressions of nonnormative sexuality to a joke (including homophobic slurs dropped by Chuck until his character undergoes a transformation). The expression of and denial of alternative identities happen simultaneously. The film also reproduces homophobic stereotypes for comic effect by reducing gayness to femme demeanor. Rodger Streitmatter gives credit to the media in the United States for the American public's shift to a more enlightened view of gay people but then acknowledges the limitations in that certain types of gay men and lesbians have been (or had been until then) embraced more readily than others by the media and subsequently by the public (2–4). He discusses the safely othered and readily digestible gay characters in films such as *My Best Friend's Wedding* (1997) and the show *Will and Grace* during the 1990s and lists their positive characteristics, which have now become stereotypes of gay representation: charming, physically attractive, possessed of impeccable taste, successful, and chaste or monogamous. These characters also often elicit laughter, which is tied to their performance of a gay identity. The slippage between gender and sexuality is also evident here in the way in which the gay characters are expected to have good taste in everything from clothes to interior decoration, to be perfectly groomed, and to be effeminate. However endearing this may make these characters, given that Chuck and Larry remain straight, the film presents gay identity without admitting to same-sex desires. The gayness is therefore made unthreatening because it is represented as nothing more than gender performance.

Let me give an example: The narrative arc of the film includes important plot points of the two male firefighters coming out as gay and getting married. When their unit finds out that they are gay, the hetero-masculine space occupied by firefighters suddenly becomes charged with suspicion and homophobia. All the potential homoeroticism, often present in all-male spaces, is rendered obvious and threatening (see fig. 4.2).

Figure 4.2. Ving Rhames singing and dancing in *I Now Pronounce You Chuck and Larry*. Source: *I Now Pronounce You Chuck and Larry* (Dennis Dugan 2007).

It isn't until Fred (Ving Rhames), another firefighter in the unit, also comes out as gay and supports Chuck and Larry in their newly avowed relationship that there is a change in outlook. The only black man in the unit, Fred is represented as intimidating—he is huge (a look that is the result of being shot from a low camera angle), always looks stern, and carries an axe. However, his transformation from straight firefighter to gay man is represented as a shift in stereotype from the dangerous hypermasculine black man to the effeminate gay man. The moment he admits to his sexual orientation, Fred lets go of his permanent scowl and axe to become a character who is highly emotional, one who now sings and dances naked in the locker room while everyone watches. The stern black man suddenly starts singing in a high-pitched voice, "I'm every woman . . ." and dancing.

A refusal to perform straight masculinity is a refusal of naturalization of such masculinity and heterosexuality and this rejection of normative masculinity is often visible in gay culture. But here, what Richard Dyer calls "gay iconography" is used to portray and safely categorize gayness as separate (*Gays and Film* 32). While at one level, the gender-bending performance of a sexual identity is used in the film to convey to audiences that a character is gay, as with Larry's son and the funny inspector played by Steve Buscemi, at another level, it is used to reduce the transgressiveness of the performance to stereotype. Moreover, Chuck and Larry remain incarnations of straight masculinity; even when Chuck transgresses those gendered boundaries, it is so excessive that his actions are seen as clearly incongruous and so rendered hilarious, an aspect that the remake channels as well. For instance, Chuck and Larry go shopping for "gay" things, which includes shampoo for permed hair; Q-tips; a DVD of *Brokeback Mountain*; and CDs of music by Liza Minnelli, Cher, Barry Manilow, the Village People, and George Michael. Their inability to grasp the difference between gender and sexuality is made astoundingly clear when Larry, following Chuck's advice to think like a girl in order to be convincing as a gay man, picks up a pack of maxi pads to add to the mix as well. This lazy shortcut (resting in mainstream conventions that underpin popular culture) to represent gay identity as a gendered one is deployed in the remake as well. While *Dostana* borrows the basic plotline of two men pretending to be gay in order to receive certain benefits, it transfers the globalized stereotypes via the remake, stereotypes that had in some measure found their place as comic relief in Bollywood already.

Cultural Transformation in *Dostana*

Dostana surprisingly did very well at the box office even though Mansukhani eschewed the songless, tight-knit structure of multiplex cinema that was beginning to find ground among the cosmopolitan westernized audiences more used to films with unconventional subject matter. It Indianizes but does so for a story dealing with nonnormative sexuality at its center. The deliberateness of the film's favoring of the queer plot is motivated by changing laws regarding homosexuality in India.

While the DOMA context affected the treatment of homosexuality in *I Now Pronounce You Chuck and Larry*, *Dostana* was released months before a new law decriminalizing sodomy was passed in India, which was a result of activist work by LGBTQ+ groups in the years prior. Shohini Ghosh discusses the two decades (the 1990s and 2000s) of activist work that enabled protests against Section 377 of the Indian Penal Code ("The Wonderful World"). As much as the queer activism wasn't as visible to the general public in India as the debates were in the United States, the Bollywood industry was registering those changes. Many Bollywood films included queer characters or even queer relationships, but they were always minor characters or minor storylines until the more recent past. *Dostana* was the first Bollywood mainstream film that made the issue of queerness so visible and central. Released in 2007, *Dostana* was produced in a climate of increasing experimentation and risk taking by filmmakers, including *hatke* (alternative) auteurs as well as mainstream filmmakers; however, it follows the dominant form of the NRI (nonresident Indian) film and the family film from the 1990s, which has produced the family as a patriarchal site sanctioned by the state via the acceptance and integration of the heterosexual couple. In *Dostana*, Sameer's mother represents that aspect of family, and its plot fits the genre where the central crisis occurs because of the parent's refusal to accept their child's desire to desire. Here, the main conflict is about sexuality instead of gender; she is shocked to find that her son is gay and desires other men. This is followed by her rejection of this truth encapsulated in a song-and-dance number, which then gives way to her eventual acceptance of her son's sexual identity and his love for his partner. While the ending reveals that her son was just pretending to be gay, for the most part, the film provides a melodramatic resolution and acceptance of queerness through the mother—the symbol of the nation in early Hindi cinema.

This transformation of the film within Bollywood codes (or as Indianization) is thus threefold:

- melodramatic structure that uses the inherited cultural codes tied to older Hindi cinema;

- remaking within the genre of the NRI film; and

- use of comedic mode to transgress the conservative aspects of the genre even as the mode allows for a disavowal of the subject matter at hand.

In this, the film exhibits the limits of media that conforms to popular preferences and opinions, particularly of a text that imagines its audiences to be an all-India (as opposed to a niche) audience and therefore an audience that is self-regulated within dominant ideologies of heteronormativity. The moments of queer potential are at the same time moments that incite laughter at these very representations and therefore allow for a denial of any queer desire. *Dostana* introduces a vocabulary surrounding same-sex desire that has become part of the popular idiom but again transacts itself via jokes that go along phobic lines. This transformation maintains the simultaneity of queer visibility and homophobia in the film and allows for polysemy in terms of its queer articulation.

Comedy and Camp in *Dostana*

As much as *Dostana*'s representation of homosexuality is problematic, it still has moments that draw attention to the performance of, and therefore highlight the instability of, naturalized categories of sexuality and gender. In this section, then, I focus on the progressive potential of the film's politics that is perhaps located in the same factors that limit it. Rajinder Dudrah discusses the film to argue that at one level, the film stereotypes and even caricaturizes the characters in their queer performance; at another level, though, it can use the myth of the pretend gay couple to present a narrative of coming out and acceptance by society and the mother (Dudrah 54–56). Even though the film uses stereotypes for comic effect, and consequently suffers from the charges of westernization as well as homophobia, it is precisely the deployment of this comic mode that gives it immunity against rejection by the majority of its audiences, for whom a serious treatment of the theme of queerness is anathema (as proved by the controversies surrounding the reception of any film that has tried to do so in India). Because the film is a comedy, it is able to sneak in representations and examination of queerness. Moreover, Mansukhani's film does not stay at the level of stereotypes—the excess that marks its comedy pushes it into the realm of carnivalesque, indeed, of camp.

I Now Pronounce You Chuck and Larry is primarily a comedy with a romantic subplot. *Dostana* is the Bollywood version of a romantic comedy in which melodrama and masala add another dimension. In both films, there is a plot of heterosexual romance that is often linked with the genre of romantic comedy. In *I Now Pronounce You Chuck and Larry*, the comic plotline of Chuck and Larry's pretense is accompanied by the romantic plotline of Chuck's pursuit of Alex, their hot female lawyer. Alex is angry with the two friends for their elaborate lie but by the time the film ends, she has forgiven Chuck and dances with him. In *Dostana*, Sameer and Kunal function as obstacles in the romantic plot of Neha and her new boss, Abhimanyu, in whom she is romantically interested. They manage to break up the couple by using Abhimanyu's son. That crisis is then resolved when they realize the effects of their mischief and decide to get the two of them back together. So, it seems that in both films, the comedy is a result of the plot of the pretend gay relationship, whereas the romance has more to do with the heterosexual pairings. However, and perhaps more so in *Dostana*, the comedy is interwoven with intimations of romance between the two men. Dugan's film constantly interrupts with reminders of the two men's heterosexuality—whether it is through the star texts of the two actors, their appearance of straight masculinity despite the pretense, the constant parade of women, and the continual nagging by Larry to remind Chuck to keep performing "gayness." In *Dostana*, on the other hand, the two metrosexual men give in with abandon to the performance of the gay relationship. The comedy thus goes hand in hand with the romance between the two men, the latter very visibly displayed for the audiences.

Popular Hindi cinema has always lent itself to queer interpretations via various subtexts. For example, Ghosh reads several films against the grain of heteronormativity to direct attention to the spaces in Hindi films that allow for the performance of nonnormative identities. Song-and-dance sequences, she argues, are examples of interruptions in popular cinema that play out Mikhail Bakhtin's notion of the carnivalesque ("Queer Pleasures" 211). Meheli Sen compares the male homosocial bondings of the Amitabh Bachchan buddy films to those in the new bromance films; the latter, she argues, replace the "indistinctness of the social, familial, and erotic energies" of the 1970s films with an "awareness of the distinctions between straight, gay, and queer cultures and subcultures" ("From *Dostana* to Bromance" 141). Ajay Gehlawat concedes that *Dostana* is doing political work in the way in which it outs queerness but then argues that the subversion gets undercut precisely because it is explicit, as opposed to such subversion in earlier films, where it is more hidden (111). *Dostana*, however, is not merely explicit and obvious. It is a bit too obvious, too melodramatic, and too over-the-top in its rendering of the queer relationship. Thus, the pleasures it provides are those of excess, and therefore its subversive potential is of its carnivalesque display and performance. Unlike the films Ghosh discusses where the queer potential is located only in the song-and-dance sequences, the carnivalesque moments in *Dostana* exist throughout the film. They also emerge through the comic interruptions.

For Bakhtin, Ghosh says, the carnival is an "expression of people's second life that shatters, symbolically at least, 'all oppressive hierarchies.' . . . [I]t is a joyful affirmation of change, a dress rehearsal for utopia that allows those on the margins to move to the center of the narrative" ("Queer Pleasures" 211). Indeed, the majority of *Dostana* is a carnivalesque exploration of the "world upside down" or rather the world inside out: the margins have come to dominate the center and threaten the heteronormativity by displacing it to the margins. The heterosexual love subplot literally frames the main plot of the two men pretending to be gay. The framing plot gets forgotten as multiple scenes function as spectacles that revel in the performance of gayness; the diegesis includes a parent's reaction to and acceptance of the news that her son is gay; and the camera lovingly gazes on the men's half-clad bodies. This latter is also an acknowledgment of gay audiences. The camera ogles John Abraham's (Kunal's) body, zooming in and lingering on his butt cheeks (especially when his underwear is slipping low), while Abhishek Bachchan's (Sameer's) body is clad in fluorescent shirts and brightly colored scarves. At the same time, the incongruity and overturning of hierarchies that accompany the carnivalesque turn decidedly campy in the film. Camp remains highly self-conscious in its celebration of the artificial and demands from its audiences an awareness of the artifice of what is construed as "natural" (Bergman 2). If the carnivalesque revels in the world upside down, camp retains the awareness of the artifice in the reversal. Like drag, the carnivalesque scenes in the film approach camp because of their stylized theatricality, their exaggerated performance of gender and sexuality, and the serious undertone to their humor.

In *Dostana*, hilarity ensues in many scenes that start as stereotypical jokes about gay performance, but the exaggerations become too pronounced and render the performance as carnivalesque revelry. In order to get into her gay boss's good graces, Neha invites him home and instructs Sameer and Kunal to behave. Clearly, she thinks she will impress him by having him meet her two gay roommates. Her boss, M, is a flamboyant gay man, and he arrives wearing a bright-yellow shirt, a shiny striped suit, and a multicolored cravat. His first comments to Neha are about her aunt, who greets him at the door; he immediately declares her to be a fashion disaster. Thus, his queerness is established through this excessive campy performance and his taste in fashion. From this point on, the scene gets more and more extravagant and over the top. Sameer, following Neha's orders, props himself against a door and strikes a pose, inviting M's gaze; the camera, aligned with M's point of view, responds by trailing over his body in close-up from his boots all the way up his embroidered vest to his face. The deliberateness of the camera's fetishistic look here enacts a reversal of Laura Mulvey's argument regarding scopophilic pleasures in Hollywood cinema where the female body is the object of the gaze of both the male characters within the diegesis and the male viewers of the film (11). Steve Neale applies Mulvey's understanding of looking and spectacle to male genres such as war films, Westerns, and gangster movies and argues that in these films, "male figures on the screen are subject to voyeuristic looking, both on the part of the spectator and on the part of the other male characters" ("Masculinity" 12). *Dostana* does not fall within the parameters of male genres like the ones Neale discusses even though it references male genres like the buddy films of past Hindi cinema. This scene overperforms Mulvey's theorization such that the fetishism and homoeroticism in play are highly visible; I would even argue that the fetishism is fetishized by the camera in the ways in which M is shown ogling Sameer before Sameer is shown. The obviousness in the scene ruptures the immersion so that the audience is very aware that it is a male body inviting the masculine homoerotic voyeuristic gaze. At the same time, the viewers gaze along with the camera at the body, thus making them complicit in identifying with the male point of view and in the objectification of the male body while aware that they are doing so. The queered gaze of the spectator—which has been so from the very beginning of the film, when John Abraham's torso and buttocks were the camera's object—cannot be fully disavowed as a result.

In the scene, M drools over Sameer, and Sameer flirts back. When Kunal comes out of his room, M takes one look at him, stumbles over to him in his excitement, and almost kisses him on the lips. An immigration officer, Javier, who is also gay, arrives on the scene at this moment for a surprise inspection. He is dressed in pink and tells Kunal suggestively, "I am here to keep an eye on you" (see fig. 4.3a). Kunal, although scared by the idea of inspection, smiles back but then drags Sameer into a room to express his fears about Javier. Sameer reassures

Kunal and tells him to think like a girl to convince Javier that they are gay. For the rest of the scene, then, Kunal performs effeminacy, which, as opposed to Western gay stereotypes, resembles the *hijras* in India and their performance of femininity at weddings and other events.[2] The ensuing scene gets more and more campy as the four men perform queerness and queer desire. M declares that he loves "dirty" dancing and starts dancing with Sameer to the song "Beedi," a known erotic item number from the film *Omkara* (Vishal Bhardwaj 2006). When the song begins, in one of the shots, M's body in the yellow shirt occupies the entire frame, thus rendering it excessively large. He looks directly at the camera for a few brief seconds when he starts dancing, thereby drawing attention to the actor, Boman Irani, performing the role. There is a directness in this self-reflexive performance as performance in this scene that is enabled by the returned gaze. He then pulls Sameer to himself, turns him around, simulates pelvic thrusts, and pinches his bottom (see fig. 4.3b). Kunal dances

Figures 4.3a and b. "Beedi" song-and-dance number from *Dostana*. Source: *Dostana* (Tarun Mansukhani 2008).

with Javier, and the scene becomes a frenzied orgiastic flurry with the four male bodies gyrating to the music, which reaches a crescendo while the two women at first watch and then dance separately, on the outside of the center, which is occupied by the men.

The camera also goes crazy in this scene, whirling around the four men as they let loose. The pleasures of this scene are of comedy because the audience is aware of the incongruity between the real and the performed and because they are in on the joke. But the cerebral pleasures of the film give way to the bodily as the music and visual display and movement of the bodies create laughter as well as (homo) erotic pleasure. The two women become stand-ins for the audience; at first, they watch the campy display but then cannot help but participate in the festivities. Finally, the performance inverts the world as the queer interruptions take center stage.

Talking about camp's connection to gay sensibility in the introduction to *Gays and Film*, Dyer emphasizes the celebration of role playing, theatricality, performance, and illusion that is discussed by Jack Babuscio in a later chapter (2). While maintaining an illusion of straightness is part of the act of passing, performing an excessively queer identity is a rejection of oppressive heteronormative ideologies and a celebration of freedom from them. This scene exemplifies the ways in which such scenes in the film interrupt the diegesis and perform a campy queerness that is dismissive of the narrative control. The narrative seeks to explain away and neutralize the queer hyperreality of the film, but the comedic interruptions reject that primacy of the narrative over the excessive moments. Further still, these moments are not simply ones of revelry and laughter. The humor of camp is one of incongruity, that between the person and the situation or context (Babuscio 47). However, asserts Babuscio, the irony that results from this incongruity "must also affect one as painful—though not as painful as to neutralize the humour" (Babuscio 47). A serious undercurrent runs through these scenes between the act and the reality, which comes to a head when Sameer's mother arrives on the scene, and all hell breaks loose. Just as M lifts Sameer in his arms while dancing, the bell rings, the door opens, and Sameer's mother enters and subsequently faints in a highly melodramatic manner. The two gay men are sympathetic to Sameer, who they believe had not yet come out to his mother. While it seems like the humor of the scene is situational, in which two straight men who are pretending to be gay get caught, the scene ends up showing how it would be played out if they actually were gay. For various reasons, they cannot explain the truth, and even as Sameer tries to tell his mother that he is not gay, he is not believed by anyone. By this point, it is not clear anyway whether Sameer and Kunal are actually still heterosexual (that is, if it their heterosexuality was ever fully assured in the film).

Dudrah interprets this scene and the ones that follow, including the mother's apology, as a pastiche of earlier scenes from Bollywood family films, especially as the score from the well-known family film *Kabhi Khushi Kabhie Gham* (*K3G*) plays as extra-diegetic background music (56). While *K3G*, and other films like it, is about respecting patriarchal family values and parents, the intertextuality with these films in *Dostana* adds another layer of incongruity. Dudrah argues that the apology scene mimics the acceptance of the heterosexual romantic couple except that here the mother gives her blessing to a queer couple. The scene therefore enacts for the audience the acceptance of queerness that has been nonexistent on the Bollywood screen. At the same time though, the film also contains the homophobic reaction of the mother that is spliced in between these scenes. The incongruity between the plot of a film such as *K3G* and that of *Dostana* is announced by the screaming overdramatic (and campy) "Nooooo" of the mother which is immediately made the subject of the song-and-dance number that follows. This number, which is performed again at the end of the film, is one in which the mother imagines seeing Sameer and Kunal together in various locations and at various ages (babies holding hands, old men in wheelchairs holding hands). Sameer is often shown wearing a saree as the bride, and multiple shots of the two of them touching, lying over, and playing with each other's bodies follow. These shots are intercut by the mother's displeasure and efforts to fix Sameer, including one where she tries to exorcise homosexuality out of him while he is asleep. Thus, the song becomes an excuse to extend the scene's carnivalesque revelry, but it also reveals the painful rejection by the mother, always portrayed excessively so that the previous scene remains funny.

Reading Queerness in the Hindi Film Industry

At the stylistic level, *Dostana*'s over-the-top comedic style and its obviousness as a remake create a distancing effect instead of immersion through identification. This excess carries the potential for audience awareness of this representation as a performance of queerness. Thus it is that the audience is simultaneously watching and reading the text—a characteristic that Horton and McDougal associate with the remake (2). The film, however, does not just remake its Hollywood predecessor; it also looks back at a whole host of Hindi buddy films in a few very brief comic exchanges between Kunal and Sameer. Sen, rightly, argues that *Dostana* does not have the affective energies of the Bachchan buddy film, in which love, intensity, and sacrifice for the male friend express a homoerotic desire ("From *Dostana* to Bromance" 158–59). Indeed, *Dostana* seems to be merely performing the tropes of melodrama and the buddy film, especially as it is shot through with an individualism marked by neoliberalism. However, it is in this performance and in its looking back that it calls into question the heteronormativity of the buddy films of past Hindi cinema.

While walking to the immigration office, Sameer and Kunal discuss some of these characters from past Hindi films, including Gabbar in *Sholay* (*Embers*) (Ramesh Sippy 1975) and Munna and Circuit in *Lage Raho Munna Bhai* (Rajkumar Hirani 2006):

SAMEER: Gabbar Singh was gay. Why else would he say "Kitne aadmi thhe re (How many men were there)?"

KUNAL: Dude, Gabbar was not gay.

SAMEER: Now, don't say that there was nothing going on between Munna and Circuit.

KUNAL: Munna used to call Circuit *bhai* (brother).

SAMEER (nudges him with a smile): So what? Even I call you *bhai* in public . . .

By drawing attention to a queer subtext in these films through this dialogue, Mansukhani is making explicit for mainstream audiences the kind of subversive readings that exist, readings that scholars have done of buddy films in Hindi cinema. The film's title intertextually invokes the 1980 film *Dostana* (Raj Khosla) by the same production company and indicates the homoerotic subtext to the male friendship in that film as well as the entire cycle of buddy films that were being produced in the 1970s and 1980s. The word *dostana* literally means "friendship" but can also suggest more than friendship, and the film demands a reading of the word that is uncircumscribed by heteronormative ideologies.

At yet another level, not only is the word *dostana* used in the Hindi film industry as well as in normal parlance as both an indicator of friendship and one of homoeroticism in the case of same-sex friendships, but it is often explicitly the subject of all-male songs (most of them from the buddy films). Thus, in the buddy film *Sholay* (*Embers* 1975), two thieves, Jai (Amitabh Bachchan) and Veeru (Dharmendra) sing this song about *dosti* or friendship:

> Yeh dosti hum nahin todenge/ todenge dum agar, tera saath na chhodenge.
> [We will never break this bond of friendship./ Even when we die, I won't leave you.]

The two alternately claim love and affection for the other as they continue the duet:

> Tera gham, mera gham, teri jaan, meri jaan/ aisa apna pyaar
> [Your sorrow is my sorrow, your life is my life, that's how our love is].

They end the song by vowing to die for one another, an event that actually happens at the end of the film when Jai dies because he wants Veeru to continue on without him. Ironically, this death also replaces their same-sex primary relationship with a heterosexual one—the one between Veeru and Basanti—which until now had been secondary. Still the homoerotic undercurrent in the song and the film is hard to ignore especially given the phrase "Tere liye lelenge" ("I will take anything from you") in the song.[3] Ashok Row Kavi interprets this as a desire for anal penetration because the word *lelenge*, he argues, is Hindi street slang for "getting fucked" (310).

Another song from this era that celebrates this friendship is "Yaari Hai Imaan Mera" ("Friendship is my religion, my friend is my life") from the film *Zanjeer* (*Shackles*) (Prakah Mehra 1973). A synonym for both *dostana* (friendship) and romantic love, *yaari* carries deeper connotations of same-sex desire here. The song and dance are performed by the character of a *pathan* played by Pran, celebrating his friendship with Amitabh Bachchan's character.[4] The song deems *yaari* as his religion, and his *yaar* (friend), his life. The highly sensual dance that Pran performs can be seen as stereotypical of a *pathan* because "pathan tribes have always been open in their display of homoeroticism" (Kavi 310). There are multiple films from this era that explore this affective relationship between two best (male) friends.

While it would be naïve to suggest that prior to *Dostana* (2008), there weren't any queer interpretations of earlier buddy films, *Dostana* does make that connection very obvious, and it is perhaps the first mainstream film to do so. Ghosh and R. Raj Rao wrote essays published prior to Mansukhani's *Dostana* that talk about queer subtexts in buddy films, such as Khosla's *Dostana, Zanjeer, Sholay, Anand (Pleasure)* (Hrishikesh Mukherjee 1971), and *Namak Haram (Traitor)* (Hrishikesh Mukherjee 1973). As much as the 2008 *Dostana* remakes the Hollywood film, it remakes it within the tropes of these buddy films, in which the male-bonding supersedes the heterosexual love interests. It makes explicit the homoerotic subtexts underlying the buddy films and thus enforces a retrospective queer reading of earlier films that have been understood by mainstream audiences as films about straight masculinity.

However, Mansukhani's rereading of the earlier *Dostana* via the comic mode simultaneously expresses the queer subtext and renders it as laughable and othered. *Dostana* (1980) is a film about two friends, Vijay (Amitabh Bachchan) and Ravi (Shatrughan Sinha), who are in love with the same woman. On finding out that Ravi loves Sheetal (Zeenat Aman), Vijay decides to sacrifice his own desires for the sake of his friend and his *dostana* ("friendship"). However, a criminal Daaga (Prem Chopra) creates misunderstanding between the two men by convincing Ravi that Vijay is involved in a relationship with Sheetal. The rest of the film explores this rift created between the two men. Karan Johar, one of the producers of *Dostana* (2008), used a similar plot in an earlier NRI film, *Kal Ho Naa Ho* (Nikkhil Advani 2003), which is in many ways a precursor to the newer *Dostana*. In *Kal Ho Naa Ho*, two men, Aman and Rohit, love Naina, but Naina loves only Aman. Aman decides to help Rohit in getting Naina to fall in love with him. The woman's desire in both cases is irrelevant; the films are about men and their relationships with each other. Vijay and Ravi in *Dostana* (1980) had been childhood friends, and their homosocial as well as homoerotic bond is in place before Sheetal enters the picture. While in *Kal Ho Naa Ho*, Aman and Rohit don't have that prior friendship, the film itself is full of jokes about their relationship conveyed through the homophobia of the maid (Kanta Bhen). A series of comic situations occur, in which she is continuously shocked by the apparent explicit homoeroticism between the two men. She keeps walking in on the two of them in compromised positions. For instance, in one scene, Aman and Rohit are snuggled together in the morning and wake up shocked. Aman explains to Rohit that he carried Rohit to his bed the previous night because Rohit was drunk, and it was too late for him to go back to his own home. Then Aman reaches across Rohit to pick up the bottle of water as Rohit stretches. The camera zooms in on Aman's buttocks as he stretches over Ravi's torso and then immediately cuts to Kanta Bhen standing with a shaking breakfast tray in her hands. She stammers out the question: "What should I get for the guest?," and Aman replies quite innocently, "Banana." While the audience is in on the joke, the obviousness of the homoerotic situation becomes part of the pleasure of the scene. Aman's shirt is unbuttoned, and his chest is bare, Rohit is wearing a sleeveless tank top, and their bodies are touching throughout the scene. Finally, catching on to her discomfort, Aman calls her as she is about to leave, and when she turns towards them, he puts his head on Rohit's shoulder and purses his lips as if he is about to kiss him, which makes her cringe and run out. Audiences are meant to laugh at Kanta Bhen in this instant and enjoy the queer pleasures, but these pleasures are distanced because of the awareness of the pretense. Thus, homophobia and visibility of queerness are present simultaneously and become even more apparent because of Kanta Bhen's homophobia.

In *Dostana* (2008), Mansukhani goes one step further. He repeats the plotline of the triangle with two men in love with the same woman, but the homoeroticism that is a subtext in the earlier *Dostana* and exists as comic interludes in *Kal Ho Naa Ho* becomes the obvious focus (although still as a joke). The 1980s theme of two friends (or brothers) on opposite sides of the law is replaced by the theme of diasporic Indians and their bourgeois lifestyles, and the intense melodramatic enactment of the rift is replaced by the comic vein that is part of the romantic comedy genre of these films following the 1990s. But the tongue-in-cheek invocation to the earlier film is there in Mansukhani's reworking. The posters of the two *Dostana*s are uncannily similar, each depicting two men on either side of a woman. The comic text of a fake same-sex relationship in the newer film thus calls attention to that unconscious subtext in the older film. And since the older *Dostana* is part of the entire genre of the buddy film in Hindi cinema with its similar plotlines and intense male-male friendships, by using the same name, *Dostana*, for his film, Mansukhani is drawing explicit attention to all these films and is queering their interpretations of straight masculinity, even if he does it via imported and caricaturized stereotypes of gayness.

From Dostana to *Dedh Ishqiya*

Dudrah astutely points to the seemingly contradictory aspects of queer representation in *Dostana*, whereby it is not clear if the two men are queer caricatures or queer beings (57). Ghosh, too, argues that the film's expression of gayness straddles the line between the erotic and the phobic ("Wonderful World" 19). The problem of the excess, performance, and play in the film is that although it allows for a free play of queer desires to be projected onto what is happening on-screen, through its very comedic excess and performance, it presents it as a lie. The film has certainly introduced a vocabulary about same-sex desire, but it is one that encompasses imported homophobic stereotypes that "other" gay identity through misogynistic reduction into effeminate masculinity. At the very least, gayness is safely othered and controlled through gendered presentation of masculinity as less than and as something to be laughed at.

I contend through using this analysis that the particular expression of queerness in the remake, resulting from this transference as well as transformation, makes it a contact zone that simultaneously expresses conflicting and paradoxical affirmation as well as rejection of homosexuality and tension between gay desire and its ideological containment. Chan uses the idea of the contact zone to discuss the clash of cultures in a remake (11). Analyzing *Dostana* as a contact zone shows how the clash between Hollywood and Bollywood makes visible a third, shared, category of global capitalism and its role in regulating nonnormative expressions of identity and desires.

Dedh Ishqiya shares with *Dostana* a few characteristics: it deploys a comedic mode and has a buddy relationship at its center. It continues the antics of Babban and Khalujaan from the previous film, *Ishqiya*. Literally meaning *Ishqiya* 1.5, or *Passionate* 1.5, *Dedh Ishqiya* announces its intertextuality as a sequel to the previous iteration via its name. It promises a similar kind of comedic ride, even though there is little continuation of the main plot from *Ishqiya*. However, its use of *1.5* already indicates something *hatke* or alternative about it. That extra 0.5 is in the alternative subplot that is a noneconomic intertextual invocation of Chughtai's story "Lihaaf." Unlike *Dostana*, *Dedh Ishqiya* reserves comedy for the heterosexual main plot and presents a serious articulation of queerness through the subplot, which decenters the hetero desires of the main plot.

Dedh Ishqiya's use of "Lihaaf" creates a palimpsest of sorts of other versions of "Lihaaf," particularly Deepa Mehta's film *Fire*. In both stories, women who are frustrated by their husbands turn elsewhere for sexual and emotional gratification. Normal, everyday close-contact experiences between women in India, like massaging oil in each other's hair, are invested with queer affect. Both texts were at the heart of censorship debates addressing female desire and lewdness; in the case of *Fire*, these debates involved religion as well. The three texts together also create a transnational relationship between Pakistan, Canada, and India, but they have an affinity that is closer to India for various reasons. Pakistan was part of India when Chughtai wrote and published "Lihaaf." Deepa Mehta is a diasporic Indian filmmaker who settled in Canada, but her films employ a more realist, indeed naturalist, mode that investigates Indian identity. *Fire* is set in the capital of India and is very evocative in its expression of the reality of a lower-middle-class family life, much more so than the globalized cosmopolitan NRI films that present diasporic fantasies in spaces that exist in the West. *Dedh Ishqiya* belongs to New Bollywood, which has several *hatke* auteurs making different kinds of films. Thus, while *Dedh Ishqiya* was made possible because of corporate funds, Abhishek Chaubey, too, eschews the typical Bollywood fare and instead makes the film adhere to a realist mode. Nostalgia-tinged mise-en-scène and cinematography often remind its viewers of Islamicate films via Begum Para who used to be a courtesan, and is now royalty, and via its use of Urdu as well as its architecture, but it does not follow Islamicate genre in the way contemporary director Sanjay Leela Bhansali is wont to do. It is more of an aesthetic call back to the genre and invites the viewer to be conversant with these other texts, including Urdu poetry and literature. Set in Lucknow, the city of the decadent and decaying past, this film, too, refuses the Bollywood globalized look and instead anchors itself within a particular location in India. *Dedh Ishqiya*'s transnational palimpsest, then, produces a localized South Asian sensibility, which becomes the vehicle for its expression of alternative desires.

Religion, Patriarchy, and Sexuality in *Fire*

Deepa Mehta's *Fire* mediates Chughtai's story but also converses with Bollywood conventions—as well as Hindu Right's beloved version of the epic *Ramayana* encapsulated in the state-funded TV series, *Ramayan* (Ramanand Sagar 1987–88)—via its adaptation into a story about two women married to two brothers. Single-handedly, *Fire* articulates queer desire and critiques religion-laced patriarchy by updating the names of Chughtai's characters. Instead of the Muslim Begum and Rabbu from "Lihaaf," Mehta names the two women after two Hindu goddesses, Radha and Sita. The series idealized the version of *Ramayana* in which Sita is so devoted to her husband, Rama, that she chooses to undergo a test by fire, *agnipareeksha*, to prove her chastity and fidelity to him.[5] Through this version of Sita, Hindu patriarchy gets regressively focused on the role of the wife as sacrificial even in the face of unjust treatment. By using the names of these two goddesses for its characters who are victims of patriarchy, and who turn to each other for love and desire, *Fire* angered several sections of the population, but particularly the adherents of Hindu Right-Wing nationalism (or Hindutva), which was in its ascendancy in the 1990s. Mehta's critique of Hindu ideology is noticeably connected to the regressive gender politics of Sagar's *Ramayan*, which is always playing on the TV in *Fire*.[6] Arvind Rajagopal talks about Congress's sanctioning of this religious TV serial, which changed the religious sentiment in the country and created a space in which Hindu fascism could develop.[7] The weight of the role of Sita that Hindu Indian women are subjected to is ultimately about being submissive and about accepting the injustice of the patriarchy that the film critiques and makes visible. By naming her protagonists after the goddesses Radha and Sita, Mehta centralizes the desire of women and shows these characters' desire for each other as a critique of patriarchy.

In *Fire*, Radha is married to Ashok, the elder brother of the family, and Sita is newly wedded to Jatin, the younger brother. They live with their ailing mother-in-law, Biji, and their servant, Mundu. Radha's life is one of serving and catering to the demands and desires of everyone in the family. She takes care of the home, cooks, and looks after the mother-in-law. Radha is sexually frustrated because her husband reveres a religious figure, a *swamiji*, who preaches against any kind of desire. Ashok therefore refuses to copulate with her but tests his sexual restraint by making her lie in bed next to him. Radha has accepted her life's reality until Sita arrives and upsets Radha's fatalistic acceptance of her life. Sita is also unhappy because Jatin has a girlfriend and is therefore not interested in her. Unlike Radha, however, Sita is irrepressible and refuses to be stifled by this life—she loves going out, which takes her away from her domestic duties inside the home; she loves dancing, which conveys her happiness instead of prioritizing others over her own emotions; and she does not shy away from expressing her desires for intimacy. She repeatedly chooses her own joy instead of sacrificing it like a dutiful wife and daughter-in-law. She finds this joy with Radha; the film shows their growing emotional and physical bond as the two fall in love with each other, thus combining its anti-patriarchal and queer politics.

Fire expands the story of Chughtai's text quite a bit but quotes from it in everyday scenes. In "Lihaaf," the begum's niece narrates:

> Perched on the couch she [Rabbu] was always massaging some part of her [begum's] body or the other. At times I could hardly bear it—the sight of Rabbu massaging at all hours . . . In fact, Begum Jaan was afflicted with a persistent itch. Despite using all the oils and balms the itch remained stubbornly there . . . "There's nothing wrong with you. It's just the heat of the body," Rabbu would say, smiling while she gazed at Begum Jaan dreamily. (37)

The child's innocent descriptions are suggestive of deeper intimacies between Begum Jaan and Rabbu, further evidenced by the mutterings of disapproval from other maids at these rituals. In *Fire*, Mehta uses everyday rituals in homosocial spaces and queers them. One such ritual, which is very common across households but also deeply reminiscent of "Lihaaf," occurs when Radha gives a head massage to Sita. The slow motions of the hand and the way in which the two women gaze at each other via the mirror in which they are reflected imbues the act with queer affect and intimacy.

In yet another scene, Sita, dressed in Jatin's clothes, draws Radha from the kitchen to the living room, where Biji, the mother-in-law, is relaxing, and the two of them dance to an older Hindi song (see figures 4.4a and 4.4b). The song, "Aa Ja Zara," like many romantic Bollywood songs, expresses the love and desire between the hero and the heroine. At first, Radha is shy as Sita lip-syncs the lyrics and dances with her, but she soon gets into the spirit of things as the song becomes more than a matter of play, turning into a vehicle for expressing the transgressive desire between them. Here, the usual ideological function of the romantic musical number in Hindi films is turned on its head when Sita and Radha dance dressed as the hero and heroine. First, this is a sort of parody of romantic songs that often function as expressions of heterosexual desire and its consummation.[8] Second, Sita in drag underscores the performativity of gender and the construction of that heterosexual desire as a construct naturalized through repetitiveness in Hindi film. Scholars of Hindi cinema have discussed other instances of cross-dressing in Hindi cinema that express the queer unconscious in family films such as *Hum Aapke Hain Koun . . . !* (Sooraj Barjatya 1994), but again these instances are contained as moments of play that end with the event.[9] In the case of Radha and Sita, the eruption or expression of queer desire does not end with the song, unlike other such instances in mainstream Hindi cinema.

If, like "Beedi" in *Dostana*, this scene is akin to a carnivalesque and campy moment that later on reverses hierarchies and centralizes queer desire, it doesn't right itself. Instead, it continues as the comic play gives way to a serious tone marked by changes in sound and editing. The earlier self-conscious laughter and play give way to the two women dancing closer and closer together.

Figures 4.4a and b. Radha and Sita dancing in *Fire*. Source: *Fire* (Deepa Mehta 1996).

The shots get shorter with close-ups of their faces together or of their faces intercut as they gaze at each other until they sink down, as if weighed by desire, and disappear from the frame; we don't get to see this part. The fictive male is taken out of the equation of desire, and the women's performance enacts female-female desire. The smiling expression on Biji's face changes to a frown, switching from conveying happiness and enjoyment to displeasure, and perhaps even to disgust. Mundu, who had been watching from the doorway, also shakes his head disapprovingly. But by this point, it is clear that the women are no longer performing for an audience. The presence and reactions of Biji and Mundu self-reflexively draw attention to audiences who similarly might have that reaction, but the film's emotional alliance is constructed with the women.

Since Deepa Mehta is a diasporic filmmaker and made the film in a form serving as an alternative to mainstream Bollywood (it is shorter, has no song-and-dance numbers, is in realist mode, and is attentive to location), the charge of being Western levied at the film attempts to establish Indiannness as staunchly heterosexual and patriarchal and lesbianism or same sex-desire as an antinational Western import. This construction of Indianness is in line with 1990s ideology, also reflected in the Bollywood family films of the decade.[10] Despite Mehta's diasporic status, however, the film is rooted culturally in India in terms of both gender and sexuality. Its accuracy angered the right-wing groups; moreover, it was threatening because it showed queer possibility in the domestic everyday spaces of ordinary people in India and not of the diaspora living elsewhere, especially in Western locations.

Surprisingly, even as the film was lauded by gay rights activists, it also resulted in public outrage by some LGBTQ+ groups in India. *Fire* does not show a development of a lesbian subjectivity, and therefore it seems as if the expression of same-sex desire is a trope used by the filmmaker just to critique patriarchy. This kind of approach can undermine the film's queer politics and rightly so because its logical progression suggests that according to the film, women become lesbians overnight simply because their husbands are awful. Such claims, however, can be as problematic as the Hindu Right's. For Hindutva followers, lesbianism is Western, and for these LGBTQ+ groups, same-sex desire as expressed by the West is the only understanding of queerness. The film's expression of homoeroticism does not fit within Western categorizations, and judging it by those standards is a colonial gesture. Gayatri Gopinath has written on "Lihaaf" and *Fire* extensively to establish their articulation of alternative sexuality as non-Western. Gopinath warns against the application of current discourses around the formation of "lesbian" or queer subjectivity that can rely upon and function in the service of familiar colonial strategies of subjectification. She argues that the film must be understood not as representative of a lesbian narrative but through the structures set up by the story that demand that female homoeroticism be located as simply one form of desire within a web of multiple, competing desires. The film's alternative homoerotic desire, very much in line with the expression of the same in "Lihaaf," by that application, then exists outside the Euro-American context. In the examples I mentioned earlier of Radha putting oil in Sita's hair, the slippages between female homosociality and homoeroticism are enabled within spaces that are sanctioned by normative sexual and gender arrangements. Thus, the story and film's queer articulation enables a critique of patriarchy and vice-versa. The two are linked.

Palimpsestic Queerness in *Dedh Ishqiya*

Both *Fire* and *Dedh Ishqiya* borrow from "Lihaaf," but *Dedh Ishqiya* more directly invokes Chughtai's story. The Islamicate setup and the relationship between a begum and her servant are clear clues to its homage. The main plot, as I mentioned before, is one of continued comedic antics by the uncle-nephew duo Khalujaan and Babban; the subplot focuses on Begum Para and her maid, Munniya. Khalujaan recognizes Begum Para as someone he was in love with in his youth and wants to pursue her, while Babban falls in love with Munniya. Like "Lihaaf" and *Fire*, *Dedh Ishqiya* slides between the heteroerotic and homoerotic planes that function like a continuum for women but centralize female desire and subjectivity.

Time and again, the cinematic machinery of *Dedh Ishqiya* tells the queer truth even as the main plot presents the heterosexual story as the only one until almost the very end. For example, in one scene (figure 4.5), the begum is dancing alone in a beautiful space inside a palace that evokes the Islamicate setups of the *mujras* from the Courtesan films of the 1980s:

Figure 4.5. *Dedh Ishqiya*, Begum Para dancing a *mujra*. Source: *Dedh Ishqiya* (Abhishek Chaubey 2014).

The begum, as we find out, was a *tawaif* (a courtesan) who married a *nawab*. Her passion for dance is highlighted earlier as well when Khalujaan reminds her of it, in words that seem like a translation from Yeats's "How Can We Know the Dancer from the Dance," that when she danced, there was no difference between her and the dance, and that her very being was defined by dance. In *mujras* (classical dance performances), usually a female dancer would be at the center, surrounded by male viewers. The courtesan figure in Islamicate films is an important context for this particular scene. In these films, several song-and-dance numbers feature a *tawaif* performing a *mujra*. In the center, surrounded by patrons, she sings of love, her own beauty, and desire, showing her awareness of her own power over the male patrons. While the *tawaif* is not simply the object of the gaze, she is nevertheless performing for the male patrons' pleasure. Here in *Dedh Ishqiya*, however, the begum dances for herself, exhibiting a certain autoeroticism in fulfilling the desire of her own body, which she satisfies herself. The fact that the dancer is Madhuri Dixit—whose filmic history since 2012, Usha Iyer argues, has continually decentered heterosexual coupling and for whom dance is an integral part of her stardom—adds to the scene's queer expression as well ("Lesbian Begums").

By removing the expected male patrons from this scopophilic space, the film writes off the primacy of their pleasure and privileges the begum's subjectivity and desire. This is further enhanced when Khalujaan and, later, Babban and Munniya, arrive outside the room. Khalujaan sees her dancing and watches from behind a window with a voyeuristic, even if love-filled, gaze. When Munniya comes looking for her, Babban tries to flirt with Munniya, but Munniya rejects him and goes to see the begum, who invites her inside and continues dancing, now with Munniya. Babban becomes one more person watching from outside the window of the room (see figures 4.6, 4.7, and 4.8). Khalujaan and Babban thus become onlookers, but they remain obviously peripheral, their unsanctioned gazes reduced to those of voyeurs. The scene constructs them as outsiders as the begum moves from her singular pleasure to inviting another participant, Munniya, and the men are literally framed outside this circuit of desire, minimized and powerless.

The dynamic between inside and outside gets reversed as the domestic space becomes the space of pleasure rather than of

Figure 4.6. *Dedh Ishqiya*, Munniya joins Begum Para, and they dance together. *Source: Dedh Ishqiya* (Abhishek Chaubey 2014).

Figure 4.7. *Dedh Ishqiya*, Khalujaan watching from outside. *Source: Dedh Ishqiya* (Abhishek Chaubey 2014).

Figure 4.8. *Dedh Ishqiya*, Babban watching from outside. *Source: Dedh Ishqiya* (Abhishek Chaubey 2014).

imprisonment, and men get framed through the crisscrossing mullions on the window as the ones who are perhaps shackled. A similar scene occurs toward the end of the film, when the women have tied up the men. The women are drunk and playing hopscotch, and the men watch them. Chained and made to witness the cavorting of the two drunk women who outsmarted them, Khalujaan says to Babban, "Lihaaf maang le" (literally meaning, "Ask for the quilt." The subtitles translate it as "let's ask them for some heat"). The phrase here functions at three levels:

- They are cold in a dank underground space and thus want to be warm; a quilt will help.

- It's a double entendre: the cavorting visible to the audiences only through the shadow play on the walls is too steamy, leaving the men cold (because they are external to the play of desire that is being exhibited). The subtitles, "let's ask them for some heat" makes more sense in this context.

- Most importantly, it is a direct intertextual reference to Ismat Chughtai's story. The English subtitles of the film, while indicating Khalujaan's awareness of the sexual temper of the play between the women, omits the actual reference to Chughtai's title, "Lihaaf."

In "Lihaaf," the narrator child, who sleeps in the same room as the begum, her aunt, is woken up by slurping sounds. She is confused and slightly scared by elephant shapes in the dark made by a quilt's shadow. In Chughtai's text, the narrator never knows but can see the movement of women under the quilt creating shadows on the wall; similarly, in the film, the camera shows the play of the women's shadows over Khalujaan as he sits in frustrated desire. Whereas in the earlier scene, Iyer's argument that "where lesbian sex is rendered invisible, dance takes its place" is applicable when the begum and Munniya dance, here the desire is made more directly explicit ("Lesbian Begums"). The shadows of the two women join and overlap several times, indicating the coming together of the two bodies (and what seems like a kiss) toward the end. The fetishization of the two women (a hetero dream) is taken away because of the shadow play at the same time as that desire is enacted and expressed.

Dedh Ishqiya shows how the women move between heteroerotic and homoerotic desires but clearly prefer each other as companions, sexual and otherwise, over the men. For them, playing at straight desire (while simultaneously articulating a possible bisexuality) is the performance and play (just as it is with the *tawaif*).

Conclusion

Multiple scholars have made distinctions regarding the ways that sexual identity is constructed differently in non-Western cultures. Binary identity constructions of sex (male/female), gender (masculine/feminine), and sexuality (heterosexual/homosexual) in the West end up reifying the boundaries of normative and nonnormative and do not leave room for identities that exist and are performed between the two poles. While certain kinds of gay and lesbian people get safely normativized through popular culture, the existing binaries leave out people who aren't always considered to fit within either of the two poles—whether bi- or pansexual, nonbinary, or transgender. Work done in queer studies in the West highlights the need to see how even within the safely binarized zones, the matrices of desire, identity, and practices give the lie to any such static and polarized understandings of identity (Matthew Stern, Chilla Bulbeck, Michael Kimmel). Homoerotic desire might exist in clearly heterosexual relationships, and homosexual practices sometimes occur in heterosexual spaces.

I am not suggesting that the contruction of queerness in the West is binaristic and that in the Indian subcontinent, it is fluid—thus creating another set of problematic binaries as a result. Rather, the patriarchal relay between Hollywood, as mainstream media, and capitalism is to blame for the ways in which sexuality gets incorporated in the West (as in the case of *I Now Pronounce You Chuck and Larry*) as well as for how *Dostana*, a Bollywood remake by a big corporatized production company, re-represents it and adds to the globalized stereotypes of LGBTQ+ identity.

While the transformation at work in *Dostana* makes queer articulation punchier, the film's fidelity to the regurgitated stereotypical tropes betrays how the remake of a mainstream film by a mainstream film industry shows the ways in which power and hierarchy in terms of global capitalism puts constraints on any real challenge to the status quo. The remake becomes a sort of contact zone because of the power differential between Hollywood and Bollywood. While Chan points to highly asymmetrical relations of power such as colonialism or its aftermath in a contact zone, and while we can see how Hollywood makes that kind of power visible via the remake's adherence to Western ideas of gayness, the Bollywood remake cannot be fully seen as a site of culture clash either. Instead, because Bollywood has been the new entrant in the global marketplace, it has joined the neocolonial landscape and functions like a continuation. *Dostana* belongs to this kind of globalized Bollywood that parrots neocolonial expressions of gender and sexuality even as it seeks to interrupt the heteronormative ideologies at its core.

However, *Dedh Ishqiya*, while it is part of Bollywood, is *hatke* in its form and content (the elevated Urdu, the explicit queer subplot, the tight narrative) and is similar to both "Lihaaf" and *Fire* in how its form is tied to its alternative ideological politics. Unlike the model of anxiety of influence or transference/transformation, its intertextual citationality functions to memorialize a particular fragment of nonnormative erotic and affective pleasures: the shadows on the wall in "Lihaaf." That citation, especially because of its double reference to Chughtai's story (content and mention of "Lihaaf"), invests this fragment with meaning that exceeds all other diegetic meanings that the film produces. It is what has been seared into the text, what makes *Dedh Ishqiya* a palimpsest whereby what is retained in all these texts via this fragment is what cannot be cleaved from the culture. The intertextuality here historicizes this alternative expression of sexual identity and desire as non-Western. In this, the transnational movement of the story "Lihaaf" provides a localized expression that contains the potential of articulation of both—queerness and same-sex desire as fluid as well as potentially a matter of queer non-Western identity.

Conclusion

IN THIS BOOK, I HAVE SITUATED the remake as one of the primary responses to Bollywood's globalization, starting from the 1990s, when the remaking trend becomes rampant in the industry. I discuss the remake as part of the industrial practices of film industries such as Hollywood and Bollywood, in which remakes, like genres and sequels, are aesthetic and ideological as well as economic products. The chapters in *Déjà Viewed* employ an approach that includes feminist and gender-studies frameworks, textual analysis, cultural studies, exhibition and reception studies, and genre theory to understand the increasingly transnational nature of Bollywood via the remake. This book, as a result, contributes to scholarship on transnational remakes as well as on Bollywood cinema. By mapping the continuities and differences between the remakes of the 1990s and those produced after 2000, *Déjà Viewed* seeks to historicize how gender and genres become translated and transformed in the Bollywood remake. The movement from earlier remakes that are Indianized to later remakes that are more liberally hybridized as cultural and industrial texts is set against the backdrop of changes in Bollywood's production, exhibition, and reception structures, thus presenting the remake as a valid form for the study of Bollywood, of its relationship with Hollywood, and of transnational cinema in general.

In the years since I started researching this trend, there has been an explosion of remaking practice in India: regional cinematic remakes of Hindi films, Bollywood remakes of Hindi films, Bollywood remakes of regional cinemas, and Bollywood remakes of Hollywood and other international films vie with cinephilic citational practices by filmmakers.[1] Repetition in its varied manifestations has become one of the key signs of postmodernity of Bollywood. Accompanying this frenzied remaking practice are variations in how filmmakers are approaching the remake, including how it is made part of promotion and marketing as well.[2] This project has situated the changing nature of Bollywood remakes within the context of Bollywood's transnationalization and Hollywood's global presence, as well as within the context of new industry practices that form New Bollywood's aesthetic. These newer trends keep shifting the terrain within which remakes are being produced and consumed and need further study.

One such trend that has been on the rise is the emergence of film franchises in Bollywood that create a universe of texts based on the appeal of one film. Neelam Sidhar Wright argues that in 2006, Bollywood production companies realized the potential for mass profit through film franchises and launched their first movie sequels, *Krrish* (Rakesh Roshan) and Sanjay Gadhvi's *Dhoom 2* (9). Many of these franchises are composed of remakes and sequels and bring together diverse kinds of remaking. *Krrish* is a Bollywood sequel of *Koi Mil Gaya* (I . . . Found Someone) (Rakesh Roshan 2003), which itself is a remake of *E.T. the Extra-Terrestrial* (Steven Spielberg 1982). Many of the remakes I discuss in the book already have sequels. *Jism 2* (Pooja Bhatt 2012) and *Murder 2* (Mohit Suri 2011) are a couple of examples; *Dostana*'s sequel is currently under production. A similar process is at work in Bollywood remakes of earlier Hindi films, too. The famous Amitabh Bachchan Hindi film *Don* (Chandra Barot 1978) was remade in 2006 as *Don: The Chase Begins Again* (Farhan Akhtar). In 2011, *Don 2: The King Is Back* (Farhan Akhtar), the sequel of the remake, hit the theaters to tremendous success. Even newer Bollywood films such as *Munnabhai M.B.B.S.* (Rajkumar Hirani 2003) and *Dhoom* (*Blast*) (Sanjay Gadhvi 2004) have sequels that were huge hits. Clearly, the franchises are capitalizing on the success of earlier films and invoking those through the sequels. In fact, while the newer franchises are owned by the same company that owned the first film, the remakes of older films involve purchase of copyright. Nariman Films, the owner of the original *Don* (1978), sued the production companies of *Don 2*, Excel Entertainment and Reliance Entertainment, for violating copyright by using the "'Don' signature tune, songs of the original movie and also copying its script, characters and music" ("*Don 2*"). Nariman Films argued that the intellectual property purchase only allowed for the remake, *Don: The Chase Begins Again*, whereas the film producers of the sequel argued that the sequel is a completely original film and has nothing to do with the remake. The remake and the sequel have been dubbed in Tamil and Telugu, and the *Don* franchise has also released video games based on the films. Within this changing scenario, remakes are not just produced differently; they even acquire more meanings within a newer contextual framework.

Similarly, these practices impact Bollywood remakes of regional cinemas, too, and make them part of this newer industrial context. Bollywood filmmakers had been heavily remaking films from regional cinemas in the 1990s; even before 1990 there are instances of these remakes. This remaking practice is cannibalistic as an Indian film industry's hegemony within India directly affects the viability of other industries. Bollywood becomes monstrous in stealing, regurgitating, and spitting out the regional films in a form that is easily sellable. The remakes would strip the films of their cultural markers and effectively undercut their profits: because of the dominance of both the Hindi language and of Hindi cinema, the remakes would take over the markets where the regional-language film would have otherwise done well. The postmillennial rise in popularity of regional cinemas (like the Telugu film industry) within India and globally has changed this dynamic. But more importantly, recent remakes of, for example, films from South Indian film industries share similarities with the franchised remakes and sequels that I discussed earlier. *Ghajini* (A. R. Murugadoss 2008), the Hindi remake of the Tamil *Ghajini* (A. R. Murugadoss 2005), which itself is a loose remake of *Memento* (Christopher Nolan 2000), was a huge box-office success. Another Tamil film, *Singam* (Hari 2010), was remade in Hindi as *Singham* (Rohit Shetty 2011). The acknowledgment of the remaking through the title is deliberate to appeal to fans of the regional films, especially given the popularity of certain regional cinema directors who have crossed over to Bollywood or straddle the two industries. Here, the remake seems to be similar to a sequel, which often uses the name of the film to indicate its intertextuality and expects the viewer to be familiar with the previous film. There is yet another level of remaking in play as a result of the movement between the South Indian film industries and the Hindi film or Bollywood industry. Award-winning director Mani Ratnam remade his Tamil film *Ayitha Ezhuthu* (2004) in Hindi as *Yuva* (*Youth*) (2004). Priyadarshan, a noted Malayali director, remade his film *Vellanakalude Naadu* (1988) in Hindi as *Khatta Meetha* (*Sour*

Sweet) (2010). As examples of the new face of Bollywood, these films announce the changing practices of remaking as Bollywood filmmakers plot different relationships with other Indian film industries.

This is very different from most remakes in the 1990s, when the filmmakers either used films from regional cinemas as inspirations or used international (not very popular) films for remaking but would refuse to acknowledge the remakes as remakes. In the past, Hindi cinema has remade Bengali, Telugu, Tamil, Marathi, and Malayalam films and has consolidated its hegemony through these remakes in a manner similar to Hollywood's. As I have discussed through this book, filmmakers such as Vikram Bhatt openly acknowledged that they were inspired by Hollywood films but used the word *inspiration* to sidestep accusations of remaking because it was thought to indicate that their films are nothing more than cheap imitations.

Sangita Gopal ("Bourgeois Extreme") and Ian Robert Smith ("Hollywood"), and to a lesser extent Rashna Richards ("Translating Cool") and Wright, have discussed intra-Asian remakes in the case of *Zinda* (Sanjay Dutt 2006), a remake of *Oldboy* (Park Chan-wook 2003), and *Kaante* (Sanjay Gupta 2002), a remake of *City on Fire* (Ringo Lam 1987) and *Reservoir Dogs* (Quentin Tarantino 1992). Where Smith looks at the movement of the films in terms of globalization ("Hollywood"), Gopal adds another nuance by looking not just at the remake but also at the "microimport"; microimports are smaller elements of a film ("Bourgeois Extreme" 101).[3] In the case of *Oldboy*, Gopal looks at the Korean revenge film, which, she argues, results in the genre of what she calls the "bourgeois extreme." She situates the middle-class man's revenge, which is propelled by a feeling of power, within the context of neoliberalism. Her analysis points to how the Bollywood remake localizes a global genre that had already been localized by another Asian film industry ("Bourgeois Extreme" 104). This transnationalism, while it includes Hollywood's influence on Asian cinema, produces other ways of looking at Bollywood's globalization through the remake.

The films I discuss here are A-circuit mainstream films with their sanitized, posh, and relatively clean narratives. Hindi cinema has a long history of remaking in the B and C circuits, which follow different production, exhibition, and reception trends. In these films, production values are low, the films are often crudely made and push at what is taboo or subject to censorship, they are screened at dilapidated theaters or have a morning show runtime when other mainstream films don't play, and their viewership usually comprises working-class males. Even the "bourgeois extreme" that Gopal discusses is a shift of a genre to the mainstream; revenge films were rich materials for the B-movie remakes. The relationship between local and global that these remakes articulate exists along different axes of gender, class, and caste than the mainstream A-circuit remakes. Their local aspect draws even more attention to the connection of Bollywood and global capitalism in Bollywood remakes of Hollywood films.

The changing context of globalization and corporatization within which Bollywood's remaking trend has been gaining momentum in the twenty-first century has also affected the way in which filmmakers understand remaking—instead of being hidden, remaking is now acknowledged as an industrial practice. Newly corporatized Bollywood's open embrace of remaking and the nuances differentiating each kind of remake have the potential to rupture the connection between nation, gender, and industry by showing these constructions as local, historically specific, and differentiated. This openness has also resulted in free play with genres and character types. For example, in May 2013, Illuminati Films released *Go Goa Gone* (Raj Nidimoru and Krishna D.K.), a parody of the zombie genre that was advertised as a zom-com. The story follows three friends who go to Goa, a westernized tourist haven in India, to have fun. They visit an island off the coast for a rave, where, after consuming an expensive drug, people turn into zombies. While running for their lives, the three friends meet Boris (Saif Ali Khan), who is a zombie slayer. After being chased by zombies and killing several of them, they manage to escape the island, only to arrive at the mainland to find it has also been infested with zombies.

The film is very interesting for its self-conscious deployment of the Hollywood genre and older Bollywood conventions, which are constantly debunked. The humor in the film arises from the audience's familiarity with these conventions. For example, Boris resembles the villains of pre-1990s Hindi cinema with his bleached-blond hair, fake Russian accent, and jewelry. He introduces himself in his exaggerated accent by saying, "I kill dead people," immediately invoking M. Night Shyamalan's *The Sixth Sense* (1999). The layers of performance in this scene make it funny but also highly self-aware. The manner in which Saif Ali Khan, a Bollywood star, plays this role would immediately make the audiences recall similar performances by villains from Hindi cinema of the 1970s and 1980s: the deliberate drawl; the fake non-Indian accent; the body language and gestures that perform hyper-masculinity; and his blond hair and tattoos that replace the gold chains, hat, and moustaches of the older villains. But then one of the friends asks him, "Are you really Russian? You look a little Desi," thus immediately calling attention to his exaggerated persona. The self-reflexivity in this scene generates laughter as its humor is a result of this exaggerated intertextual performance.

The zombie genre is also used obviously to poke fun at it. The film's trailer includes a scene that reveals the film's tongue-in-cheek awareness of Hollywood films. When the three friends see a zombie on the island, they are scared but also confused.

> Luv: India has a lot of *bhoot pret* [Indian supernatural creatures]; where did these zombies come from?
>
> Bunny: Globalization. These foreigners have screwed us up. First, they brought HIV, now zombies.

This scene, part of the trailer, targets audiences who, like these three friends, are familiar with the zombie genre. Meheli Sen, while analyzing the zombie as part of Bollywood horror, draws attention to how swiftly the zombie figure entered the Indian consciousness and claims that the "zombie as a global entity is instantly recognizable and readily available for its Bollywood debut. The audience to whom such a figure would signify was similarly in place by 2013," the year that *Go Goa Gone* and another Bollywood zombie film, *Rise of the Zombie* (Luke Kenny and Devaki Singh), was released (*Haunting* 140). The fact that Luv immediately recognizes the zombie as a zombie betrays the audience's familiarity with the Hollywood cinematic type, as well as the film's attempts to play with the genre's characteristics. The genre is also announced in the intertitles: "The Makers of . . . Cocktail . . . Love Aaj Kal . . . Now Bring you a Zom-Com." Given that this is one of the first Bollywood films—remake or otherwise—that participates in the zombie genre, its politics of rejection of the Western horror film have larger implications. All the zombies in the trailer (and most zombies in the film) are white, thus indicating that they are a metaphor of westernization as a disease. Bunny's response that globalization and foreigners have "screwed us up" also functions at a metalevel. It points to the globalization of Bollywood because of which a zom-com is being produced as a Bollywood film.

At yet another level, the self-reflexivity in the film extends to its use of zombies as a metaphor for the neo-colonial exercise at play under global capitalism; it indicates the entry of Western industries and people that are feeding on and zombifying India. In *Bride and Prejudice* (Gurinder Chadha 2004), an adaptation of Jane Austen's *Pride and Prejudice*, Goa is the place where Darcy's mother wants to launch their company's new hotel so that they can sell a luxury experience to the moneyed Western tourists. This location is where the central couple, Lalita (Lizzy) and Darcy, watch Ashanti perform a Hindi song. Goa thus stands as the tourist space in India that is for international—largely white and Western—consumption. That is why the island in *Go Goa Gone* is full of mostly white people who can afford the expensive drug. If the zom-com recognizes that globalization has screwed India, and is so highly aware of Bollywood's transnationalization, it also perhaps points to Hollywood's entry into India as a kind of zombification.

Hollywood studios have been showing a lot of interest in Bollywood and have merged with Hindi filmmakers and production companies to tap India's markets (Ganti, *Producing Bollywood* 360). In 2009, Fox Star Studios, an Indian subsidiary of 20th Century Fox, purchased the global distribution rights for *My Name Is Khan* (Karan Johar 2010). The last decade has also revealed Bollywood's increasing presence in the US media. For a few days in November 2011, when *Don 2* was released in the United States, the IMDB homepage sported the poster for it. The Fox show *So You Think You Can Dance* has Bollywood as one of its staple dance styles. Ann Taylor Loft advertised a bright pink dress for a time, and its color was named "Bollywood Pink." Heineken came out with a commercial set to a musical number from the Hindi film *Gumnaam* (*Anonymous*) (Raja Nawatha 1965), "Jaan Pehchaan Ho," which had previously appeared in the Hollywood film *Ghost World* (Terry Zwigoff 2001). Baz Luhrmann has acknowledged the influence of Hindi cinema on his film *Moulin Rouge* (2001), which includes a Bollywood number, "Chamma Chamma." The list could go on and on.

At another level, Bollywood films released in the US are now often screened in mainstream theater chains such as Regal Cinemas instead of being relegated to independent theaters. Moreover, there have been talks of Hollywood remaking Bollywood films, as in the case of *Johnny Gaddaar*, whose remake rights were purchased by Ray Haboush's Automatic Media. In 2011, at a University of Westminster conference titled "What's New in Indian Cinema," 21st Century Fox executives expressed their plans to produce a Hindi film with the intent of remaking it as a Hollywood musical. Nitin Govil draws attention to this trend of Hollywood copying Hindi cinema as well as part of its financial entry into the Indian marketplace. He mentions that "as part of a larger development deal with Reliance BIG Pictures, Brett Ratner's reedited English version of the Hindi film *Kites* (2010) was released simultaneously with the 'original' in May 2010" (*Orienting Hollywood* 70). The implications for Bollywood remakes of Hollywood films and Hollywood remakes of Bollywood films thus demand a larger analysis in terms of transnationalization and hegemony of the two industries, as well as the negotiations between them given the messy mergers that already defy easy separations of Bollywood and Hollywood and of India and the West.

The coming years will reveal whether these projects will come to successful fruition and will show the changing nature of remaking when Hollywood remakes Bollywood, and as purchases of intellectual property involving transnational remakes take hold of the Bollywood remaking practice, too. The historical and textual analysis that I have presented in this book contributes to and anticipates future research in these directions. Bollywood remakes of Hollywood films constantly negotiate inherited conventions, changing codes of gender, imported foreign themes and aesthetics, Bollywood and Hollywood genres, and experimentation by Hindi filmmakers. By charting the shifting nature of remaking within a rapidly changing industrial context from the 1990s onward, this book has explored the ideological and economic motivations and the implications of the Bollywood remake in the global market, which contributes to conversations in the field of transnational remakes as well as of Bollywood. New and continuing research on Bollywood remakes by Ganti, Mehta, Richards, Smith, Wright, and others in the last few years in some ways parallels the rise in the remakes, and it points to the validity and importance of studying the Bollywood remake as a new aesthetic and industrial form. *Déjà Viewed* is a contribution to this exciting field of knowledge that is still growing. No doubt, more work is needed on domestic remakes, intra-Asian remakes, and remakes within other circuits. My sincere hope is that this book adds in important ways to the consideration of intertextuality, gender, and genre within remake studies.

jalāo sham.a se sham'eñ ujālo bazm-e-hunar
udhār māñgne se nuur kam nahīñ hotā

—Ajmal Siddiqui

Notes

Introduction

1. See *Rekhta*, https://www.rekhta.org/couplets/hain-aur-bhii-duniyaa-men-sukhan-var-bahut-achchhe-mirza-ghalib-couplets.
2. *Mirza Ghalib* (1988) was written and produced by Gulzar.
3. An example is the second line of his couplet: "ham ko ma.alūm hai jannat kī Haqīqat lekin, dil ke khush rakhne ko 'ġhālib' ye khayāl achchhā hai." The first line is about how the idea of heaven or God is not real. The second line then adds to it by saying that this belief (in an afterlife) makes living life a little easier. The second line, unmoored from the context of the first one, however, is quite popular and in everyday usage is often used jokingly to simply mean the equivalent of "whatever helps you sleep better at night." Another one of his couplets, "Ishq par zor nahin," was used in the title song of Mani Ratnam's film *Dil Se* (1988). The same phrase was used as a title for a Hindi film from the 1970s and of a TV series.
4. Other poets have echoed this kind of thinking as well by using Ghalib's very phrase, "*andāz-e-bayāñ*." Saifuddin Saif explicitly denies any reality of originality at all:

> 'saif' andāz-e-bayāñ rañg badal detā hai . . . varna duniyā meñ
> koī baat na.ī baat nahīñ
> (Saif, the style of expression gives new color and new meaning;
> otherwise, there is no newness or uniqueness in this world)

See Saifuddin Saif, https://www.rekhta.org/couplets/saif-andaaz-e-bayaan-rang-badal-detaa-hai-saifuddin-saif-couplets.

5. In Urdu, *shayari*, *tazmeen* is a literary practice that collapses the difference between copying and originality as well and enforces a recognition of deriving from precursors a necessary aesthetic practice. Parekh describes

tazmeen as a kind of "emulation, a figure of rhetoric, wherein a line or couplet from a well-known poet is inserted, with or without minor changes, in one's poetry. It is a kind of borrowing to either give the emulated line or couplet a new meaning in a deeper context or to add something to one's own ideas. When skillfully used, this technique can bring in wonderful results, adding to the joy of poetry, both the original and the quoted one" ("Literary Notes").

6. Creekmur's phrase, here, is a play on Ramanujan's saying that he uses as an epigraph: "No Hindu ever reads *Mahabharata* for the first time" (qtd. in Creekmur, "Repetition" 173). The repetition of stories in the Sanskrit epics *Ramayana* and *Mahabharata* in Hindi cinema is also common knowledge. The pleasure of rewatching these stories in different guises is not based on originality of the story itself but the repetition itself is part of the pleasure. Thus, there are numerous examples beyond just that of Ghalib in Indian culture of alternative ways of appreciating repetition.

7. See Zengin, p. 311, about Bakhtin's influence of Julia Kristeva's notion of intertextuality.

8. The list has since been updated to include more titles and is comprised of one hundred films at this time.

9. By "loose remakes," I mean films that perhaps copy one scene from a source text or take so much liberty with the plot that calling them remakes might be incorrect.

10. For example, *Kaante*, a remake of several Hollywood films (but most notably Quentin Tarantino's *Reservoir Dogs*), employed several Hollywood technicians to produce the Hollywoodesque action film style (see Govil, "Orienting Hollywood," pp. 64–65, and Neelam Sidhar Wright, pp. 173–75). I discuss this in more detail in chapter 3.

11. Khan had already started playing with similar tropes in her film *Main Hoon Na* (2004). Other films, such as *Johnny Gaddaar*, which I discuss in chapter 3, also has a dominant mode of neo-noir and pastiche and was released a few months prior to *OSO*. The difference is that that film is not mainstream and in the popular vein like *OSO*. *Johnny Gaddaar*, despite its slick production quality, remains an auteur-driven, *hatke* film with a much smaller viewership. See Wright (*Bollywood and Postmodernism*) for an extended examination of Khan's auteurism in terms of postmodernity and Iyer ("Looking for the Past in Pastiche") for their discussion of the complicated relationship that Bollywood films, particularly *OSO*, articulate with their past.

12. Indian cinema scholars such as Tejaswini Ganti and Sangita Gopal have explored the status of Bollywood as one that now attracts foreign capital because of financial stability granted through bank loans and newer, more profitable, markets of the multiplexes. See Tejaswini Ganti, *Producing Bollywood* (Duke UP, 2012), and Sangita Gopal, *Conjugations: Marriage and Form in New Bollywood* (U of Chicago P, 2011).

13. See John Harlow quoted in Govil. Govil points to the economic standpoint by referencing Harlow: "One Hollywood studio lawyer noted that, 'until now it has not been worth our time tangling with filmmakers in a Mumbai court. But if this *Reservoir Dogs* rehash starts making serious money in the East, then we shall have to start investigating how closely such movies are copying the originals'" (69).

14. As I will discuss later, Bollywood was granted industry status by the state in 1998. The industry remained based in a producer system, and older systems of finance remained in place until 2005, when the effects of the industry status and the entry of new production, distribution, and exhibition companies precipitated changes in a number of practices related to financing, production, distribution, and exhibition (Ganti, *Bollywood* 58)

15. The industry has very few non-value-added people such as executives, lawyers, agents, professional managers (Ganti, *Bollywood* 60).

16. The only works I could find then were the articles by Tejaswini Ganti and Sheila Nayar.

17. See Ganti (*Producing Bollywood*) and Punathambekar for a discussion of corporatization of the industry.

18. In fact, Bollywood has come to be associated with post-1990s Hindi cinema. Scholars and filmmakers of Indian cinema distinguish popular Hindi cinema from Bollywood to indicate the change in the industry and the product. Bollywood is thus associated with the glitzy films described here that attract a bourgeois and diasporic audience through the spectacle they provide.

19. As in includes the film industry but is more than just industrial practices (Rajadhyaksha), 27.

20. There were loose genres and repetition of certain aspects to films in Hindi cinema. It is an industry where repetition is not understood as plagiarism the way that modernity's expression of individualism and art does in Western culture. However, the ways in which certain genres are intentionally produced since the 1990s, how producers become associated with certain genres and start branding their later films with, for example, music from earlier films as a score, and so on expose the capitalist intent that bulwarks the film industry.

21. Vasudevan discusses how as a domestic commercial cinema in the "third world," Hindi cinema "has successfully marginalized Hollywood's position in the domestic market" and has also been "influential in certain foreign markets" (305).

22. The film had been remade by Anant Thakur once before, as *Chori Chori* (*Stealthily*), in 1956. The remakes after the nineties, however, are not occasional, and Bhatt is a director who has become notorious for producing (unacknowledged) remakes.

23. Sheila Nayar cites Anupama Chandra, a writer for the weekly magazine *India Today*, to claim that in August 1993, 90 percent of Hindi films in production were remakes (74).

24. See Chakravarty; Thomas, "Melodrama"; and Ganti, *Bollywood* for a discussion of these influences on Hindi cinema.

25. Many scholars in postcolonial studies have talked about this gendered split between tradition and modernity. Partha Chatterjee, in his seminal work, *The Nation and Its Fragments*, talks about the divide between home and the material world. That is, the place of the woman is within the home where she becomes the beholder of tradition so that the men can deal with the corrupt material world. Women become the preserver of national culture that should then remain uncorrupted by the public and westernized world (120–21). Zillah Eisenstein, a postcolonial feminist scholar, argues that Indian women symbolically represent the community and the nation (*Against Empire*). Another scholar of Third World feminism, Uma Narayan, seeks to undo this binary of tradition and Western, which automatically labels feminism as a "symptom of Westernization" because it goes against the ideology of ideal femininity (*Dislocating Cultures*).

26. See Chakravarty, *National Identity in Indian Popular Cinema, 1947–1987*.

27. Jyotika Virdi complicates this notion by tracing religious discourses after partition that feed into the notion of women as bearers of religious identity. Therefore, she argues that "the symbol of woman as home and nation turns out to be an unstable signifier" (*Cinematic ImagiNation* 72) However, whether the woman is a signifier of a secular nation or of religious tradition, she becomes the site of contestation over religioethnic identities that end up regulating femininity as traditional and "othering" a sexualized and individualist westernized notion of femininity.

28. See Thomas ("Melodrama" 165–66). *Dharma*, literally meaning "duty," refers to the ethical codes of conduct that characters believe in and live by in popular Hindi cinema. These codes are as much conventions of Hindi cinema as they resonate culturally with the audience as well.

29. Mankekar discerns a shift in the way this imagined Indianness gets reconfigured in 1990s films (such as *Phir Bhi Dil Hai Hindustani*, *Pardes*, and *DDLJ*)—it now becomes a quality that can be carried within westernized Indians. While Mankekar is talking about Bollywood films that are not remakes, I am arguing that remakes articulate these concerns even more directly.

30. Part of the impulse behind 1990s films such as *DDLJ* and *Pardes* is about how Indianness can be carried. In the 1950s film *Shree 420*, the song "Phir Bhi Dil Hai Hindustani" ("And Yet My Heart Is Indian") presents the global Raj who sings about his clothes and accessories: "Mera joota hai japani,

yeh patloon inglistani, sar pe lal topi roosi, phir bhi dil hai Hindustani." The lyrics convey that his shoes are from Japan, pants from England, hat from Russia, but that his heart remains Indian. Discussions of postindependence films focus on the tension between modernity and tradition, and Raj is the modern man but with an Indian heart. Modernity also indicates globalization in these films, but the use of the term *globalization* gained more currency in the 1990s because of economic liberalization of the country; relaxing of rules governing Western imports; popularity of foreign, especially American entertainment, via satellite TV; and the large wave of migration of professional class. Thus, the films of the 1990s often resurrect such oppositions, which are then complicated as it becomes difficult to separate out the lived reality of the local and the global as they interpenetrate.

31. Gopal's argument is very nuanced in how she contends that the forces of Bollywoodization are apparent in the early 1970s but that they come to fruition in the 1990s (*Conjugations* 14). She further traces New Bollywood's beginnings to the 1990s, but as is clear from her discussion, the films from the 1990s have both impulses: those of classic Hindi cinema and of Bollywood as well as those that have the emergent characteristics of New Bollywood, which is more obvious after 2000 (*Conjugations* 18). For example, her distinction of the new couple form, concerned more with intimacy than with traditional romance's focus on external obstacles such as fathers, places some of the 1990s family films in the realm of Bollywood instead of New Bollywood. I discuss these films in chapter 1.

32. See Sangita Gopal, *Conjugations*, for a discussion of gender and New Bollywood.

33. It was considered a "Super Hit" by Box Office India, coming second only to *Kuch Kuch Hota Hai* (https://web.archive.org/web/20120825211319/ http://www.boxofficeindia.com/showProd.php?itemCat=126&catName= MTk5MC0xOTk5).

34. This formula both involves the industry—the songs, stars, and foreign locations ensure profits—and involves the trend started by films such as *DDLJ*, which exploits the audience's fascination with the diaspora and their negotiation of their Indian identity.

35. Carolyn Durham uses the example of Euro Disney to discuss the politics of Frenchness and Americanness that it generates. Cultural concerns regarding national identity coalesce on this amusement park about whether it will be yet another example of American imperialism or if it will assimilate into French culture: "One could say that America offered France its 'version' of Euro *Disney*: a Disneyland, translated, that is, transferred, intact, from California to Marne-la-Vallée. France, in contrast, wanted its own 'version' of *Euro* Disney: a Disneyland translated, that is, *transformed*, into Frenchness itself" (5).

Chapter 1

1. Leitch does not discuss cross-cultural remakes, but he provides four possible relationships between texts that adapt or remake a previous text. Of these, the first two, readaptation and update, are about adapting from a literary source to film. A readaptation treats earlier cinematic adaptations as inconsequential in its drive to be more faithful to the literary source (45), whereas an update accommodates it for contemporary relevance (48). Homage and true remakes are the remake equivalents of the two, where the true remake also tries to make the original relevant by updating it (49). The cross-cultural remake is like the update because the difference in form is so stark; at the same time, it is like a true remake because it is a makeover from film to film. The cross-cultural Bollywood remake involves an update in formal and temporal terms but also in terms of the industry and cultural codes. Thus, it straddles both the update and the true remake.

2. Weirdly enough, no one does the "Macarena" dance steps.

3. *Masala* literally means a mix of spices. The term is used to refer to films of the 1970s and 1980s that combined aspects of several genres (comedy, melodrama, romance, action, etc.).

4. While Thomas primarily focuses on the masala films of the 1970s and 1980s, she does trace these ideas in terms of larger melodramatic frameworks for Hindi cinema, while adding caveats about exceptions. For example, she discusses how control of female sexuality was not as strict anymore but continued to exert a force on representations of the heroine. Therefore, it is not a surprise when it becomes so central in the 1990s—it is both a reversal because it's so excessive and a continuation of the weakened strain.

5. Priya Village Roadshow (PVR), established in 1997, was the first multiplex in New Delhi. Other multiplexes in Delhi, Pune, Bombay, and other cities followed in the next few years.

6. Filmmakers did not necessarily have to make films that would please one big market (such as when the all-India hit was a primary goal for pre-1990s films, and the Indian and South Asian diaspora was the desired audience for films in the late 1990s) (Ganti, *Producing Bollywood* 354–55). Experiments with genre films and films that bucked the dominant trends attracted different audience bodies.

7. See Siddiqui, "Behind Her Laughter . . . Is Fear: Domestic Abuse and Transnational Feminism in Bollywood Remakes."

8. See Lalitha Gopalan for a discussion of the avenging-women films.

9. See Mehta ("Globalizing") for a discussion of the involvement of the state in the production of clean entertainment as encapsulated by the family film.

Other forms of media that more actively produce the Indian state as Hindu are the war films in the 1990s that constantly represent Pakistan as the enemy and mark the Indian Muslim as the enemy within. TV shows *Ramayan* (Ramanand Sagar 1987–88) and *Mahabharat* (B. R. Chopra 1988–1990), based on sacred Hindu epics, became very popular in the late 1980s and early 1990s. Of these two, *Ramayan* propagated a regressive Hindu identity. I discuss it in chapter 4 in the context of Deepa Mehta's *Fire*, which actively critiques the combination of Hindutva, patriarchy, and heterosexism that *Ramayan* popularized and that was used by Rashtriya Swayamsevak Sangh (RSS)—the fundamentalist arm of the political party, Bharatiya Janta Party (BJP)—to aggravate communal tensions for political gain.

10. See Gopalan, *Cinema of Interruptions*. Lalitha Gopalan argues for the simultaneity of immersion and awareness in audiences for Hindi films.

11. Linda Williams claims that melodrama "is the dominant form of popular moving-image narrative" in Hollywood (54).

12. Ganti's ethnographic research shows how a film such as *Fatal Attraction* would be hard to remake because it does not gel with the tastes of audiences of Hindi cinema ("And Yet My Heart"). I discuss this in the next chapter.

13. See Thomas, "Indian Cinema."

14. See Thomas, "Melodrama."

15. Sumita Chakravarty argues that Hindi cinema was involved in nation building in postindependence India.

16. I use the term *Bollywood* here as a subset of popular Hindi cinema as it refers to post-1990s Hindi cinema. Dissanayake, however, complicates the term and says it is larger than the film industry because, like Rajadhyaksha, he includes all kinds of industries and events (like DVDs, film festivals, etc.) connected to the film industry as part of Bollywood ("Globalization" 144).

17. Benegal's cinema bridges mainstream fictional film and art cinema (also known as India's parallel cinema).

18. Jyotika Virdi argues that in the romance films of the 1980s, "the new enemy was the authoritarian patriarch, a response to the consciousness spread by the women's movement" (16).

19. The lyrics of certain songs were banned and changed. Derek Bose mentions a few significant ones, such as "Choli ke Peeche" and "Sexy, Sexy, Sexy Mujhe . . ." (*Bollywood Uncensored*).

20. Mankekar talks about the state seeking wealthy NRI investment in India and connects this with representations of NRIs as knights who will save damsels: "These NRIs appear in elite discourses as male, affluent, and peripatetic" (Mankekar 744).

21. Peter Krämer is talking mostly about the films in the 1960s and 1970s and indicates their appeal to children. Robert Allen, however, includes

younger teen audiences in this categorization. He talks about the echo boom in the 1980s and the VCR's popularity creating a profitable market for these films targeted at the children ages fifteen and younger.

22. Festivals and weddings are common events around which song and dance numbers and melodramatic moments of familial love are often organized.

23. Pervasiveness of Hindu culture is central to Hindi cinema even as it imagines the country's understanding of secularism as one that is anchored in acceptance and respect of all religions. Even films, such as *Mother India* and *Deewaar*, while having strong Muslim minor characters, create the dominant world view via the family as Hindu. In *Shree 420*, the state gets modernized through Raj as the saree-wearing Vidya anchors the Indian culture, a move followed by NRI films. In the family films of the 1990s, however, rituals such as Karwachauth and the Hindu wedding with its festivities including sangeet couch the Hindu patriarchal norms within the new liberal romance. So, they become more than a mere continuation especially when considered alongside the general Hindutva tide of the decade. Mostly however, it is cultural, rather than religious aspects of Hinduism that get emphasized in the family films. The 1990s remakes tend to replicate that, but so do most later remakes. Muslim protagonists are rare or are incorporated within a genre like the Islamicate film, which is associated overwhelmingly with a certain kind of Muslim culture.

24. For example, Frank Capra's *It Happened One Night* (1934) was remade twice; once as *Chori Chori* (1956) and then in the nineties as *Dil Hai Ke Manta Nahin* (*The Heart Is Such, It Disagrees*) (Mahesh Bhatt 1991).

25. Cited in Steve Neale, "The Big Romance or Something Wild? Romantic Comedy Today."

26. See Eva Illouz, *Consuming the Romantic Utopia*.

27. Jyotika Virdi talks about films such as *Dil* (*Heart*) (Indra Kumar 1990), which makes fun of the patriarch, and *Qayamat Se Qayamat Tak* (*Eternity to Eternity*) (Mansoor Khan 1988), which blames the families for the tragic deaths of the lovers.

28. Thomas argues that often heroes of Hindi films were associated with villainy and loose morals but that even then, this would be temporary; it would be revealed that the hero's dharma required it or the hero would be punished for it even if he transformed his ways ("Melodrama" 172–77).

29. In *French Kiss*, Luc is very similar to the hero of women's romances. Two incidents related to Luc's character get changed in the remake, and both are related to his sexuality. The first happens when Luc takes Kate to Bob's place to retrieve her bag and the necklace he stole. Just before they arrive, a skimpily dressed woman excitedly hugs him and kisses him on the cheek. The body language indicates a sexual familiarity between the two. The scene establishes Luc's appeal as a romantic hero but also, crucially, recalls Kate's

joke about his inability to perform sexually and reestablishes his masculinity. In *Pyaar To Hona Hi Tha*, this scene is replaced with one in which cops are chasing someone, and Shekhar guiltily lifts his hands in the air thinking it is him. The scene establishes Shekhar as a crook and on the wrong side of the law. The change in this detail is significant because being overfamiliar with women would have implied that he lacked respect for women instead of emphasizing his sexual prowess and manliness. In both films, these scenes indicate the male protagonist's unsuitability as a romantic object, and yet in both, his potential to be the right guy remains plausible.

30. Peter Evans lists various conventions of romantic comedies and argues that in the 1990s there is an absence of sex before the realization of true love (233).

31. In this case, the film ignores Nisha's Indian and Sanjana's French citizenship; instead, it prefers the ideological understanding of Sanjana's Indianness and Nisha's Westernness in presenting Sanjana as the ideal. I explore the contradictoriness of this situation later in the chapter.

32. The phrase *brides who travel* is used by Mankekar to talk about gender in these films. These brides reject arranged marriage, and each falls in love with an NRI whose heart is, however, Indian.

33. Shandley argues that unlike the postwar runaway romances, *French Kiss* is evidence of a newer relationship between America and the Old World. Therefore, unlike the earlier heroines of these romances, Kate can decide to stay in France and get married in France instead of returning to America.

Chapter 2

1. Since Bipasha Basu, the female star of *Jism*, and Anurag Basu, the director of *Murder* have the same last name, I will use their complete names in the chapter.

2. She does not change the will to name herself as the sole beneficiary. Instead, the will she manufactures still divides Edmund's fortune between her and his sister. But she deliberately prepares it improperly as that will result in the will being considered null and void. As a result, all the property reverts to her as Edmund's surviving widow, and Ned, with his history of being incompetent, seems to be the one on whom rests the blame for this injustice.

3. In an interview for *Rediff.com*, Rohini Iyer questions Bipasha Basu on the shocking promos of the film, which Bipasha Basu keeps denying, saying that it's not a pornographic film and that she would never do any vulgar roles. Taran Adarsh notes the film's biggest strength is in defying stereotypes and ends his review by claiming that Bipasha Basu steals the show: "Her sexy look and seductive deep voice, in contrast with her cold and calculating

personality, makes her the most impressive femme fatale since Zeenat Aman and Parveen Babi" (*Bollywood Hungama*).

4. India gained independence in 1947. The films under discussion here are from 1930 onwards.

5. Partha Chatterjee discusses the formal education required for the new *bhadramahila*, which insisted on cultural refinement and borrowed from British values but also ensured a distinction so the *bhadramahila* would never be in danger of becoming a memsahib (a British lady) (128).

6. See Gopalan for a deeper discussion of Carol Clover's work on B films and for how Gopalan relates it to the Hindi rape-revenge films of the 1980s.

7. See Radha Kumar, who discusses the feminist outcry against the public rape of a woman by policemen in 1972.

8. Except that in the domestic-abuse films the women are abused by their husbands. These films fall into the regressive patriarchal dynamic of the 1990s and critique it at the same time. In them, instead of allowing the woman to enact her revenge, the narrative privileges the nicer patriarch, another man, who helps by rescuing her. At the same time, these films provide an alternative to abusive masculinity, and almost "all the films in this cycle . . . are anti-romantic critiques of the institution" of marriage (Siddiqui "Beyond Her Laughter is Fear . . ." 4).

9. This was the decade when the item number emerged as a convention. An item number is a sexualized dance number in a film, known for its hot and steamy scenes, often presenting the spectacle of the female body, and having little or nothing to do with the rest of the diegesis.

10. In the movement from the vamp played by Helen to the item girl, the association with villainy and evil lessens while the sexualization becomes more pronounced. This movement betrays the attempt to control such deviant femininity by containing it within the item number so that the rest of the diegesis remains uninfected. The item number is an essential ingredient in the 1990s because it is Bollywood's response to threats posed by MTV and is a major source of revenue on its own. Therefore, it has a life before the film and is often what draws audiences to the theaters. Moreover, the appeal of the item number often makes it overwhelm the popularity of the film and become the main attraction. The item number also circulates independently of the film, as it is performed at weddings and at parties by professionals, as well as by girls for certain functions like the *sangeet*. The item girls become famous too, and their sexuality as displayed in the item numbers becomes part of their star text.

11. See Mini, "Locating the 'B,'" and Amit Kumar, "The Lower Stall."

12. See Mini, "Locating the 'B,'" for a discussion of A-circuit and B-circuit films. Splintering the too-easy equivalence between the B circuit, B-grade films, and sleaze, she argues that B-circuit theaters are defined as such

for various reasons, including their location (far away from urban centers or within urban areas but where films are released after a lag), their lack of access to the most up-to-date technology for exhibition, and the physical condition of their equipment and space (usually below par due to low-quality screens and sound as well as a lack of adequate funds for maintenance). B-circuit theaters often screen films that are cheaply produced and low in quality, but while sleaziness is associated with these theaters, not all films released in them are pornographic. For this chapter's purposes, the correlation between sleaze, B-grade films, and the B circuit is relevant, but that is not all that these theaters cater to.

13. Staiger talks about the vamp in *A Fool There Was*, who does not have to pay a penalty for her crimes (147). Classic femme fatales were always punished. For example, Vera (*Detour*), Cora (*The Postman Always Rings Twice*), Phyllis (*Double Indemnity*), and Kathie (*Out of the Past*) all die. Mildred (*Mildred Pierce*) is "returned to her proper place in patriarchy" (Kaplan 18).

14. Susan Bordo connects the misogynistic representations of powerful women as responses to feminism (Grossman 97).

15. In *Postmodernism*, Jameson argues that *Body Heat*'s lack of reference to the 1980s and to Florida, where it is set, makes it nothing more than pastiche—a mere postmodern play on noir elements (68). I talk more about it in the next chapter, which addresses neo-noir.

16. Polanski deployed the figure of the femme fatale in *Chinatown* (1974), another neo-noir before *Body Heat*, only to subvert audience expectations by showing her as the victim.

17. Chabrol's heroines tend to be more like Hitchcock's heroines, who, nevertheless, are similarly drawn from the vamp. These women are often fetishized as well as punished for their sexual power. Chabrol's camerawork, however, sympathizes with Hélène by representing her life as one of dreary suburban lifelessness.

18. Bipasha Basu had by then established herself as an actor. Sherawat had been known for doing hot and sexy scenes because of her appearance in the music videos "Maar dala," by Nirmal Pandey, and "Lak tunu tunu," by Surjit Bindrakhiya. "Maar dala" is similar to item numbers and introduces her with a close-up of her navel; the rest of the music video shows her being subjected to the advances of a perverse predatory man. "Lak tunu tunu" shows the daydreaming of a tennis umpire as he watches a game between two women, one of them played by Sherawat. His fantasized dreams are of dancing with the two women. In the first one, Sherawat is wearing a revealing black dress as the two of them engage in a very hot dance alone. While this dance expresses lust, the other one functions in opposition and expresses love. Here, the dance with the other girl uses the conventions of the Hindi film song with the heroine: she is dressed in Indian clothes and

dances with other girls, and the gaze that she is subjected to does not objectify her body. Sherawat's only film before *Murder*, *Khwahish* (Govind Menon 2003), promised titillating scenes and made her notorious for doing several kissing scenes; the poster is similar to that of *Jism* in suggesting a skin flick.

19. Doane argues that the femme fatale is equipped with a body that is itself given agency independent of consciousness. In a sense, the femme fatale has power *despite herself* (2). While I do not agree with Doane's generalization, it does apply to certain femme fatales like Gilda but not to someone like Phyllis.

20. See Andrew Horton and Stuart McDougal.

21. See Horton and McDougal.

22. See Meheli Sen (*Haunting Bollywood*) for more on the *nagin* heroine in Hindi cinema.

23. Kasdan claims in an interview that he wanted the last shot of Matty on her island to be deliberately ambiguous. Kathleen Turner reads this as Matty's unhappiness because she has lost the only real love she had (see "Special Features," *Body Heat*).

24. Wood and Walker argue that Hélène has needs that Charles cannot satisfy and that the affair supports their marriage by satisfying Hélène's needs (118). However, the film does not allow the audience any confident view of the matter—we don't know if Charles is emotionally and sexually unavailable because he already suspects his wife of infidelity or for some other reason. On the other hand, his immediate suspicion of his wife based on her guilty start while talking on the phone (to the extent that he hires a private investigator to spy on her) already indicates his lack of faith in her.

25. The genre of roman policier to which this film belongs is also similar to Hollywood crime films like films noir or Hitchcock's films.

26. In an interview, Chabrol says that the blue in the film is the color of madness:

> Blue is above all the color of madness, a form of madness. A psychiatrist once told me that the dominant color in the drawings and paintings of the mentally deranged is blue. I thought it was strange: "How could it be blue, which is such a calm color?" And he said: "No, think about it; try to imagine living perpetually in blue." It's the most unbalanced, and unbalancing, color. Voila! So, when I wanted to show imbalance, I used blue to please that psychiatrist, whom I like quite a bit . . . And it's true that it has a strange effect. (Yakir and Chabrol 12)

27. Doane argues that the femme fatale is represented as the antithesis of the maternal (1).

28. Jans Wager uses the term *femme attrapee* for the domestic antithesis of the femme fatale (4). Janey Place calls her the "innocent sister of the dark woman" (49).

29. See my discussion of the film and its censorship in "New Womanhood."

30. This scene references the scene between Mickey Rourke and Kim Basinger in *9½ Weeks* (I'm grateful to Tejaswini Ganti for telling me about this allusion). The scene is similar in how Sonia is blindfolded, wearing a white shirt, and in how Kabir uses ice in a glass to tease her. However, in *9½ Weeks*, the play with ice moves between Kim Basinger's mouth and chest, whereas here, the navel becomes the main focus of the foreplay.

31. I discuss Abraham's queer fandom in the next chapter.

32. See Studlar for a discussion of the editing of this scene. Neff tells Phyllis that she can never get away with this murder. Then the scene cuts to the present, when Neff is recording the story. When it cuts back to Neff and Phyllis again, Neff tells her that he will help her with the murder. Studlar explains that this change in him, which is obfuscated by the flashforward, is easy for audiences to understand (392–93). They fill in the gap created by editing by what the scene also reveals when it cuts back to Ned and Phyllis; that Phyllis is applying her lipstick and Neff has lit a cigarette discloses the occurrence of a sexual act in the interim.

33. Helen Hanson comments on the feminist influence on neo-noir. She says, "The period of the 1970s was marked by an increasing fluidity and exchange between radical activist feminist discourses on women's place and more popular, commodified images of the 'liberated woman'" (144).

34. Pooja Bhatt and her father have been known to speak out against the censorship laws against nudity in India. Pooja Bhatt even appeared on the cover of a film glossy, covered only in body paint (Bose 148–49).

35. "'Bits' is a few feet of celluloid containing pornographic or sexually explicit scenes" lifted from other films which filmmakers insert to satiate the carnal desires of the audience: "Since [the bit] can appear and disappear at will it is used by the filmmakers to bypass censorship guidelines" (Subba 227).

36. Bose argues that for actresses to remain in the reckoning in post-globalized Bollywood is for them to play the temptress or something similar that results in display of the skin and body. He sees *Jism* as similar to films that objectify female bodies for profit except for the fact that it is disguised as a feminist film (173).

37. Amit Kumar argues that to avoid legal and moral problems, another publicity strategy unique to the sleaze films is the use of "written-text" in place of "visual-images" in posters (33).

38. While the term *skin flick* shares similarity with the Hollywood genre of skin flicks, its usage indicates a lack of awareness of Hollywood soft-porn films. It references mainstream films that are more erotic than the

usual fare because of the amount of (mostly female) skin that is shown and the occasional suggestion of sex.

39. Writing in 2008, Govindan and Datta explain how the item number was helping in the competition against the likes of MTV: "Hindi films now have started to compete with the look of music and entertainment channels. Thus, song-and-dance sequences are staged and directed to look like music videos precisely so that they can be aired on music video channels as advanced film publicity" (183).

40. See Somini Sengupta.

41. For example, members of RSS attacked a few people, mostly women, in a Mangalore pub in 2009. Its founder, P. Muthalik called the incident minor and defended the RSS attackers by saying, "In that pub, women were indulging in obscenity, they were taking drugs . . . why is the media making it a big issue?" (qtd. in *Economic Times*). This incident is not a one-off either; for instance, RSS members routinely harass couples on Valentine's Day.

42. Many of these women have a secondary career in Bollywood.

43. Many scholars have connected the rise of religious fundamentalism in the past decade to the eroding of native cultures because of globalization and its attendant westernization.

44. Shrivastava uses the example of the item number to discuss the problem of filming women in Bollywood: "There's the item song that objectifies women . . . This type of song has no connection with the narrative; there are just shots of the woman's body, accompanied with weird lyrics and a group of men trying to maul the woman; and this is supposed to be entertainment. This sort of male gaze has shaped popular Hindi cinema for decades. There have been too few women who have been behind the camera . . . I have to keep telling technicians sometimes that they should not shoot in a certain way" (qtd. in Arora, Sanos, and Siddiqui).

45. See the section on "Spectators Haggle with the Movie" in Naficy, "Theorizing 'Third-World' Film Spectatorship," 7–16.

46. See Patricia Pisters, *The Neuro-Image: A Deleuzian Filmphilosophy for Digital Screen Culture* (forthcoming), and Elena del Río *Deleuze and the Cinemas of Performance: Powers of Affection*.

47. These experiments are undertaken by older production companies and long-standing directors as well.

Chapter 3

1. The term Bollywood has a contentious history (which I lay out in the introduction). I use it for the most part to indicate post-1990s Hindi cinema films. However, later on in this chapter, I also complicate ideas of

Bollywood to include the transnational and corporatized aspects of Hindi cinema.

2. Monika Mehta analyzes *Kaante*'s production and promotion contexts to point to the contradictory ways in which the influence of *Reservoir Dogs* is denied as well as used for marketing. Rumors about Tarantino's film as the "original" were deliberately used to make *Kaante* more appealing to viewers (Mehta, "Affective Logics" 440–44). On the other hand, Sanjay Gupta denied that his film is a remake of *Reservoir Dogs*, instead citing several heist films like it as his inspiration; he mentions *City on Fire*, *The Asphalt Jungle*, and *The Killing* in this list for the generic plot his film follows (Mehta, "Affective Logics" 441).

3. Kakar claims that the Indian male lacks complete separation from the mother, and in that, experiences a desire to be female in the desire to be one with the mother.

4. Please see chapter 1 for a discussion of the ideological construction of Indianness.

5. In this, the film is harking back to earlier films such as *Mother India* and *Deewaar* (which I discuss in this chapter) as well. Films of the1990s, as I've mentioned in chapter 1, increasingly give prominence to the patriarch.

6. See Rosie Thomas, "Melodrama," for a discussion of dharma. I also discuss her argument about melodramatic gendered codes in chapter 1.

7. The figure of the mother is an important trope in Hindi cinema. She is the one inviolable figure, and she is on the highest pedestal. From *Mother India* to *Deewaar*, a mother's forgiveness and her sense of justice is often used as a dharmic code in Hindi cinema.

8. We can perhaps already see the kind of beginnings of the vengeful middle-class character that Sangita Gopal identifies in the genre of "Bourgeois Extreme," a character that she sees as a microimport from Asian vengeance films such as *Oldboy* within a context of neoliberalism.

9. Several scholars, including Ganti (*Producing Bollywood*) and Mehta ("Globalizing"), discuss the shift to diasporic and bourgeois audiences in the 1990s.

10. Shah Rukh Khan no longer remains the antihero; his star text changes as he becomes the much beloved yuppie NRI.

11. This hero figure is connected with the appeal of the NRI groom in India because of the increasing migration of Indians abroad to earn money in US dollars and English pounds and due to the increasingly large percentage of profits that are secured by Bollywood films in overseas territories.

12. Paunksnis discusses postmilennial Hindi noir films by directors such as Anurag Kashyap within a context of neo-liberalism and Hindutva, tracing the anxiety of the noir protagonist to the late 1980s (98). He differentiates the paranoia in these noir films as one based in not knowing where the

destination is as opposed to one that arises from knowing that the destination is forever out of reach (98). His rich discussion of these noir films, however, does not include the specific neo-noir aspects of global noir, a genre that he discerns is in ascendance in Asia at the same time as in India. Cinephilia and intertextual invocations of noir films are also important facets of other global noir films; these aspects are more clearly evident in films that are remakes or pastiches of noir, and it is this cross-cultural homage and negotiation that I am pursuing in this chapter.

13. The genre of Bombay noir, produced by the likes of Ram Gopal Varma, is an example of gangster films produced by the Hindi film industry. But Varma's films, with their gritty style, are very different from the spectacle of the gangster film that Hollywood represents in the contemporary Indian imagination. Mehta argues that the film provides a dystopic vision of diaspora ("Affective Logics" 452).

14. *Reservoir Dogs* is a classic example of how neo-noir does heist films because the heist goes wrong, and it goes wrong because of backstabbing and distrust. See Mark Bould (4).

15. Mak justifies his shooting of Bali by saying that Bali was about to kill him as well as the policeman and run away with the money. But the viewer knows that Mak is lying, and Ajju and Marc refuse to believe that Bali would ever do this.

16. These include diaspora and urban cosmopolitan audiences familiar with Western genres as well as domestic mass audiences looking for a Western-style spectacle.

17. See Srinivas. "The Quentin Conversation."

18. Mehta traces the term *cinephilia* back to France in the 1950s and connects it with transatlantic passages between Europe and the United States.

19. Chase's work is argued to be heavily influenced by the works of American pulp fiction writers, James M. Cain and Raymond Chandler.

20. Bombay noir represents the gritty Bombay underworld and uses the noir style to represent the city (see Mazumdar).

21. Ram Gopal Varma's films have been different from regular Bollywood fare. Ranjani Mazumdar argues that Varma's film *Satya* (*Truth*) (1998) is a gritty and psychological exploration of the city (Bombay) that often uses an experimental documentary style to create a remarkably different aesthetic mode (150–75). As in many Hollywood noirs, Satya's protagonists do not have a past (Mazumdar 151).

22. In the interview that's part of the DVD bonus material, Raghavan says that the film is a homage to all the Johnny films ever made.

23. The use of the name Johny by Vijay Anand is also crucial since most villains and vamps in earlier Hindi cinema have westernized names such as Johnny, Don, Mona, and so on. Therefore, the adoption of this

particular name adds another layer to the way in which the film negotiates the Indian/Western binary.

Chapter 4

1. I'm using Kenneth Chan's conceptualization of the remake as a contact zone here, a term he borrows from Mary Louise Pratt. Chan analyzes the remake in terms of a cultural contact zone, where disparate cultures meet, clash, and grapple with each other often in highly asymmetrical relations of domination and subordination" (11).
2. The *hijra* community is one of the social groups that are considered as belonging to the third gender in South Asia.
3. The lyrics for that stanza follow:

Jaan pe bhi khelenge, tere liye le lenge (I will risk my life, I will take for you)
Jaan pe bhi khelenge, tere liye le lenge (I will risk my life, I will take for you)
Sab se dushmani (enmity with everyone)

I have written down the literal translation. The complete stanza recontextualizes "tere liye le lenge" in terms of picking a fight with anyone for the friend. But the way it is sung, twice without the last phrase (Sab se dushmani/ enmity with everyone), provocatively presents the meaning Kavi has presented.
4. Playback singing is common in Hindi cinema. The songs are sung by playback singers and are lip-synched by the actors.
5. The TV series was based on the Sanskrit epic *Ramayana* by Valmiki and *Ramcharitmanas* (also influenced by Valmiki's *Ramayana*) by Tulsidas.
6. There are other references as well; for instance, the servant Mundu keeps fantasizing about Radha, imagining that she, like Rama's wife, Sita, is subservient to him.
7. He discusses the emergence of a Hindu public and Hindu militancy as tied with the TV show (31).
8. Usha Iyer discusses the centrality of "libidinal and political affect of song and dance numbers" in South Asian cinemas ("Song and Dance Sequence" 174). These interludes often express what is denied, in this case, romantic and sexual desire. Mehta adds another layer by wresting it out of heterosexual context and making it a vehicle for expression of queer desire, a reading that has always existed in reception of these song numbers.
9. See Ghosh, "Queer Pleasures."
10. See Monika Mehta, "Globalizing Bombay Cinema."

Conclusion

1. See Ramna Walia for Bollywood remakes of Hindi films and Kathryn Hardy for Bhojpuri remakes of Hindi films.
2. See Mehta, "Affective Logics."
3. Gopal looks at the importation of "smaller elements of storytelling conventions, narrative construction, mise-en-scène, framing, cinematography, editing, sound, and so on from one cultural form to another that enables existing genres to reorient and refresh themselves in relation to emerging social dynamics" (101). In this case, she is looking at the Korean film's concept of revenge—one that is not confined to a particular social strata—as being important to how it makes its way into Bollywood and has implications for the figure of the middle-class avenger (101).

Bibliography

Adarsh, Taran. "*Jism.*" *Bollywood Hungama*, 17 Jan. 2003, 14:55 IST. *Internet Archive*, web.archive.org/web/20160610055149/http://www.bollywoodhungama.com/moviemicro/criticreview/id/201876/.
Allen, Robert C. "Home Alone Together: Hollywood and the Family Film." *Identifying Hollywood's Audiences: Cultural Identity and the Movies*, edited by Melvin Stokes and Richard Maltby, London: BFI, 1999.
Altman, Rick. "A Semantic/Syntactic Approach to Film Genre." *Film Theory and Criticism*, edited by Leo Braudy and Marshall Cohen, New York: Oxford UP, 2004, pp. 680–90.
Anwer, Megha, and Anupama Arora, editors. *Bollywood's New Woman: Liberalization, Liberation, and Contested Bodies*. New Brunswick, NJ: Rutgers UP, 2021.
Arora, Anupama, Sandrine Sanos, and Gohar Siddiqui. "Filming Women: A Conversation with Alankrita Shrivastava." *Journal of Feminist Scholarship*, vol. 21, Fall 2022, pp. 80–92.
Athique, Adrian M. "The 'Crossover' Audience: Mediated Multiculturalism and the Indian Film." *Continuum*, vol. 22, no. 3, 2008, pp. 299–311.
Babuscio, Jack. "Camp and the Gay Sensibility." *Gays and Film*, edited by Richard Dyer, London: BFI, 1977, pp. 40–57.
Baird, Robert M., and Stuart E. Rosenbaum, editors. *Same-Sex Marriage: The Moral and Legal Debate*, Amherst, NY: Prometheus Books, 2004.
Bannerjee, Kanchan. "Cloning Hollywood." *The Hindu*, 3 Aug. 2003, A1. http://www.hindu.com/thehindu/mag/2003/08/03/stories/2003080300090400.htm.
Barker, Jennifer M. *The Tactile Eye: Touch and the Cinematic Experience*. Berkeley: U of California P, 2009.
Bergman, David. *Camp Grounds: Style and Homosexuality*. Amherst: U of Massachusetts P, 1994.

Bhaskar, Ira. "Desire, Deviancy and Defiance in Bombay Cinema (1930s–1950s)." *Bad Women of Bollywood Films: Studies in Desire and Anxiety*, edited by Saswati Sengupta, Shampa Roy, and Sharmila Purkayastha, Cham, Switzerland: Palgrave-Macmillan, 2019, pp. 27–44.

Bhaskaran, Suparna. "The Politics of Penetration: Section 377 of the Indian Penal Code." *Queering India: Same-Sex Love and Eroticism in Indian Culture and Society*, New York: Routledge, 2002. 15–29.

Bhowmik, Someswar. *Cinema and Censorship: The Politics of Control in India*. New Delhi: Orient Blackswan, 2009.

Bindrakhiya, Surjit. "Lak Tunu Tunu." *YouTube*, uploaded by T-Series Apna Punjab, 15 Feb. 2012. www.youtube.com/watch?v=-8vXkK31jbA. Accessed 5 May 2024.

Boaz, David. "Privatize Marriage: The Simple Solution to the Gay-Marriage Debate." *Slate*, April 1997. Accessed 7 Oct. 2012.

Bordwell, David, Janet Staiger, and Kristin Thompson, editors. *The Classical Hollywood Cinema*. New York: Columbia UP, 1985.

Bose, Derek. *Bollywood Uncensored: What You Don't See on the Screen and Why*. New Delhi: Rupa, 2006.

Bose, Nandana. "The Hindu Right and the Politics of Censorship: Three Case Studies of Policing Hindi Cinema, 1992–2002." *The Velvet Light Trap*, vol. 63 (2009): 22–33.

Bould, Mark, Kathrina Glitre, and Greg Tuck, editors. *Neo-Noir*. London: Wallflower, 2009.

Braudy, Leo. Afterword. *Play It Again, Sam: Retakes on Remakes*, edited by Andrew Horton and Stuart Y. McDougal, Berkeley: U of California P, 1998, pp. 327–34.

Brooks, Peter. *The Melodramatic Imagination: Balzac, Henry James, Melodrama, and the Mode of Excess*. New Haven, CT: Yale UP, 1974.

Bulbeck, Chilla. "Sexual Identities: Western Imperialism?" *Beyond Borders: Thinking Critically about Global Issues*, edited by Paula S. Rothenberg, NY: Worth, 2006, pp. 224–45.

Bygrave, Mike. "Farewell Rambo, Hello Romeo." *The Guardian*, 6 June 1991, p. 30.

Chakravarty, Sumita S. *National Identity in Indian Popular Cinema, 1947–1989*. Austin: U of Texas P, 1993.

Chan, Kenneth. *Remade in Hollywood: The Global Chinese Presence in Transnational Chinese Cinemas*. Hong Kong: Hong Kong UP, 2009.

Chatterjee, Partha. *The Nation and Its Fragments: Colonial and Postcolonial Histories*. Princeton: Princeton UP, 1993.

Chatterji, Shoma A. *Subject Cinema, Object Women: A Study of the Portrayal of Women in Indian Cinema*. Calcutta: Parumita, 1998.

Chawla, Devika. "*I Will Speak Out*: Narratives of Resistance in Contemporary Indian Women's Discourses in Hindu Arranged Marriages." *Women and Language*, vol. 30, no. 1, Spring 2007, pp. 5–19.
Chhabra, Aseem. "Dear Bollywood: Gay Jokes Are NOT FUNNY." *Rediff Movies*, 10 July 2012. www.rediff.com/movies/report/column-dear-bollywood-gay-jokes-are-not-funny/20120710.htm. Accessed 11 July 2012.
Chhibber, Kavita. "Bipasha Basu: Loosening Up . . . on Her Feet." *Kavita Chhibber.com*, 6 Jan. 2010. Accessed 10 Mar. 2010.
Chibnall, Steve. "Travels in Ladland: The British Gangster Film Cycle 1998–2001." *The British Cinema Book*, edited by Robert Murphy, London: BFI, 2001, pp. 281–91.
Chughtai, Ismat. "Lihaaf ("The Quilt")." Translated by M. Asaduddin. *Manushi*. 3rd edition, no. 110, 1996, pp. 36–40.
Clover, Carol. "Her Body, Himself: Gender in the Slasher Film." Misogyny, Misandry, and Misanthropy, edited by R. Howard Bloch and Frances Ferguson, Los Angeles: U of California P, 1989, 187–221.
Creekmur, Corey K. "*C.I.D.*" *Indian Cinema: Notes on Indian Popular Cinema by Philip Lutgendorf with Additional Contributions from Corey Creekmur.* https://indiancinema.sites.uiowa.edu/cid.
Creekmur, Corey K. "Remembering, Repeating, and Working through *Devdas*." *Indian Literature and Popular Cinema: Recasting Classics*, edited by Heidi R. M. Pauwels, New York: Routledge, 2007, pp. 173–90.
Creekmur, Corey K., and Jyotika Virdi. "India: Bollywood's Global Coming of Age." *Contemporary Asian Cinema*, edited by Anne Tereska Ciecko, New York: Berg, 2006, pp. 133–43.
Cunningham, Stuart. "The 'Force-Field' of Melodrama." *Film and Theory*, edited by Robert Stam and Toby Miller, Oxford: Blackwell, 2000, pp. 179–90.
Dasgupta, Shamita Das. "Feminist Consciousness in Woman-Centered Hindi Films." *Journal of Popular Culture*, vol. 30, no. 1, 1996, pp. 173–89.
Dawtery, Adam. "Polygram Yearns for a Blockbuster Prize." *Variety*, January 29, 1996–February 4, 1996, 13. Accessed 26 June 2011.
del Río, Elena. *Deleuze and the Cinemas of Performance: Powers of Affection*. Edinburgh UP, 2008.
Derné, Steve. *Movies, Masculinity, and Modernity: An Ethnography of Men's Filmgoing in India*, Westport, CT: Greenwood 2000.
Desai, Radhika. "Imagi Nation: The Reconfiguration of National Identity in Bombay Cinema in the 1990s." *Once upon a Time in Bollywood: The Global Swing in Hindi Cinema*, edited by Gurbir Jolly, Zenia Wadhwani and Deborah Barretto, Toronto: TSAR, 2007, pp. 43–60.

Deshpande, Sudhanva. "The Consumable Hero of Globalised India." *Bollyworld: Popular Indian Cinema through a Transnational Lens*, edited by Raminder Kaur and Ajay J. Sinha, New Delhi: Sage, 2005, pp. 186–206.
Desser, David. "Global Noir: Genre Film in the Age of Transnationalism." *Film Genre Reader III*, edited by Barry Keith Grant, Austin: U of Texas P, 2003, pp. 516–36.
Dhawan, Himanshi. "'Pink Chaddi' Campaign a Hit, Draws over 34,000 Members." *The Times of India*. 14 Feb. 2009. Accessed 10 May 2011.
Dissanayaake, Wimal. "Globalization and Cultural Narcissism: Note on Bollywood Cinema." *Asian Cinema*, vol. 15, no. 1, Mar. 2004, pp. 143–50.
Dissanayaake, Wimal, editor. *Melodrama and Asian Cinema*, edited by Wimal Dissanayaake, Cambridge UP, 1993.
Dixon, Wheeler Winston. *Straight: Constructions of Heterosexuality in the Cinema*, Albany: SUNY P, 2003.
Doane, Mary Ann. *Femmes Fatales: Feminism, Film Theory, Psychoanalysis*, London: Routledge, 1991.
"*Don 2:* HC refuses to stay release of film for copyright violation." *The Economic Times*, 19 Dec. 2011. economictimes.indiatimes.com/industry/media/entertainment/don-2-hc-refuses-to-stay-release-of-film-for-copyright-violation/articleshow/11171273.cms.
Doty, Alexander. *Making Things Perfectly Queer: Interpreting Mass Culture*. Minneapolis: U of Minnesota P, 1993.
Dudrah, Rajinder. *Bollywood Travels: Culture, Diaspora and Border Crossings in Popular Hindi Cinema*, London: Routledge, 2012.
Durham, Carolyn A. *Double Takes: Culture and Gender in French Films and Their American Remakes*, Hanover, NH: UP of New England, 1998.
Durham, Meenakshi Gigi. "Sex in the Transnational City: Discourses of Gender, Body and Nation in the 'New Bollywood.'" *Cinema, Law, and the State in Asia*, edited by Corey K. Creekmur and Mark Sidel, New York: Palgrave Macmillan, 2007, pp. 45–62.
Dwyer, Rachel, and Divia Patel. *Cinema India: The Visual Culture of Hindi Film*, London: Reaktion Books, 2002.
Dyer, Richard. "Entertainment and Utopia." *Only Entertainment*, 2nd ed., New York: Routledge, 2002, pp. 19–35.
Dyer, Richard. *Pastiche*. New York: Routledge, 2006.
Dyer, Richard. "Resistance through Charisma: Rita Hayworth and Gilda." *Hollywood Heroines: Women in Film Noir and the Female Gothic Film*, New York: I. B. Tauris, 2007, pp. 115–22.
Dyer, Richard, editor. *Gays and Film*. London: BFI, 1977.
Eisenstein, Zillah. *Against Empire: Feminisms, Racism, and the West*. London/New York: Zed Books, 2004.

Ettelbrick, Paula. "Since When Is Marriage a Path to Liberation?" *Lesbian and Gay Marriage: Private Commitments, Public Ceremonies*, edited by Suzanne Sherman, Philadelphia: Temple UP, 1992, pp. 20–28.

Evans, Peter William. "Meg Ryan, Megastar." *Terms of Endearment: Hollywood Romantic Comedy of the 1980s and 1990s*, edited by Peter William Evans and Celestino Deleyto, Edinburgh UP, 1998, pp. 188–208.

Forrest, Jennifer, and Leonard R. Koos, editors. *Dead Ringers: The Remake in Theory and Practice*. Albany: SUNY P, 2002.

Gahlaut, Kanika. "Mallika Sherawat Debuts with 17 Kisses in *Khwaish*." *India Today*, 24 Feb. 2003. https://www.indiatoday.in/magazine/eyecatchers/story/20030224-mallika-sherawat-debuts-with-17-kisses-in-khwaish-793169-2003-02-23.

Gangoli, Geetanjali. "Indian Feminisms: Issues of Sexuality and Representation." *Popular Culture in a Globalized India*, edited by K. Moti Gokulsing and Wimal Dissanayake, New York: Routledge, 2008, pp. 53–65.

Ganti, Tejaswini. "'And Yet My Heart Is Still Indian': The Bombay Film Industry and the (H)Indianization of Hollywood." *Media Worlds: Anthropology on New Terrain*, edited by Faye D. Ginsburg, Lila Abu-Lughod, and Brian Larkin. Berkeley: U of California P, 2002, pp. 281–300.

Ganti, Tejaswini. *Bollywood: A Guidebook to Popular Hindi Cinema*. 2nd ed., New York: Routledge, 2013.

Ganti, Tejaswini. "The Limits of Decency and the Decency of Limits: Censorship and the Bombay Film Industry." *Censorship in South Asia: Cultural Regulation from Sedition to Seduction*, edited by William Mazzarella and Raminder Kaur, Bloomington: Indiana UP, 2009, pp. 87–122.

Ganti, Tejaswini. "No Longer a Frivolous Singing and Dancing Nation of Movie-Makers: The Hindi Film Industry and Its Quest for Global Distinction." *Visual Anthropology*, vol. 25, 2012, pp. 340–65.

Ganti, Tejaswini. *Producing Bollywood: Inside the Contemporary Hindi Film Industry*, Durham, NC: Duke UP, 2012.

Garwood, Ian. "The Songless Bollywood Film." *South Asian Popular Culture*, vol. 4, no. 2, 2006, 169–83.

Gehlawat, Ajay. *Reframing Bollywood: Theories of Popular Hindi Cinema*. Thousand Oaks, CA: Sage, 2010.

Genette, Gérard. *Palimpsests: Literature in the Second Degree*. Translated by Channa Newman and Claude Doubinski, 2nd ed., Lincoln: U of Nebraska P, 1997.

Ghosh, Shohini. "Queer Pleasures for Queer People: Film, Television, and Queer Sexuality in India." *Queering India: Same-Sex Love and Eroticism in Indian Culture and Society*, edited by Ruth Vanita, New York: Routledge, 2002, pp. 207–21.

Ghosh, Shohini. "The Wonderful World of Queer Cinephilia." *BioScope*, vol. 1, no. 1, 2010, pp. 17–20.
Gledhill, Christine. *Home Is Where the Heart Is: Studies in Melodrama and the Woman's Film*, edited by Christine Gledhill, London: BFI, 1987.
Gledhill, Christine. "Rethinking Genre." *Reinventing Film Studies*, edited by Christine Gledhill and Linda Williams, London: Arnold, 2000, pp. 221–43.
Gopal, Sangita. "Bourgeois Extreme: Cultural Flows and the Microimport. *Cultural Critique*, no. 114, Winter 2022, pp. 101–26.
Gopal, Sangita. *Conjugations: Marriage and Form in New Bollywood*, U of Chicago P, 2011.
Gopalan, Lalitha. "Bombay Noir." *Journal of the Moving Image*, vol. 13, Dec. 2015, pp. 64–90.
Gopalan, Lalitha. *Cinema of Interruptions: Action Genres in Contemporary Indian Cinema*, London: BFI, 2002.
Gopinath, Gayatri. "Bollywood Spectacles: Queer Diasporic Critique in the Aftermath of 9/11." *Social Text*, vol. 23, no. Fall–Winter 3–4, 2005, pp. 157–69.
Gopinath, Gayatri. "Queering Bollywood: Alternative Sexualities in Popular Indian Cinema." *Journal of Homosexuality*, vol. 39, no. 3–4, 2000, pp. 283–97.
Govil, Nitin. "Hollywood's Effects, Bollywood FX." *Contracting Out Hollywood: Runaway Productions and Foreign Location Shooting*, edited by Greg Elmer and Mike Gasher, New York: Rowman and Littlefield, 2005, pp. 92–116.
Govil, Nitin. *Orienting Hollywood: A Century of Film Culture between Los Angeles and Bombay*, New York: New York UP, 2015.
Govil, Nitin, et al. "Hollywood's Global Rights." *Global Hollywood 2*, by Toby Miller et al., London: BFI, 2005, pp. 213–58.
Govindan, Padma, and Bisakha Dutta. "'From Villain to Traditional House-wife!': The Politics of Globalization and Women's Sexuality in the 'New' Indian Media." *Global Bollywood*, edited by Anandam P. Kavoori and Aswin Punathambekar, New York: New York UP, 2008, pp. 180–202.
Grant, Barry Keith, editor. *Film Genre Reader II*. Austin: U of Texas P, 1995.
Grossman, Julie. "Film Noir's 'Femme Fatales' Hard-Boiled Women: Moving beyond Gender Fantasies." *Quarterly Review of Film and Video*, vol. 24, no. 1, 2007, pp. 19–30.
Grossman, Julie. *Rethinking the Femme Fatale in Film Noir: Ready for Her Close-Up*. Basingstoke, Hampshire: Palgrave Macmillan, 2009.
Groves, Don. "Action Pix Burn Up O'seas B.O." *Variety*, September 4, 1995–September 10, 1995, p. 15. Accessed 26 June 2011.
Guneratne, Anthony R., and Wimal Dissanayake, editors. *Rethinking Third Cinema*. New York: Routledge, 2003.

Gunning, Tom. "The Cinema of Attractions: Early Film, Its Spectator and the Avant-Garde." *Early Cinema: Space, Frame, Narrative*, edited by Thomas Elsaesser and Adam Baker. London: BFI, 1990, pp. 56–62.
Hanson, Helen. *Hollywood Heroines: Women in Film Noir and the Female Gothic Film*. New York: I. B. Tauris, 2007.
Hardy, Kathryn. "Spectators from the Past: Remakes, Development, and the Bhojpuri Audience." *A Companion to Indian Cinema*, edited by Neepa Majumdar and Ranjani Mazumdar, Hoboken, New Jersey: John Wiley and Sons, 2022, pp. 60–77.
Holmlund, Chris. "Postfeminism from A to G." *Cinema Journal*, vol. 44, no. 2, 2005, pp. 116–21.
Horton, Andrew, editor. *Comedy, Cinema, Theory*. Berkeley: U of California P, 1991.
Horton, Andrew, and Stuart McDougal. Introduction. *Play It Again, Sam: Retakes on Remakes*, edited by Andrew Horton and Stuart Y. McDougal, Berkeley: U of California P, 1998, pp. 1–11.
Hunt, Leon. "Asiaphilia, Asianisation and the Gatekeeper Auteur: Quentin Tarantino and Luc Besson." *East Asian Cinemas: Exploring Transnational Connections on Film*, edited by Leon Hunt and Leung Wing-Fai, New York: I. B. Tauris, 2008, pp. 226–36.
Hutcheon, Linda. *A Theory of Parody: The Teachings of Twentieth-Century Art Forms*. London: Methuen, 1985.
"I Am Too Old to Be Wild." *Rediff Movies: Kaante Special*, 2002, www.rediff.com/entertai/2002/dec/18dutt.htm. Accessed Oct. 31 2011.
Illouz, Eva. *Consuming the Romantic Utopia: Love and the Cultural Contradictions of Capitalism*, Berkeley: U of California P, 1997.
Iyer, Rohini. "People Approach Bipasha Because She Is the Only One Who Will Take Risks." *Rediff.com*, 14 Jan. 2003, 14:13 IST. https://www.rediff.com/entertai/2003/jan/14bipasha.htm.
Iyer, Usha. *Dancing Women: Choreographing Corporeal Histories of Hindi Cinema*, New York: Oxford UP, 2020.
Iyer, Usha. "Lesbian Begums and Maja Ma Mothers: An Older Madhuri Dixit in Newer Media Ecologies." *Critical Collective*, Jan. 2023. https://criticalcollective.in/.
Iyer, Usha. "Song and Dance Sequence." *BioScope: South Asian Screen Studies*, vol. 12, no. 1–2, 2021, pp. 174–77.
"Jacqueline Uninhibited in *Murder 2*." *YouTube*, uploaded by Zoom, 2 Dec. 2010. www.youtube.com/watch?v=aJrXZgnveRo. Accessed 10 May 2011.
Jaikumar, Priya. "Bollywood Spectaculars." *World Literature Today*, vol. 77, no. 3/4, 2003, pp. 24–29.
Jameson, Fredric. *Postmodernism or the Cultural Logic of Late Capitalism*, London: Verso, 1991.

Jess-Cooke, Carolyn. *Film Sequels: Theory and Practice from Hollywood to Bollywood*, Edinburgh UP, 2009.
Jha, Priya. "Lyrical Nationalism: Gender, Friendship, and Excess in 1970s Hindi Cinema." *The Velvet Light Trap*, vol. 51, spring 2003, pp. 43–53.
Jha, Subhash K. "'I Can't Do Another *Jism*': Bipasha Basu." *India Glitz*, 6 Oct. 2004. Accessed 6 Jan. 2010.
Jha, Subhash K. "Jacqueline Fernandez Plays Centerspread Model in *Murder 2*." *Bollywood Hungama*, 2 Feb. 2011. Accessed 10 May 2011.
Jha, Subhash K. "*Jism* Is No Sex Romp, Says Pooja Bhatt." *IANS*, 14 Jan. 2003. Accessed 6 Jan. 2010.
Johnston, Claire. "Feminist Politics and Film History." *Screen*, vol. 16, no. 3, 1975, pp. 115–24.
Johnston, Claire. "The Subject of Feminist Film Theory/Practice." *Screen*, vol. 21, no. 2, Summer 1980, pp. 27–34.
Kabir, Nasreen Munni. "The Villains and the Vamps." *Bollywood: The Indian Cinema Story*, London: Channel 4 Books, 2001, pp. 81–102.
Kakar, Sudhir. "Masculine/Feminine: A View from the Couch." *Intimate Relations: Exploring Indian Sexuality*, New Delhi: Viking, 1989, pp. 129–40.
Kavi, Ashok Row. "The Changing Image of the Hero in Hindi Films." *Journal of Homosexuality*, vol. 39, no. 3–4, 2000, pp. 307–12.
Kesavan, Mukul. "Urdu, Awadh and the Tawaif: The Islamicate Roots of Hindi Cinema." *Forging Identities: Gender, Communities, and the State*, edited by Zoya Hasan, New Delhi: Kali for Women, 1994, pp. 244–57.
Khubchandani, Lata, and Mahesh Manjrekar. "Amitabh's Energy Level Was Higher than All of Us." *Rediff Movies: Kaante Special*, 2002. Accessed 31 Oct. 2011.
Kimmel, Michael. "Ritualized Homosexuality in a Nacirema Subculture." *Sexualities*, vol. 9, no. 1, 2006, pp. 95–105.
Kinsley, Michael. "Abolish Marriage: Let's Really Get the Government out of Our Bedrooms." slate.com/news-and-politics/2003/07/let-s-really-get-the-government-out-of-our-bedrooms.html.
Klein, Amanda. *American Film Cycles: Reframing Genres, Screening Social Problems, and Defining Subcultures*. Austin: U of Texas P, 2011.
Krämer, Lucia. "Hollywood Remade: New Approaches to Indian Remakes of Western Films." *Remakes and Remaking: Concepts, Media, Practices*, edited by Rüdiger Heinze and Lucia Krämer, Bielefeld: Transcript Verlag, 2015, pp. 81–96.
Krämer, Peter. *The New Hollywood: From* Bonnie and Clyde *to* Star Wars, London: Wallflower, 2005.
Kumar, Amit. "The Lower Stall: The Sleaze-Sex Film Industry in India: An Introduction." *Spectator*, vol. 26, no. 2, Fall 2006, pp. 27–41.

Kumar, Radha. *The History of Doing: An Illustrated Account of Movements for Women's Rights and Feminism in India, 1800–1990*, New Delhi: Zubaan, 2003.

Leitch, Thomas. "Twice-Told Tales: Disavowal and the Rhetoric of the Remake." *Dead Ringers: The Remake in Theory and Practice*, edited by Jennifer Forrest and Leonard Koos. Albany: SUNY P, 2002, pp. 37–62.

Lutgendorf, Philip. "Is There an Indian Way of Filmmaking?" *International Journal of Hindu Studies*, vol. 10, no. 3, 2006, pp. 227–56.

"Mallika Sherawat to SEDUCE in *Jism 2*." *YouTube*, uploaded by Bollywood Backstage. Accessed 10 May 2011.

"Mangalore Pub Attack: 17 Held, Ram Sena Unapologetic." *The Economic Times*. 26 Jan. 2009. https://economictimes.indiatimes.com/news/politics-and-nation/mangalore-pub-attack-17-held-ram-sena-unapologetic/articleshow/4033613.cms.

Mankekar, Purnima. "Brides Who Travel: Gender, Transnationalism, and Nationalism in Hindi Film." *Positions: Asia Critique*, vol. 7, no. 3, 1999, pp. 731–61.

Manorama Six Feet Under. 2007. www.manoramasixfeetunder.com/main. Accessed 30 Oct. 2011.

Masci, David. "An Overview of the Same-Sex Marriage Debate." *Pew Research Center*, 21 Nov. 2008. www.pewresearch.org/religion/2008/04/01/an-overview-of-the-same-sex-marriage-debate.

Mazdon, Lucy. *Encore Hollywood: Remaking French Cinema*. London: British Film Institute, 2000.

Mazumdar, Ranjani. *Bombay Cinema*. Minneapolis: U of Minnesota P, 2007.

Mehta, Monika. "Affective Logics: Re-Making Fidelity and Homosociality in *Kaante*." *A Companion to Indian Cinema*, edited by Neepa Majumdar and Ranjani Mazumdar, Hoboken, New Jersey: John Wiley and Sons, 2022, pp. 433–55.

Mehta, Monika. *Censorship and Sexuality in Bombay Cinema*. Austin: U of Texas P, 2011.

Mehta, Monika. "Globalizing Bombay Cinema: Reproducing the Indian State and Family." *Cultural Dynamics*, vol. 17, no. 2, 2005, pp. 135–54.

Mehta, Monika. "Reading Cinephilia in *Kikar Ha-Halomot/Desperado Square*, Viewing the Local and Transnational in *Sangam/Confluence*." *South Asian Popular Culture*, vol. 4, no. 2, Oct. 2006, pp. 147–62.

Mini, Darshana Sreedhar. "Locating the 'B' in B-Circuit Cinema." *Film Studies: An Introduction*, edited by Vebhuti Duggal, et al., Delhi: Worldview, 2022, pp. 319–28.

Mishra, Vijay. *Bollywood Cinema: Temples of Desire*. New York: Routledge, 2002.

Mohanty, Chandra Talpade. *Feminism without Borders, Decolonizing Theory, Practicing Solidarity*. Durham, NC: Duke UP, 2003, pp. 295–314.
Mohanty, Chandra Talpade. "Under Western Eyes." *Third World Women and the Politics of Feminism*, edited by Chandra Talpade Mohanty, Ann Russo, and Lourdes Torres, Indianapolis: Indiana UP, 1991, pp. 51–80.
Mukherjee, Silpa. "Behind the Green Door: Unpacking the Item Number and Its Ecology." *Bioscope: South Asian Screen Studies*, vol. 9, no. 2, 2018, pp. 208–32.
Mulvey, Laura. "Visual Pleasure and Narrative Cinema." *Screen*, vol. 16, no. 3, 1975, pp. 6–18.
Murty, Madhavi. *Stories That Bind: Political Economy and Culture in New India*. New Brunswick, NJ: Rutgers UP, 2022.
Naficy, Hamid. "Theorizing 'Third-World' Film Spectatorship." *Wide Angle*, vol. 18, no. 4, 1996, pp. 3–26.
Narayan, Uma. *Dislocating Cultures: Identities, Traditions, and Third-World Feminism*. New York: Routledge, 1997.
Nayar, Sheila J. "The Values of Fantasy: Indian Popular Cinema through Western Scripts." *The Journal of Popular Culture*, vol. 31, no. 1, summer 1997, pp. 73–90.
Neale, Steve. "The Big Romance or Something Wild? Romantic Comedy Today." *Screen*, vol. 33, no. 3, 1992, pp. 284–99.
Neale, Steve. *Genre and Hollywood*. New York: Routledge, 2000.
Neale, Steve. "Masculinity as Spectacle: Reflections on Men and Mainstream Cinema." *Screening the Male: Exploring Masculinities in Hollywood Cinema*, edited by Steven Cohan and Ina Rae Hark, New York: Routledge, 1993, pp. 2–16.
Neale, Steve. "Questions of Genre." *Film Genre Reader III*, edited by Barry Keith Grant, Austin: U of Texas P, 2003, pp. 160–84.
Orfall, Blair. "Bollywood Retakes: Literary Adaptation and Appropriation in Contemporary Hindi Cinema." U Oregon, PhD dissertation, 2009.
Oza, Rupal. *The Making of Neoliberal India: Nationalism, Gender, and the Paradoxes of Globalization*. New York: Routledge, 2006.
Pandey, Nirmal. "Maar Dala." *YouTube*, uploaded by noidsama, 1 Nov. 2008, https://www.youtube.com/watch?v=76vjLzzQACk.
Parekh, Rauf. "Literary Notes: Tazmeen, Urdu and Persian Poetry and Omar Khayyam." *Dawn*, 24 July 2023. https://www.dawn.com/news/amp/1766505.
"Partner Gets Sued by Producers of *Hitch*." *Bollyspice*, 9 Aug. 2007, 20 Dec. 2012. http://bollyspice.com/7121/partner-gets-sued-by-producers-of-hitch.
Patel, Geeta. "On *Fire*: Sexuality and Its Incitements." *Queering India: Same-Sex Love and Eroticism in Indian Culture and Society*, edited by Ruth Vanita, New York: Routledge, 2002, pp. 222–33.

Patil, Vimla. "Bollywood Heroes Tone Down Their Masculinity Because of Gay Directors?" *SAWF News*, 23 June 2005. Accessed 25 Feb. 2012.

Pattnaik, Sonali. "Outside the Frame: The Representation of the *Hijra* in Bollywood Cinema." *Intersections: Gender and Sexuality in Asia and the Pacific*, no. 22, Oct. 2009. intersections.anu.edu.au/issue22/pattnaik.htm. 25 Feb. 2012.

Paunksnis, Šarūnas. "Film Noir and the Dark Spaces of New Hindi Cinema." *Dark Fear, Eerie Cities: New Hindi Cinema in Neoliberal India*, New Delhi: Oxford UP, 2019, pp. 90–122.

Peterson, Kavan. "California Gay Marriage Sparks New Debate." *Stateline*, 16 May 2008. Accessed 22 July 2012.

Pharr, Suzanne. "Homophobia: A Weapon of Sexism." *Race, Class, and Gender in the United States*, edited by Paula Rothenberg, New York: Worth, 2009, pp. 162–71.

Pisters, Patricia. "The Neuro-Image in Contemporary Digital Screen Culture." Humanities Center, Syracuse University, 9 Feb. 2011, seminar.

Place, Janey. "Women in Film Noir." *Women in Film Noir*, edited by E. Ann Kaplan, London: BFI, 1980, pp. 47–68.

Preston, Catherine L. "Hanging on a Star: The Resurrection of the Romance Film in the 1990s." *Film Genre 2000: New Critical Essays*, edited by Wheeler Winston Dixon, Albany: SUNY P, 2000, pp. 227–44.

Punathambekar, Aswin. *From Bombay to Bollywood: The Making of a Global Media Industry*. New York: New York UP, 2013.

Rajadhyaksha, Ashish. "The 'Bollywoodization' of the Indian Cinema: Cultural Nationalism in a Global Arena." *Global Bollywood*, edited by Anandam P. Kavoori and Aswin Punathambekar, New York: New York UP, 2008, pp. 17–40.

Rajagopal, Arvind. *Politics after Television: Hindu Nationalism and the Reshaping of the Public in India*. Cambridge UP, 2001.

Rao, R. Raj: "Memories Pierce the Heart: Homoeroticism, Bollywood-Style." *Journal of Homosexuality*, vol. 39, no. 3–4, 2000, pp. 299–306.

Raymond, Diane. "Popular Culture and Queer Representation." *Gender, Race, and Class in Media*, edited by Gail Dines and Jean Humez, California: Sage, 2003, pp. 98–110.

Richards, Rashna Wadia. "(Not) Kramer vs. Kumar: The Contemporary Bollywood Remake as Glocal Masala Film." *Quarterly Review of Film and Video*, vol. 28, no. 4, 2011, pp. 342–52.

Richards, Rashna Wadia. "Translating Cool: Cinematic Exchange between Hong Kong, Hollywood, and Bollywood." *Transnational Film Remakes*, edited by Iain Robert Smith and Constantine Verevis, Edinburgh UP, 2017, pp. 118–29.

Saifuddin, Saif. "saif andaz-e-bayan rang badal deta hai." *Rekhta*. https://www.rekhta.org/couplets/saif-andaaz-e-bayaan-rang-badal-detaa-hai-saifuddin-saif-couplets.

"Same-Sex Marriage, Civil Unions, and Domestic Partnerships." *The New York Times*, n.d. Accessed 7 Oct. 2012.

SammyManiac. "Bollywood Remakes of Hollywood Movies." *IMDb*, 2013. www.imdb.com/list/ls009466984.

Sedgwick, Eve Kosofsky. *Between Men: English Literature and Male Homosocial Desire*. New York: Columbia UP, 1985.

Sen, Meheli. "From *Dostana* to Bromance: Buddies in Hindi Commercial Cinema Reconsidered." *Reading the Bromance: Homosocial Relationships in Film and Television*, edited by Michael Deangelis, Detroit: Wayne UP, pp. 139–64.

Sen, Meheli. *Haunting Bollywood: Gender, Genre, and the Supernatural in Hindi Commercial Cinema*. Austin: U of Texas P, 2017.

Sen, Raja. "*Manorama*: A Well-Executed Thriller." *Rediff India Abroad*, 21 Sept. 2007. im.rediff.com/movies/2007/sep/21man.htm. 3 Dec, 2012.

Sengupta, Somini. "Careers Give India's Women New Independence." *The New York Times*, 23 Nov. 2007, www.nytimes.com/2007/11/23/world/asia/23india.html. Accessed 10 May 2011.

Shandley, Robert R. *Runaway Romances: Hollywood's Postwar Tour of Europe*. Philadelphia: Temple UP, 2009.

Sharma, Nupur. "Discourse of Desire." *The Hindu*, 29 June 2011. www.thehindu.com/features/metroplus/discourse-of-desire/article2145029.ece. Accessed 1 July 2012.

"Sher of Mirza Ghalib." *Rekhta*. Rekhta Foundation, www.rekhta.org/couplets/hain-aur-bhii-duniyaa-men-sukhan-var-bahut-achchhe-mirza-ghalib-couplets. Accessed 26 June 2023.

Siddique, Salma. "The Partition Doppelgänger: Rattan Kumar and the Pakistani Charbas." *Evacuee Cinema: A Partition History of Cinema in South Asia*, Cambridge UP, 2022, pp. 176–219.

Siddiqui, Gohar. "Behind Her Laughter . . . Is Fear: Domestic Abuse and Transnational Feminism in Bollywood Remakes." *Jump Cut: A Review of Contemporary Media*, no. 55, Fall 2013. www.ejumpcut.org/archive/jc55.2013/SiddiquiDomesAbuseIndia.

Siddiqui, Gohar. "Making the Past Present: Intertextuality and Pastiche in Bollywood Neo-Noir." *Pop Empires: Transnational and Diasporic Flows of India and Korea*, edited by S. Heijin Lee et al., Honolulu: U of Hawai'i P, 2019, pp. 72–88.

Siddiqui, Gohar. "New Womanhood and #Lipstick Rebellion: Feminist Consciousness in *Lipstick Under My Burkha*." *Bollywood's New Woman: Liberalization, Liberation, and Contested Bodies*, edited by Megha Anwer and Anupama Arora, New Brunswick, NJ: Rutgers UP, 2021, pp. 79–91.

Singh, Greg. *Feeling Film: Affect and Authenticity in Popular Cinema.* New York: Routledge, 2014.
Singh, Greg. "The Kitsch Affect; Or, Simulation, Nostalgia and the Authenticity of the Contemporary CGI Film." *Cinephilia in the Age of Digital Reproduction: Film, Pleasure and Digital Culture,* edited by Scott Balcerzak and Jason Sperb, vol. 2, Columbia UP, 2012.
Singh, Pawan. "Visibly Queer Bollywood." *Open Space,* 25 Feb. 2011. Accessed 22 Mar. 2012.
Smith, Iain Robert. "Hollywood and the Popular Cinema of India." *The Hollywood Meme: Transnational Adaptations in World Cinema,* Edinburgh UP, 2016, pp. 102–42.
Smith, Iain Robert, and Constantine Verevis. Introduction. *Transnational Film Remakes,* edited by Iain Robert Smith and Constantine Verevis, Edinburgh UP, 2017, pp. 1–18.
"Special Features." *Body Heat.* Directed by Lawrence Kasdan, performances by William Hurt, Kathleen Turner, Richard Crenna, Ted Danson, and J. A. Preston. The Ladd Company, 1981.
Srinivas. "The Quentin" Conversation, *Naachgana,* 23 Sept. 2007. www.naachgaana.com/2007/09/23/the-quentin-conversation. Accessed 12 Oct. 2008.
Srinivasan, Rama. "'Gaylords' of Bollywood: Politics of Desire in Hindi Cinema." *Economic and Political Weekly,* vol. 46, no. 7, 12 Feb. 2011, pp. 73–78.
"Staff Report to the Committee on Oversight and Investigations." *Domestic but Not Equal,* Council of City of New York, June 2003.
Staiger, Janet. *Bad Women: Regulating Sexuality in Early American Cinema,* Minneapolis: U of Minnesota P, 1995.
Stern, Matthew. "Dudes, Bros, Boyfriends and Bugarrones: Redistributing the Stigma of Same-Sex Desire." *Sprinke: A Journal of Sexual Diversity Studies,* vol. 3, Apr. 2010, pp. 144–53. Accessed 1 July 2012.
Stoddard, Thomas. "Why Gay People Should Seek the Right to Marry." *Lesbian and Gay Marriage: Private Commitments, Public Ceremonies,* edited by Suzanne Sherman, Philadelphia: Temple UP, 1992, pp. 13–19.
Straayer, Chris. "Femme Fatale or Lesbian Femme: Bound in Sexual *Difféance.*" *Women in Film Noir,* edited by E. Ann Kaplan. London: BFI, 1980, pp. 151–63.
Streitmatter, Rodger. *From "Perverts" to "Fab Five": The Media's Changing Depiction of Gays and Lesbians,* New York: Routledge, 2009.
Studlar, Gaylyn. "*Double Indemnity*: Hard Boiled Film Noir." *Film Analysis: A Norton Reader,* edited by Jeffrey Geiger and R. L. Rutsky, New York: Norton 2005, pp. 380–99.
Subba, Vibhushan. "The Bad-Shahs of Small Budget: The Small-Budget Hindi Film of the B Circuit." *BioScope: South Asian Screen Studies,* vol. 7, no. 2, 2016, pp. 215–33.

Sullivan, Andrew. "Here Comes the Groom: A (Conservative) Case for Gay Marriage" *The New Republic*, 28 Aug. 1989. https://archive.org/details/gay-history-here-comes-the-groom. Accessed 5 Jan. 2012.
Sundar, Pavitra, *Listening with a Feminist Ear: Soundwork in Bombay Cinema*, U of Michigan P, 2023.
Thomas, Rosie. "Indian Cinema: Pleasures and Popularity—An Introduction." *Screen*, vol. 26, no. 3–4, 1985, pp. 116–31.
Thomas, Rosie. "Melodrama and the Negotiation of Morality in Mainstream Hindi Film." *Consuming Modernity: Public Culture in a South Asian World*, edited by Carol A. Breckenridge, Minneapolis: U of Minnesota P, 1995, pp. 157–82.
Thompson, Kristin. "The Concept of Cinematic Excess." *Film Theory and Criticism*, edited by Leo Braudy and Marshall Cohen, New York: Oxford UP, 2004, pp. 513–24.
Thottam, Jyoti. "India's Historic Ruling on Gay Rights." *Time*, 2 July 2009. time.com/archive/6947199/indias-historic-ruling-on-gay-rights/.
Travers, Peter. "*French Kiss*." *Rolling Stone*, no. 708, 18 May, 1995. Accessed 7 July 2012.
Trivedi, Harish. "From Bollywood to Hollywood: The Globalization of Hindi Cinema." *The Postcolonial and the Global*, edited by Revathi Krishnaswamy and John C. Hawley, Minneapolis: U of Minnesota P, 2008, pp. 200–210.
Vanita, Ruth. Introduction. *Queering India: Same-Sex Love and Eroticism in Indian Culture and Society*, edited by Ruth Vanita, New York: Routledge, 2002, pp. 1–14.
Vasudevan, Ravi. "Addressing the Spectator of a Third World National Cinema: The Bombay 'Social' Film of the 1940s and 1950s." *Film and Theory*, edited by Robert Stam and Toby Miller, Oxford/Malden: Blackwell, 2000, pp. 381–402.
Verevis, Constantine. *Film Remakes*, New York: Palgrave Macmillan, 2005.
Virdi, Jyotika. *The Cinematic ImagiNation: Indian Popular Films as Social History*, New Brunswick, NJ: Rutgers UP, 2003.
Virdi, Jyotika, and Corey K. Creekmur. "India: Bollywood's Global Coming of Age." *Contemporary Asian Cinema: Popular Culture in a Global Frame*, edited by Anne Teresa Ciecko, Oxford, UK: Berg, 2006, pp. 133–43.
Wadia, Riyad Vinci: "Long Life of a Short Film." *Journal of Homosexuality*, vol. 39, no. 3–4, 2000, pp. 313–23.
Wager, Jans B. *Dames in the Driver's Seat: Rereading Film Noir*. Austin: U of Texas P, 2005.
Walia, Ramna. "Recycle Industry: The Visual Economy of Remakes in Contemporary Bombay Film Culture." *Synoptique—An Online Journal of Film and Moving Images Studies*, vol. 3, no. 1, Spring 2014, pp. 30–66.
Wang, Yiman. *Remaking Chinese Cinema: Through the Prism of Shanghai, Hong Kong, and Hollywood*. Honolulu: U of Hawai'i P, 2013.

Waugh, Thomas. "'I Sleep Behind You': Male Homosociality and Homoeroticism in Indian Parallel Cinema." *Queering India: Same-Sex Love and Eroticism in Indian Culture and Society*, edited by Ruth Vanita, New York: Routledge, 2002, pp. 193–206.

Williams, Linda. "The American Melodramatic Mode." *Playing the Race Card: Melodramas of Black and White from Uncle Tom to O. J. Simpson*, Princeton, NJ: Princeton UP, 2001, pp. 10–44.

Williams, Linda. "Film Bodies: Gender, Genre, Excess." *The Film Genre Reader III*, edited by Barry Keith Grant, Austin: U of Texas P, 2003, pp. 141–59.

Wood, Robin, and Michael Walker. *Claude Chabrol*, New York: Praeger, 1970.

Wright, Neelam Sidhar. *Bollywood and Postmodernism: Popular Indian Cinema in the 21st Century*. Edinburgh UP, 2017.

Yakir, Dan, and Claude Chabrol. "The Magical Mystery World of Claude Chabrol: An Interview." *Film Quarterly*, vol. 32, no. 3, 1979, pp. 2–14.

Zengin, Mevlüde. "An Introduction to Intertextuality as a Literary Theory: Definitions, Axioms and The Originators." *Sosyal Bilimler Enstitüsü Dergisi (Journal of the Institute of Social Sciences)*. Number 25/1. 2016, pp. 299–326.

Filmography

À bout de souffle (*Breathlesss*) (Jean-Luc Godard 1966)
Achhut Kanya (Franz Osten 1936)
Anand (*Pleasure*) (Hrishikesh Mukherjee 1971)
Asphalt Jungle (John Huston 1950)
Aayitha Ezhuthu (Mani Ratnam 2004)
Baazigar (*Gambler*) (Abbas-Mustan 1993)
Body Heat (Lawrence Kasdan 1981)
Bonnie and Clyde (Arthur Penn 1967)
Bride and Prejudice (Gurinder Chadha 2004)
Bunty Aur Babli (*Bunty and Babli*) (Shaad Ali 2005)
C. I. D. (Raj Khosla 1956)
Chinatown (Roman Polanski 1974)
Chori Chori (Anant Thakur 1956)
City on Fire (Ringo Lam 1987)
Company (2002)
Coyote Ugly (David McNally 2000)
Darr (*Fear*) (Yash Chopra 1993)
Devdas (Bimal Roy 1955)
Dedh Ishqiya (Abhishek Chaubey 2014)
Deewaar (Yash Chopra 1975)
Detour (Edgar G. Ulmer 1945)
Dhoom (*Blast*) (Sanjay Gadhvi 2004)
Dhoom 2 (Sanjay Gadhvi 2006)
Dil (*Heart*) (1990)
Dil Hai Ke Manta Nahin (*The Heart Is Such, It Disagrees*) (Mahesh Bhatt 1991)
Dil Se (Mani Ratnam 1988)
Dillagi (A. R. Kardar 1949)
Dilwale Dulhania Le Jayenge (*The Bravehearted Will Win the Bride*) (Aditya Chopra 1995)

213

Don (franchise)
Don (Chandra Barot 1978)
Don: The Chase Begins Again (Farhan Akhtar 2006)
Don 2 (Farhan Akhtar 2011)
Dostana (Friendship) (Tarun Mansukhani 2008)
Double Indemnity (Billy Wilder 1944)
E.T. the Extra-Terrestrial (Steven Spielberg 1982)
Fatal Attraction (Adrian Lyne 1987)
Fire (Deepa Mehta 1996)
A Fool There Was (Frank Powell 1915)
French Kiss (Lawrence Kasdan 1995)
Ghajini (A. R. Murugadoss 2005)
Ghajini (A. R. Murugadoss 2008)
Ghulam (Slave) (Vikram Bhatt 1998)
Gilda (Charles Vidor 1946)
Go Goa Gone (Raj Nidimoru and Krishna D. K.)
Heer (Hameed Butt 1956)
Home Alone (Chris Columbus 1990)
Hum Aapke Hain Koun . . . ! (What Am I to You . . . ?) (Sooraj Barjatya 1994)
I Now Pronounce You Chuck and Larry (Dennis Dugan 2007)
Ishqiya (Abhishek Chaubey 2010)
It Happened One Night (Frank Capra 1934)
Jism (Body) (Amit Saxena 2003)
Jism 2 (Pooja Bhatt 2012)
Johnny Gaddaar (Johnny the Traitor) (Sriram Raghavan 2007)
Kabhi Khushi Kabhie Gham (Sometimes Happiness, Sometimes Sorrow) (Karan Johar 2001)
Kaante (Thorns) (Sanjay Gupta 2002)
Kal Ho Naa Ho (There May Be No Tomorrow) (Nikhil Advani 2003)
Khatta Meetha (Sour Sweet) (2010)
Khwahish (Govind Menon 2003)
Kill Bill (Quentin Tarantino 2003 & 2004)
The Killing (Stanley Kubrick 1956)
A Kiss Before Dying (Gerd Oswald 1956)
A Kiss Before Dying (James Dearden 1991)
Kiss Me Deadly (Robert Aldrich 1955)
Koi . . . Mil Gaya (I . . . Found Someone) (Rakesh Roshan 2003)
Krrish (Rakesh Roshan 2006)
Kuch Kuch Hota Hai (Karan Johar 1998)
La Femme infidèle (The Unfaithful Wife) (Claude Chabrol 1969)
Lage Raho Munna Bhai (Rajkumar Hirani 2006)

Laura (Otto Preminger 1944)
Lipstick Under My Burkha (Alankrita Shrivastava 2016)
Lock, Stock, and Two Smoking Barrels (Guy Ritchie 1998)
Main Hoon Na (Farah Khan 2004)
Manorama Six Feet Under (Navdeep Singh 2007)
Memento (Christopher Nolan 2000)
Mother India (Mehboob Khan 1957)
Moulin Rouge (Baz Luhrmann 2001)
Mughal-e-Azam (*The Great Mughal*) (K. Asif 1960)
Munnabhai M.B.B.S. (Rajkumar Hirani 2003)
Murder (Anurag Basu 2004)
Murder 2 (Mohit Suri 2011)
Namak Haram (*Traitor*) (Hrishikesh Mukherjee 1973)
Oldboy (Park Chan-wook 2003)
Om Shanti Om (Farah Khan 2007)
Omkara (Vishal Bhardwaj 2006)
On the Waterfront (Elia Kazan 1954)
Out of the Past (Jacques Tourneur 1947)
Pakeezah (*The Pure One*) (Kamal Amrohi 1972)
Pardes (*Foreign Land*) (Subhash Ghai 1997)
The Parent Trap (Nancy Meyers 1998)
Parwaana (*Moth*) (Jyoti Swaroop 1971)
Phir Bhi Dil Hai Hindustani (*And Yet the Heart Is Indian*) (Aziz Mirza, 2000)
The Pirate (Vincente Minnelli 1948)
The Postman Always Rings Twice (Tay Garnett 1946)
Pyaar To Hona Hi Tha (*Love Had to Happen*) (Anees Bazmee 1998)
Pyaar Tune Kya Kiya (Ram Gopal Varma 2001)
Qayamat Se Qayamat Tak (*Eternity to Eternity*) (1988)
Ramayan (Ramanand Sagar 1987–88)
Reservoir Dogs (Quentin Tarantino 1992)
Rise of the Zombie (Luke Kenny and Devaki Singh 2013)
Satya (*Truth*) (1998)
Sholay (Ramesh Sippy 1975)
Shree 420 (Raj Kapoor 1955)
Singam (Hari 2010)
Singham (Rohit Shetty 2011)
Singin' in the Rain (Gene Kelly and Stanley Donen 1952)
The Sixth Sense (M. Night Shyamalan 1999)
Sleepless in Seattle (Nora Ephron 1993)
So You Think You Can Dance (Fox show)
Some Kind of Wonderful (Howard Deutsch 1987)

Tarana (Ram Daryani 1951)
Trimurti (Mukul Anand 1995)
Umrao Jaan (Muzaffar Ali 1981)
Unfaithful (Adrian Lyne 2002)
Vellanakalude Naadu (Priyadarshan 1988)
Yuva (Youth) (Mani Ratnam 2004)
Zinda (Sanjay Dutt 2006)

Index

Note: Figure locations are set in **bold** type.

Abbas–Mustan (Abbas and Mustan Burmawalla). See *Baazigar (Gambler)* (Abbas–Mustan)
À bout de souffle (Breathless) (Godard), 101–102, 122
Abraham, John, 62, 88–90, 133, 146–47, 191n31
Ali, Shaad: *Bunty Aur Babli*, 4
Allen, Robert, 39, 185n21
Aman, Zeenat, 68, 75, 153, 187n3
Anand, Dev, 128–29, 131
Anand, Vijay, 124–25; *Johny Mera Naam (My Name Is Johny)*, 99–100, 127, 129, 131, 194–95n23
andāz-e-bayañ, 1–2, 4, 179n4
Anderson, Benedict, 15
angry-young-man films, 38, 67–68, 74, 106, 110, 129
antiheroes, 67–68, 124; Shah Rukh Khan as, 104–12, 193n10
Anwer, Megha, 17
Arora, Anupama, 17
audience imaginaries, 115
auteurism, 20, 22, 32, 34, 82, 143, 156; in neo-noir, 100–102, 119–22, 127, 180n11

avenging women films, 32, 69–70, 188n8. See also domestic-abuse films; revenge films
Azmi, Shabana, 86–87

Baazigar (Gambler) (Abbas–Mustan), 22–23, 102; *A Kiss Before Dying* (Oswald; Dearden) and, 101, 104, 107–10; masculinity in, 100, 104–12, 131
Babi, Parveen, 68, 74–75, 85, 187n3
Babuscio, Jack, 149
Bachchan, Abhishek, 133–**34**, 136, 145–51
Bachchan, Amitabh, 3, 113, 145, 151–53, 170; stardom of, 38, 67–68, 106, 115, 127–29
Bakhtin, Mikhail, 3, 145–46
Barjatya, Sooraj: *Hum Aapke Hain Koun . . . ! (What Am I to You)*, 11, 39, 159
Basu, Anurag. See *Murder* (Basu)
Basu, Bipasha, 61–62, 80–81, 89–92, 96, 187nn1–2, 189–90n18
Bazmee, Anees. See *Pyaar To Hona Hi Tha (Love Had to Happen)* (Bazmee)

217

B-circuit movies in India, 69–70, 87–89, 173, 188n12
Benegal, Shyam, 38, 185n17
Bhansali, Sanjay Leela, 156; *Devdas*, 3, 67, 125
Bhaskar, Ira, 65–66
Bhatt, Mahesh, 71, 77, 87, 89, 91–92; *Dil Hai Ke Manta Nahin (The Heart Is Such, It Disagrees)*, 5, 13, 186n24
Bhatt, Pooja, 87, 90–91, 191n34; *Jism 2 (Body 2)*, 91, 170
Bhatt, Vikram, 9, 172, 181n22; *Ghulam (Slave)*, 5, 108
Bloom, Harold, 19, 134–35
Body Heat (Kasdan), 22, 59, 61–62, 73, 76–77, 79–80, 88, 189nn15–16, 190n23
Bollywood film industry, 18, 21, 184n1, 185n16; B-circuit movies and, 69–70, 87–89, 172–73, 188n12; Bollywoodization and, 11–12, 33, 57, 183n31; corporatization of, 5–14, 20, 101, 118, 127, 156, 166, 173, 181n18, 181nn14–15, 192–93n1; film franchises in, 170–71; Hollywood's interest in, 175–76; New Bollywood and, 11, 17, 60–61, 127, 156, 170, 183n31; regional cinemas and, 9, 115, 169–72. See also Hindi cinema; *individual films*
Bombay, 12, 25, 39, 42, 86, 106, 184n5
Bombay noir, 121, 129–30, 194n13, 194nn22–23
Bonnie and Clyde (Penn), 4
Bordo, Susan, 189n14
Braudy, Leo, 20
Brooks, Peter, 34, 45
Bunty Aur Babli (Bunty and Babli) (Ali), 4
Bygrave, Mike, 41

camp, 34, 125, 144–50, 159
carnivalesque, 23, 144–46, 150, 159
caste, 32–33, 40, 104, 173
censorship, 156, 172, 191n34, 191n35; by Central Board of Film Certification (CBFC), 86–89, 133–34; feminism and, 76, 87–89, 91–92; kissing scenes and, 133–34; by Production Code Administration (PCA), 71–73, 76, 86, 88; song-and-dance performances and, 38, 89, 92, 185n19
Central Board of Film Certification (CBFC), 86–89, 133–34
Chabrol, Claude: *La Femme infidèle (Unfaithful Wife)*, 22, 59, 63, 73–74, 81–85, 189n17, 190n24, 190n26
Chakravarty, Sumita, 15, 38, 185n15
Chan, Kenneth, 135, 155, 167, 195n1
Chandra, Anupama, 182n23
Chase, James Hadley, 100, 125, 194n19
Chatterjee, Partha, 37, 65, 182n25, 188n5
Chatterjee, Sarat Chandra: *Devdas* novel, 3
Chaubey, Abhishek: *Ishqiya (Passionate)*, 137, 156. See also *Dedh Ishqiya (Passionate 1.5)* (Chaubey)
Chibnall, Steve, 130
Chinatown (Polanski), 101, 120–24, 189n16
Chopra, Aditya: *Dilwale Dulhania Le Jayenge* or *DDLJ (The Big-Hearted Will Win the Bride)*, 11, 39–40, 45–46, 51–53, 55–56, 182nn29–30
Chopra, Yash: *Deewaar (The Wall)*, 68, 106, 108–109, 186n23, 193n5, 193n7

Index   219

Chughtai, Ismat: "Lihaaf," 23, 134, 136–37, 156–59, 161–62, 165, 167
cinephilia, 6, 22–23, 81–83, 100–103, 119–28, 193–94n12, 194n18
City on Fire (Lam), 119, 172, 193n2
comedy: queerness and, 23, 144–45, 148–49. See also romantic comedies; individual films
Constantine, Verevis, 20
copyright disputes, 8–9, 21, 170–71
Creekmur, Corey, 3, 125, 180n6

darsán, 95–97
Dearden, James: *A Kiss Before Dying*, 101, 104, 107–10
Dedh Ishqiya (Passionate 1.5) (Chaubey), 135, 155, 163–64, 166; *Fire* (Mehta) and, 23, 134, 136–37, 156–57, 162, 167; "Lihaaf" (Chughtai) and, 23, 134, 136–37, 156–57, 162, 165, 167
Deewaar (The Wall) (Chopra), 68, 106, 108–109, 186n23, 193n5, 193n7
defamiliarization, 19–20, 22, 61, 63, 75–77, 82, 85, 97–98, 126
Defense of Marriage Act (DOMA) of 1996, 137–38, 142
déjà vu, 3–4, 37, 134
Deleuze, Gilles, 97
Desai, Radhika, 39
Desser, David, 102, 119
Devdas novel (Chatterjee), 3; film adaptations and remakes of, 3–4, 67, 125
dharma (duty to society and community), 14, 16, 36, 42, 103–105, 182n28, 186n28
Dharmendra, 128–29, 131, 152
diaspora, Indian, 106, 111–12, 181n18, 184n6; family films and, 11–12, 21, 27, 31, 37, 39–40, 51–52, 56, 71, 104, 183n34;

Hollywood spectacle and, 116–17, 120, 194n13, 194n16; NRI (nonresident-Indian) films targeting, 39, 46, 51–54, 143, 153, 156, 185n20, 186n23, 187n32, 193nn10–11; queer representation and, 154, 156, 161
Dilwale Dulhania Le Jayenge or *DDLJ (The Big-Hearted Will Win the Bride)* (Chopra), 11, 39–40, 45–46, 51–53, 55–56, 182nn29–30
Dissanayake, Wimal, 56, 185n15
Dixit, Madhuri, 162–**64**
Doane, Mary Ann, 65, 71–72, 84, 190n19, 190n27
domestic-abuse films, 32–33, 69, 130, 188n8. See also avenging women films; revenge films
Dostana (Friendship) (Khosla), 151–55
Dostana (Friendship) (Mansukhani), 23, 133–34, 143, 145–47, 149, 167, 170; "Beedi," 148, 159; compared to Raj Khosla's 1980 film, 151–55; gay stereotypes in, 135–38, 142, 144, 148, 155, 166; homophobia in, 138, 144, 150, 154–55
Double Indemnity (Wilder), 22, 59–62, 73–74, 76–78, 80, 88, 189n13
Dudrah, Rajinder, 144, 150, 155
Dugan, Dennis. See *I Now Pronounce You Chuck and Larry* (Dugan)
Durham, Carolyn, 7, 22, 75, 114, 135, 183n35
Durham, Meenakshi Gigi, 85, 93
Dutt, Guru: remakes of *Devdas*, 3
Dutt, Sanjay, 9; in *Kaante (Thorns)*, 113, 115; *Zinda*, 172
Dyer, Richard, 55–56, 126, 141, 149

East/West binary. See Indian/Western binary

eroticism, 63, 69, 77, 88–90, 92, 94, 105, 145, 191–92n38; homoeroticism, 138, 140, 147–49, 151–55, 161–63, 166–67
Ettelbrick, Paula, 139
Evans, Peter, 43–47, 187n30

family films, 5, 26–29, 34–35, 41–43, 45, 54–55; caste in, 32–33, 40; diasporic audiences and, 11–12, 21, 27, 31, 37, 39–40, 51–52, 56, 71, 104, 183n34; femininity in, 17, 49, 51, 69–71; Hinduism in, 31–33, 186n23; patriarchy in, 37–39, 47, 51–53, 56, 143, 150, 183n31; queerness in, 160–61. *See also individual films*
femininity, 44, 47–48, 53, 148, 182n25; angel/whore binary, 51, 64–65, 85–86, 92–93, 182n27; *bhadramahila* (respectable woman), 65, 188n5; defamiliarization of, 22, 61, 63, 75–77, 85, 97–98; in family film genre, 17, 49, 51, 69–71; *femme attrapée*, 85, 191n28; femme fatale trope (*see* femme fatales); intertextuality and, 22, 43, 59–63, 95; mother figures, 15–16, 30, 105, 111–12, 143, 193n7; New Woman, 17, 72–74; *tawaif* (courtesan) trope, 67, 69, 156, 162–63, 166; vamp trope (*see* vamps)
feminism, 32, 56, 95, 98, 182n25, 189n14, 191n33, 191n36; censorship and, 76, 87–89, 91–92; femme fatale trope and, 63, 69, 72–73, 76, 85–89, 92–94; New Woman and, 17, 72–74; outcry against rape, 69, 188n7; Pink Chaddi (panties) Campaign, 93; revenge films and, 68–69, 188n6

femme fatales, 64–65, 82, 86, 102, 123, 187n3, 189n13, 189n16, 190n19, 190–91nn27–28; Hollywood Production Code Administration and, 71–73, 76, 86, 88; in *Jism (Body)*, 22, 59–63, 71, 74–81, 85, 87–89, 92, 96–97; in *Murder*, 22, 59, 62–63, 74–75, 81, 84–85, 87–89, 92–97. *See also* vamps
Femme infidèle, La (Unfaithful Wife) (Chabrol), 22, 59, 63, 73–74, 81–85, 189n17, 190n24, 190n26
fetishization, 69, 86–89, 92, 94, 97 147, 165–66, 189n17. *See also* sexual objectification
film franchises, 170–71
film noir: aesthetics of, 76–78, 81, 100, 102–103, 116, 120–22, 125–31, 194n13, 194nn22–23; Bombay noir, 121, 129–30, 194n13, 194nn22–23; cinephilia and, 22–23, 81–83, 100–103, 119–28, 193–94n12, 194n18; masculinity in, 23, 100–103, 111–12, 114, 128–31; misogyny in, 73, 85, 92, 102; pastiche and, 22–23, 101–103, 114, 119–31, 180n11, 189n15, 193–94n12; Production Code Administration (PCA) and, 71–73, 76, 88. *See also* femme fatales; neo-noir; *individual films*
Fire (Mehta), 136–37, 172, 184n9; "Aa Ja Zara," 159–60; queerness in, 23, 134, 156–62, 167, 195n8
Forrest, Jennifer, 13, 19, 34
French cinema, 7, 125, 135; French New Wave, 22, 59, 81–83, 101–102, 122
French Kiss (Kasdan), 21, 25, 33, 35–36, 41, 43–45, 47–48, 51, 54–56, 186n29, 187n33

Ganti, Tejaswini, 8–9, 29, 70–71, 86, 115, 176, 180n12, 181n16, 185n12, 191n30, 193n9
gay stereotypes: in *Dostana* (Mansukhani), 135–38, 142, 144, 148, 155, 166; in *I Now Pronounce You Chuck and Larry* (Dugan), 138, 140–42, 166. See also homophobia; queer representation
Gehlawat, Ajay, 145
Genette, Gérard, 18–19
genre, 3–7, 11, 13–14, 116–17, 169, 181n20, 184n6; angry-young-man films, 38, 67–68, 74, 106, 110, 129; audience imaginaries and, 115; body genres, 110; buddy films, 145, 147, 151–56; cinephilia and, 81–83, 100–102, 119–28, 193–94n12, 194n18; domestic-abuse films, 32–33, 69, 130, 188n8; intertextuality and, 18–20, 43, 100–102, 119–24, 128, 193–94n12; Islamicate films, 67, 156 162–63, 186n23; *masala* films, 12, 29, 34, 42, 144, 184nn3–4; NRI (nonresident-Indian) films, 39, 46, 51–54, 143, 153, 156, 185n20, 186n23, 187n32, 193nn10–11; parallel cinema, 38, 127, 185n17; revenge films, 68–69, 105, 172–73, 188n6, 188n8, 193n8, 196n3; romantic comedies, 21, 29, 33–34, 41–48, 54–56, 81, 144, 154, 187n30; skin flicks, 90–91, 189–90n18, 191–92n38; sleaze films, 69–70, 87, 89–92, 187n3, 188n12, 191nn35–37; zombie movies, 173–75. See also family films; film noir; neo-noir
Ghai, Subhash: *Pardes (Foreign Land)*, 39, 45, 52–53, 104, 182nn29–30

Ghalib, Mirza, 1–3, 179nn2–5, 180n6
ghazal poetry, 1–3
Ghosh, Shohini, 142, 145–46, 153, 155
Gopal, Sangita, 17, 172–73, 180n12, 183n31, 193n8, 196n3
Gopalan, Lalitha, 68–69, 96, 185n10
Gopinath, Gayatri, 161
Govil, Nitin, 10, 12, 176, 181n13
Grossman, Julie, 72
Gulzar: *Mirza Ghalib* TV series, 179n2
Gupta, Sanjay: *Kaante (Thorns)*, 9, 18, 22–23, 100–103, 112–21, 123–24, 131, 172, 180n10, 193n2

Hanson, Helen, 73, 191n33
hatke (alternative) cinema, 17, 22–23, 101, 118–27, 129, 156, 167, 180n11. See also *individual films*
Hindi cinema, 20, 54–56, 93, 181nn20–21; B-circuit movies in, 69–70, 87–89, 172–73, 188n12; dharma in, 14, 16, 36, 103–105, 182n28, 186n28; distinguished from Bollywood, 12, 100–102, 114, 181n18, 192–93n1; dominance of melodrama in, 9, 14–16, 29–30, 34–36, 80–81, 85, 103, 105, 143, 151, 184n4; film noir and (see film noir; neo-noir); Hinduism and, 40, 184n9, 186n23; Hollywood's interest in, 175–76; Indian/Western binary in (see Indian/Western binary); Islamicate films, 67, 156, 162–63, 186n23; masculinities in, 88, 103–105, 107, 114, 128–29, 131, 145, 155; moral codes in, 9, 30, 36–37, 42, 45, 72, 80–81, 103–106,

Hindi cinema *(continued)*
111–14, 123, 186n28; mother
trope in, 15–16, 30, 105, 111–12,
143, 193n7; nationalism and,
6, 9, 14–17, 21, 37–38, 52, 55,
64–65, 105, 112, 127, 185n15; in
postindependence India, 15, 36–
38, 40, 65, 94, 182n30, 185n15;
queer representation in (*see* queer
representation); regional cinemas
and, 169–72; repetition as motif
in, 2–4, 10, 13, 27, 61, 116–17,
126, 180n6; sexualization in,
15–16, 37, 46–48, 51, 80, 85–88,
94–96, 147, 188n10, 192n44;
song-and-dance performances
in, 6–7, 14, 27, 67, 95–96, 145,
152, 159–60, 189–90n18, 192n39,
195n4, 195n8; vamps in, 15–16,
61–68, 70–71, 74–75, 80–81, 87,
97, 194–95n23; verisimilitude
in, 15–17, 30, 34, 36, 76, 103,
115–16. *See also* Bollywood film
industry; Indianization; *individual
films*
Hollywood film industry, 19–20, 77,
127, 137, 155, 166–67, 180n10,
181n21; Bollywood's resistance
to, 8, 11, 13; cinephilia and, 6,
81–83, 100–103, 119–22, 124,
193–94n12, 194n18; family films
in, 39; Hollywoodization, 114–18;
influence on Bombay noir, 121–
22, 194n13, 194nn21–22; interest
in Bollywood, 170, 175–76,
181n13; melodrama in, 30, 34–36,
45, 185n10; Production Code
Administration (PCA) and, 71–73,
76, 86, 88; romantic comedy in,
21, 29, 33–35, 41, 43, 45–47,
54, 56, 81, 144, 154, 187n30;

sexualizing gaze in, 47, 87, 90–92,
94–97, 147; silent cinema, 64–65,
72; transnational borrowing and,
6–8, 10, 14, 21–22, 29, 100–102,
118–20, 124–25, 169–70, 172,
175–76; verisimilitude in, 15, 34–
35, 103, 116. *See also individual
films*
homoeroticism, 138, 140, 147–49,
151–55, 161–63, 166–67
homophobia, 23, 138, 140, 144,
150, 154–55
Hong Kong cinema, 8, 118–19,
124–25
Hooper, Gerard, 129
Horton, Andrew, 19, 22, 61, 75–76,
151
*Hum Aapke Hain Koun . . . ! (What
Am I to You)* (Barjatya), 11, 39, 159
Hunt, Leon, 119

Indianization: gender and, 5, 9, 11,
17, 20–22, 31–33, 37, 40, 43–47,
57, 74–77, 83, 101, 114, 169;
globalization and, 5, 17, 20–22,
29–33, 37, 51, 54–57; as (H)
Indianization, 9; as industrial
transformation, 5–6, 8–9, 14, 17,
20, 25–26, 33, 35, 44, 135, 169;
melodramatic mode in, 6, 9, 29–
33, 51, 115–16, 143; nationalism
and, 6, 9, 14–17, 21, 37–38, 52,
55, 64–65, 105, 112, 127, 185n15;
sexuality and, 32, 51, 71, 74, 136,
142–44; star actors and, 10, 43,
47, 49, 53, 115–16, 127–28. *See
also individual films*
Indian/Western binary, 3, 17, 31,
57, 104, 118, 176, 187n31, 194–
95n23; sexualization of women
and, 15–16, 37, 48, 50–52,

Index 223

64–66, 75, 80, 90–92. See also Indianization; westernization
I Now Pronounce You Chuck and Larry (Dugan), 23, 133, 136–37, 139, 144–46; gay stereotypes in, 138, 140–42, 166
intertextuality, 2–4, 8, 55, 75–76, 95, 126–27, 171, 174; femininities and, 59–63; genre and, 18–20, 43, 100–102, 119–24, 128, 193–94n12; masculinities and, 20, 22–23, 100–102, 131, 174; queer representations and, 20, 134, 150–56, 165, 167
Ishqiya (Chaubey), 137, 156
item numbers, 92, 94, 97, 124, 148, 188nn9, 192n39, 192n44; item girls, 63, 67, 69–70, 74, 89, 95, 188n10, 189–90n18
Iyer, Usha, 128, 163, 165, 180n11, 195n8

Jaikumar, Priya, 37
Jameson, Fredric, 73, 189n15
Jism (Body) (Saxena), 91, 93–95, 98, 187n1, 191n30; femme fatale and, 22, 59–63, 71, 74–81, 85, 87–89, 92, 96–97; "Jadoo Hai Nasha Hai" in, **77**, 90; male gaze and, 63, 88–89, 189–90n18, 191n37; triangulation in, 59–61
Jism 2 (Body 2) (Bhatt), 91, 170
Johar, Karan, 153; *Kabhi Khushi Kabhie Gham/K3G (Sometimes There's Happiness, Sometimes Sadness)*, 39–40, 150; *Kuch Kuch Hota Hai*, 30–31, 35, 39–40, 183n33; *My Name Is Khan*, 175
Johnny Gaddaar (Johnny the Traitor) (Raghavan), 22–23, 99–103, 120–22, 124–31, 176, 180n11, 194n22

Kaante (Thorns) (Gupta), 9, 18, 22–23, 100–103, 112–21, 123–24, 131, 172, 180n10, 193n2
Kabhi Khushi Kabhie Gham/K3G (Sometimes There's Happiness, Sometimes Sadness) (Johar), 39–40, 150
Kabir, Nasreen Munni, 68
Kajol, 41–42, 44–46, 48–56, 109, 187n31
Kakar, Sudhir, 105, 193n3
Kal Ho Naa Ho (Advani), 153–54
Kapoor, Raj: *Shree 420*, 40, 66, 182n30, 186n23
Kasdan, Lawrence: *Body Heat*, 22, 59, 61–62, 73, 76–77, 79–80, 88, 189nn16–17, 190n23; *French Kiss*, 21, 25, 33, 35–36, 41, 43–45, 47–48, 51, 54–56, 186n29, 187n33
Kashyap, Anurag, 121, 129, 193–94n12
Kavi, Ashok Row, 152–53, 195n3
Kesavan, Mukul, 66–67, 69
Khan, Farah: *Om Shanti Om / OSO*, 6, 23, 124–25, 128, 180n11
Khan, Mehboob: *Mother India*, 15, 105–106, 108–109, 186n23, 193n5, 193n7
Khan, Saif Ali, 173–74
Khan, Shah Rukh, 53, 104–12, 193n10
Kiss Before Dying, A (Oswald; Dearden), 101, 104, 107–10
Kiss Me Deadly (Aldrich), 101, 120–21, 123
Koos, Leonard R., 13, 19, 34
Krämer, Lucia, 10–11
Krämer, Peter, 185n21
Kuch Kuch Hota Hai (Johar), 30–31, 35, 39–40, 183n33
Kumar, Amit, 89, 191n37

Lage Raho Munna Bhai (Hirani), 151
Lam, Ringo: *City on Fire*, 119, 172, 193n2
Leitch, Thomas, 19, 25, 59, 184n1
LGBTQ+ rights advocacy, 137–39, 142, 161
Lutgendorf, Philip, 94–95
Lyne, Adrian: *Fatal Attraction*, 70, 185n12; *Unfaithful*, 22, 59, 62–63, 73–75, 81–85, 88

Mahabharata epic, 180n6; TV series adaptation (Chopra), 184n9
Malini, Hema, 70
Manjrekar, Mahesh, 113, 115, 194n15
Mankekar, Purnima, 16, 182n29, 185n20, 187n32
Manorama Six Feet Under (Singh), 22–23, 100, 102, 125, 128, 131; *Chinatown* (Polanski) and, 101, 120–24, 189n16; *Kiss Me Deadly* (Aldrich) and, 101, 120–21, 123
masala films, 12, 29, 34, 42, 144, 184nn3–4
masculinity, 117, 128, 166, 186n29, 188n8; "gangster light," 130–31; heroism and, 45, 52, 68–70, 103–14, 129, 131; intertextuality and, 20, 22–23, 100–102, 131, 174; queer representation and, 88, 140–42, 145, 147, 153, 155; vamp trope and, 68–70
Mazdon, Lucy, 7
Mazumdar, Ranjani, 129, 194n21
McDougal, Stuart, 19, 22, 61, 75–76, 151
Mehta, Deepa. See *Fire* (Mehta)
Mehta, Monika, 16, 38–39, 122, 176, 193n2, 193n9, 194n13, 194n18

melodrama, 38, 41, 45–48, 54, 111, 113, 149–50, 154; dominant in Hindi cinema, 9, 14–16, 29–30, 34–36, 80–81, 85, 103, 105, 143, 151, 184n4; in Hollywood, 30, 34–36, 185n10; in Indianization, 6, 9, 29–33, 51, 115–16, 143; masala films and, 29, 34, 144, 184nn3–4; Parsi theater and, 14, 36; song-and-dance performances and, 30, 36, 55–56, 143, 186n22
microimports, 172
Mirza, Aziz: *Phir Bhi Dil Hai Hindustani (And Yet the Heart Is Indian)*, 104, 182nn29–30
misogyny, 70, 73, 85–86, 92, 102, 107, 138, 155, 189n14
moll trope, 63, 67–68. *See also* vamps
Mother India (Khan), 15, 105–106, 108–109, 186n23, 193n5, 193n7
mujra (classical dance performance), 67, 162–**64**
Mukherjee, Silpa, 69–70
Mulvey, Laura, 94, 96, 147
Murder (Basu), 71, 83, 187n1, 189–90n18; femme fatale in, 22, 59, 62–63, 74–75, 81, 84–85, 87–89, 92–97; triangulation in, 59–63
Murder 2 (Suri), 91, 170
Murty, Madhavi, 32

Naficy, Hamid, 96
Narayan, Uma, 182n25
Nayar, Sheila, 8–9, 29, 101, 107, 110, 181n16, 182n23
Neale, Steve, 147
neoliberalism, 32–33, 111, 151, 172, 193n8
neo-noir: aesthetics of, 19, 76, 79, 99, 103, 120–22, 125–26, 128, 131, 194n14; auteurism and,

100–102, 119–22, 127, 180n11; feminist influence on, 72–73, 76, 88–89, 189n14, 191n33; femme fatales in, 72–73, 76–77, 89, 102, 189n16; as global noir, 102, 193–94n12; misogyny of, 73, 85, 92, 102, 107, 189n15; pastiche and, 73, 102–103, 119–22, 126, 128, 131, 180n11, 193–94n12. *See also* film noir; *individual films*

New Bollywood, 11, 17, 60–61, 127, 156, 170, 183n31

New Woman, 17, 72–74

nostalgia, 6, 54, 124–26, 128–29, 156

Om Shanti Om / OSO (Khan), 6, 23, 124–25, 128, 180n11

Orfall, Blair, 10

Oswald, Gerd: *A Kiss Before Dying*, 101, 104, 107–10

Oza, Rupal, 17

Pardes (Foreign Land) (Ghai), 39, 45, 52–53, 104, 182nn29–30

parody, 19, 28–29, 125, 128, 159, 173

pastiche, 6, 20, 27, 114, 150, 189n15, 193–94n12; *Johnny Gaddaar* and, 22, 101, 103, 121–22, 124–31, 180n11; *Kaante* and, 22–23, 101–103, 119; *Manorama Six Feet Under* and, 22, 101, 120–25

pathan tribes, 152–53

patriarchy, 32–33, 104, 137, 185n18; in families, 16, 105, 111, 137, 139, 188n8, 193n5; in family film genre, 37–39, 47, 51–53, 56, 143, 150, 183n31; in *Fire* (Mehta), 137, 157–58, 161–62, 184n9; Hinduism and, 157, 184n9, 186n23; queer representation and, 157–58, 161–62, 166; vamp as threat to, 64–66, 75, 84–86, 189n13

Paunksnis, Šaruñas, 102–103, 193–94n12

Phir Bhi Dil Hai Hindustani (And Yet the Heart Is Indian) (Mirza), 104, 182nn29–30

Pink Chaddi (panties) Campaign, 93

Postman Always Rings Twice, The (Garnett), 62, 72, 189n13

Pratt, Mary Louise, 195n1

Preston, Catherine, 43

Production Code Administration (PCA), Hollywood, 71–73, 76, 86, 88

Pyaar To Hona Hi Tha (Love Had to Happen) (Bazmee), 18, 21, 34–36, 42–43, 48, 186n29; "Ajnabi Mujhko Itna Bata" in, 55–56; "Duniya ri Duniya" ("Oh World, you are good") in, 49–50; globalization and, 31–33, 40–41, 51, 53–57; "Jo Hona Hai Woh Hona Hai" ("What will happen will happen)," 25–29

queer representation: camp and, 34, 125, 144–50, 159; carnivalesque and, 23, 144–46, 150, 159; in *Fire* (Mehta), 23, 134, 156–62, 167, 195n8; gay stereotypes, 135–38, 140–42, 144, 148, 155, 166; homoeroticism, 138, 140, 147–49, 151–55, 161–63, 166–67; homophobia and, 23, 138, 140, 144, 150, 154–55; kissing scenes, 133–34

Raghavan, Sriram: *Johnny Gaddaar (Johnny the Traitor)*, 22–23, 99–103, 120–22, 124–31, 176, 180n11, 194n22

Index

Rajadhyaksha, Ashish, 11–12, 57
Rajagopal, Arvind, 157
Ramayana epic, 180n6; TV series adaptation (Sagar), 157, 184n9, 195n5
Rao, R. Raj, 153
remakes: anxiety of influence and, 7, 19, 101, 134–35, 167; as close copies, 4, 18–20, 25–26, 35, 73, 77, 119, 134, 181n13; as contact zones, 135–36, 155, 167, 195n1; copyright and, 7–10, 21, 170–71, 176; defamiliarization in, 19–20, 22, 61, 63, 75–77, 82, 85, 97–98, 126; *Devdas* and, 3–4, 67, 125; genre-crossing in, 34, 61, 76, 116, 119, 124–25; geopolitical searing and, 118, 135, 167; as loose copies, 4, 8, 20, 35, 59, 107, 120, 180n9, 181n20; repetition and, 2–4, 10, 61, 135, 169–70, 181n20; transference and, 7, 22, 75–76, 82–83, 85, 97, 117, 135–42, 155, 167, 183n35. *See also* Indianization; transformation; *individual films*
Reservoir Dogs (Tarantino), 102, 181n13, 194n14; *Johnny Gaddaar* (Raghavan) and, 100–101, 125–26; *Kaante* (Gupta) and, 9, 101, 103, 112–16, 118–19, 172, 180n10, 193n2
revenge films, 68–69, 105, 172–73, 188n6, 188n8, 193n8, 196n3. *See also* avenging women films; domestic-abuse films
Richards, Rashna Wadia, 10, 30, 172, 176
Richardson, Helen, 66, 68, 75, 188n10
Ritchie, Guy: influence on *Johnny Gaddaar* (Raghavan), 100, 125,
130; *Lock, Stock, and Two Smoking Barrels*, 102
romantic comedies, 81, 144, 154, 187n30; *Pyaar To Hona Hi Tha* and, 21, 29, 33–35, 41–48, 54–56. *See also* comedy; *individual films*
Roy, Bimal: *Devdas*, 67
RSS (Rashtriya Swayamsevak Sangh), 93, 184n9, 192n41
Ryan, Meg, 41, 43–50, 54–55, 186n29, 187n33

SammyManiac, 4–5
Sanskrit epics, 14, 184n9; *Mahabharat*, 180n6; *Mahabharata*, 180n6; *Ramayan*, 180n6; *Ramayana*, 157, 195n5
Saxena, Amit. See *Jism (Body)* (Saxena)
self-reflexivity, 20, 95, 148, 159, 173–75; in noir films, 70, 76, 97, 101–103, 120–21, 123–24, 126, 128
Sen, Meheli, 145, 151, 174
sexual objectification, 15, 47–48, 68, 93, 182n27, 191–92n38; femme fatale and, 62, 72, 80, 85, 87; as fetishization, 69, 86–89, 92, 94, 97 147, 165–66, 189n18; in item numbers, 69–70, 89, 95, 188nn9–10, 189n13; male gaze and, 63, 69, 88–89, 94–97, 147, 163, 189–90n18, 191n37, 192n44; sleaze films and, 69–70, 87, 89–92, 191nn35–37
Shah, Kishan, 89, 191n35
Shandley, Robert, 47, 54, 187n33
Sherawat, Mallika: as an "item girl," 63, 74, 89, 189–90n18; in *Murder*, 63, 74–75, 83–85, 88–89, 91–97, 189–90n18
Shetty, Sunil, 113, 115, 117, 194n15
Sholay (Embers) (Sippy), 151–53

Index

Shree 420 (Kapoor), 40, 66, 182n30, 186n23
Shrivastava, Alankrita, 95, 192n44; *Lipstick Under My Burkha*, 87
Singh, Greg, 126
Singh, Navdeep, 128; *Manorama Six Feet Under*, 22–23, 100–102, 120–25, 128, 131
Sippy, Ramesh: *Sholay (Embers)*, 151–53
sleaze films, 69–70, 87, 89–92, 187n3, 188n12, 191nn35–37. See also individual films
Smith, Iain Robert, 10, 172, 176
song-and-dance performances, 6–7, 14, 44, 127, 150, 195n4, 195n8; "Aa Ja Zara" in *Fire*, 159–60; "Ajnabi Mujhko Itna Bata" in *Pyaar To Hona Hi Tha*, 55–56; "Beedi" in *Dostana*, 148, 160; censorship and, 38, 89, 92, 185n19; in *Dedh Ishqiya*, 162–65; "Duniya ri Duniya" in *Pyaar To Hona Hi Tha*, 49–50; as interruptions, 96, 145–49, 185n10; "Jadoo Hai Nasha Hai" in *Jism*, **77**, 90; "Jo Hona Hai Woh Hona Hai" in *Pyaar To Hona Hi Tha*, 25–29; "Macarena" and, 27, 29, 184n2; masala films and, 42; melodrama and, 30, 36, 55–56, 143, 186n22; *mujra* (classical dance performance), 67, 162–**64**; *pathan* identity and, 152–53; "Phir Bhi Dil Hai Hindustani" in *Shree 420*, 182n30; *So You Think You Can Dance* and, 175; "Tujhe Dekha Toh Yeh Jaana Sanam" in *DDLJ*, 55–56. See also item numbers
stardom, 10, 63, 115–16, 145, 173; Amitabh Bachchan and, 38, 67, 106, 115, 127–29, 170; Amrish Puri and, 53; Bipasha Basu and, 80–81, 89–90, 92, 96; *darsán* and, 95–97; Helen Richardson and, 66, 68, 75, 188n10; Hema Malini and, 70; John Abraham and, 88–90, 146–47; in *Johnny Gaddaar*, 127–29, 131; Kajol and, 49, 51; Madhuri Dixit and, 163; Mallika Sherawat and, 74, 89, 92, 96, 189–90n18; Meg Ryan and, 43, 47, 49; Parveen Babi and, 68, 74–75, 85, 187n3; Shah Rukh Khan as antihero, 104–12, 193n10; Theda Bara and, 64–65, 72; Zeenat Aman and, 68, 75, 153, 187n3
Straayer, Chris, 72
Streitmatter, Rodger, 140
Swaroop, Jyoti: *Parwana (Moth)*, 99–100, 125, 127–31

Tarantino, Quentin: influence on *Johnny Gaddaar* (Raghavan), 100–101, 125–26; influence on *Kaante* (Gupta), 9, 101, 103, 112–16, 118–19, 172, 180n10, 193n2; *Kill Bill*, 119. See also *Reservoir Dogs* (Tarantino)
tawaif (courtesan) trope, 67, 69, 156, 162–63, 166
Thomas, Rosie, 8–9, 14–16, 25, 29–30, 76, 103, 105, 184n4, 186n28
transformation, 7–9, 14, 18, 114, 116, 118–19, 169, 183n35; family films and, 21, 25–26, 32–37, 44–45, 54, 56–57; queer representation and, 134–38, 140–44, 155, 166–67; vamp, femme fatale tropes and, 22, 68, 71, 73–77, 83, 85, 97. See also Indianization; remakes

Unfaithful (Lyne), 22, 59, 62–63, 73–75, 81–85, 88
Urdu poetry, 1–3, 179nn2–5, 180n6

vamps, 20–22, 30, 194–95n23; feminism and, 63, 69, 72–73, 86–87, 92–94; in film history, 15–17, 64–72, 75, 82, 95, 188n10, 189n17; in *Jism (Body)*, 61–63, 71, 74–75, 80–81, 85, 87, 92, 97–98; in *Murder*, 62–63, 71, 74–75, 81, 84–85, 92, 97; patriarchy and, 64–66, 75, 84–86, 189n13. *See also* femme fatales
Varma, Ram Gopal, 121, 194n13; *Pyaar Tune Kya Kiya (Love . . . What Have You Done?)*, 70; *Satya (Truth)*, 129, 194n21
Vasudevan, Ravi, 13, 34, 94, 103, 181n21

Virdi, Jyotika, 14–16, 66, 68–69, 182n27, 185n18, 186n27

Wang, Yiman, 7–8, 118, 135
westernization, 106, 127–28, 142–44, 182n25, 182n29, 192n43; capitalism and, 26, 52–56, 173; globalization and, 20–21, 26, 37, 54, 104, 112, 173–74; sexualization of women and, 15, 37, 46–48, 65–66, 80, 90–93, 95, 182n27; through character names, 194–95n23
West/Other binary. *See* Indian/Western binary
Williams, Linda, 35, 110, 185n11
Wright, Neelam Sidhar, 10, 114, 117, 135, 170, 172, 176

yaari, 152–53

www.ingramcontent.com/pod-product-compliance
Lightning Source LLC
Chambersburg PA
CBHW052049220426
43663CB00012B/2500